Callas & di Stefano

'LUCIA DI LAMMERMOOR' 18th January 1954 LA SCALA
A kiss for Lucia from Edgardo

Callas & di Stefano

THE YEARS OF GLORY

JOHN PETTITT

THE ODDA PRESS
2002

First published in 2002
The Odda Press
Home Farm House
Menston, Ilkley
West Yorkshire LS29 6BB

ISBN 0 9539006 1 4

Designed, printed and bound by
SMITH SETTLE
Ilkley Road, Otley, West Yorkshire LS21 3JP

By the same author
Maria Callas: A Record Obsession

The posthumous history of **Callas** the artist strengthens and clarifies the conviction of her greatness. In life, appreciation had to co-exist with apprehension: throughout the glorious decade we heard the voice deteriorate and watched as the human-being came under increasing stress. What we have now…is the achievement: the artistic object, free of contingences and the dutiful incubus of critical concern.

John Steane, *Gramophone*, February 2002

Di Stefano is my idol. *There* is a solar voice – very solar – that's never wanted anything. It's like it is because it is like that, and in expression it comes as close to the truth as any voice. It was the most incredible, open voice you could hear. The musicality of di Stefano is as natural and beautiful as the voice is phenomenal.

Luciano Pavarotti, *Opera*, January 2002

CONTENTS

ACKNOWLEDGEMENTS

The 25th anniversary of the death of Maria Callas in 2002 will inevitably add new material to an already huge output. Conversely, hardly a word has appeared in print about her best-known operatic partner, Giuseppe di Stefano. This may in part be explained by Callas' reputation being, since 1977, at the mercy of any pen to paper whilst the tenor himself, now in his eighty-first year, can guard his own. In any case, Mr di Stefano, has characteristically, and in the nicest possible way, expressed to me his indifference to books so long as we have the recordings – an attitude which, of course, I respect.

But equally, I would certainly like to thank those who have enabled me to attempt to shed new light on a little-known area of familiar ground: to my editor, Peter Dewes' ever watchful and helpful eye, to Susan Hoyle and Bradford Central Library's ever available and invaluable source material, to the Henry Watson Music Library, Manchester and the University of London Library for specialist material, to João Malatian in São Paulo and Theo Hernadez in Mexico City for local assistance, to Peter Howe in London and Jack Morrell in Bradford for miscellaneous information, to Frank Abe in Amsterdam and the Editor of *Opera*, John Allison and his colleagues for help with illustrative material, to Ken Smith, Terry Nicholson and Smith Settle for their continuing patience and expertise, and above all to my wife and family for their endless forbearance.

John Pettitt
1st July 2002

PROLOGUE

'…A pair so famous.' was Shakespeare's celebrated description of Antony and Cleopatra. And so they were, immortal lovers of Roman times. And so, of course, were many others. Did not the same hand remind us: 'For never was a story of more woe, Than this of Juliet and her Romeo', the tragedy of one partner embedded in the other? Lady Macbeth's 'dearest partner of greatness' on the other hand did not live to see his 'dearest chuck' and himself dismissed by the English epicures as a 'dead butcher and his fiendlike queen'. The destiny of one is so often entwined with the other as yet another Shakespearean pair, Troilius and Cressida, found to their cost. But there is much compensating satisfaction here. Would the ingrained pride and prejudice of Jane Austen's Darcy and Elizabeth Bennet have ever been resolved in isolation? Would Elinor and Marianne have ever learned about the true value of sense and sensibility without each other? So often the joy or anguish of an individual is compounded as it relates to another's as witnessed in the epic dramas of our literature. From the Bible, Samson and Dalila, or from later troubles, Porgy and Bess; Hansel and Gretel survived, but Dido and Aeneas and the greatest of them all, Tristan and Isolde, did not.

From the real world, too, we have our famous pairs. Don't many of us start out with Punch and Judy, even if most teenagers today would quickly pass on to the attractions, say, of Posh and Becks. They would probably still enjoy the ballads of Simon and Garfunkel and thrill to the criminal adventures of Bonnie and Clyde. After a laugh with Morecombe and Wise, we might fondly remember the hypnotic dancing of Ginger Rogers and Fred Astaire or the silent antics of Laurel and Hardy. Great performers they were, like the creative partnerships of Rodgers and Hammerstein (composer and librettist) or Benjamin Britten and Peter Pears (composer and beloved interpreter): champions Torvell and Dean on ice, or Richard Burton and Elizabeth Taylor on screen, or Theatreland's post-war golden couple Laurence Olivier and Vivien Leigh, at the ballet Fonteyn and Nureyev, and what Frank Granville Barker described as the finest operatic duo since Caruso and Melba: Callas and di Stefano.

Of course, there are greater and lesser lights in many of the examples cited above. Richard Burton drank too much and Liz Taylor probably had too many husbands; poor Dame Margot died penniless caring for her crippled husband and Rudolf sadly died of AIDS. Vivien Leigh's exquisite beauty was destroyed by obstinately seeking to match her husband's cruel expertise on the stage and Callas' all-consuming genius set impossible standards which exasperated lesser mortals. Nevertheless as this book will seek to show, her most famous partnership – that with the great tenor Giuseppe di Stefano – aroused a degree of excitement rarely witnessed in the opera house. Her art is legendary, her place in operatic history assured. By bringing weight and feeling to light coloratura roles and, conversely, musicality and refinement to heavier verismo roles, she changed the face of opera for ever. And so in his way, as Peter Hutchinson has recently explained, did di Stefano. By the middle of the last century, Mr Hutchinson wrote, the Italian approach to opera had become 'largely a matter of imitative adherence to what one deemed to be the eternal gospel of the past, of leaving nothing to chance and doing anything but what better informed authorities like Wagner and Verdi had always urged: that the task of artistic creation devolves mainly on the performer, that having mastered the material they should go out and do spontaneously what seems to be the right thing at any given moment. It was nothing less than their right, indeed their duty to improvise. Di Stefano's performances had an atmosphere of unfettered, spontaneous rightness which is the hallmark of the creative genius. Whilst others looked only backwards, di Stefano became the spring board from which every distinguished tenor in recent times such as the so-called three tenors has launched themselves.'[1]

Both singers, the great Greek diva and the volatile Sicilian maestro, pursued their aims as individuals and it is scarcely any wonder that their exceptional gifts, when combined, prompted a very rare potency in performance, as they did on one particular evening nearly fifty years ago.

Chapter One

18th JANUARY 1954

There have been many memorable operatic nights and 18th January 1954 was certainly one of them, as next day's newspaper headlines made abundantly clear: "La Scala in delirium – a rain of red carnations – four minutes of applause after the first part of the Mad Scene". The occasion was a new production of *Lucia di Lammermoor* with the mighty Karajan, conductor and director, in the pit and Callas and di Stefano on stage. It was not the first performance of Donizetti's tragic masterpiece at La Scala since the war: Margherita Carosio and Gianni Poggi had appeared under Franco Capuana in March 1949. But it was very different and there were several reasons for this.

First, during performances of *Lohengrin* in January/February 1953, the Scala's director, Antonio Ghiringhelli, had unexpectedly tempted [with a tape of EMI's recently recorded *Lucia*] the conductor to present this Italian opera at La Scala. The German maestro was doubtful but was persuaded both by his interest in the new Callas phenomenon and by his recollections of pre-war performances of the opera by Toscanini. He took advantage of his engagement with the Philharmonia to the Edinburgh Festival that year to visit the Scottish borders to absorb the atmosphere of Walter Scott country, to study the architecture and the light, and to visit Sir Walter Scott's home, Abbotsford. He immediately decided to stage the opera with a minimum of reliance on conventional scenic effects and a maximum concentration on the use of atmospheric lighting, with Callas herself as the central focus. After some understandable worries on the part of the short-sighted diva, their mutual commitment to the undertaking was total. Callas herself had previously sung the role on four occasions in Italy since the sensational success of her debut as Lucia in Mexico City on 10th June 1952. She was partnered then by di Stefano, as she was subsequently in Florence and Genoa. He had first sung Edgardo in San Francisco opposite Lily Pons two years previously on 28th September 1950. Both singers were therefore well placed to take advantage of the high calibre conditions being offered at La Scala.

However, there was another factor which vastly contributed to the success of this particular January evening in 1954, stemming from the Mexico City performance, which was one of five operas – *I Puritani, La Traviata, Lucia, Rigoletto, Tosca* – that the soprano and tenor sang together in as many weeks. Truly that season gave birth to the Callas/di Stefano phenomenon. It might,

nevertheless, have remained a nine days wonder but for another twist of fate. Their final performance [*Tosca*] took place on 1st July 1952. Three weeks later in Verona, Maria signed her EMI contract to record complete operas in La Scala on the new LP format, due to start the very next month, alongside the tenor who had so impressed her in Mexico. Three recordings [*I Puritani, Tosca, Lucia di Lammermoor*] released in 1953 soon became the talk of the operatic world. Two were conducted by Tullio Serafin, two included Tito Gobbi in the cast; only Callas and di Stefano were in all three. Thus it was against this intoxicating background that the Scala curtains rose that night in January 1954 on the new golden couple, the toast of a proud, ecstatic and grateful audience.

For Callas, now in her third season at La Scala, this *Lucia* was probably her most formidable success to date. Having opened the first two seasons, she gave way to Renata Tebaldi, but both the Italian diva and *La Wally* were somewhat overshadowed by what followed three days later: Callas' most recent manifestation, Medea, a role she quickly made her own. If Lucia was to be better than this it would have to be very good indeed. Few doubted that it was. Sandro Sequi, the Italian producer, analysed the magic: 'Certain artists are gifted with something special. After watching Callas many times on the stage in many roles, I realised she had a secret few theatre people know. The brain needs to send tension to every muscle of the body – a tension of the mind, the intelligence, which would travel to every limb, to the fingers, the toes, the face, everywhere. But then there must be a sudden relaxation, which gives the impression of a break of energy, a kind of fall. The effect is extraordinary, a kind of climax, like when people die. This alternation of tension and relaxation can exert an incredible hold over the public. I believe that this was the key to Callas' magnetism, why her singing and acting were so compelling. Think of the movements in her arms in the Mad Scene of *Lucia*. They were like the wings of a great eagle, a marvellous bird. When they went up, and she often moved them very slowly, they seemed heavy, not airy like a dancer's arms, but weighted. Then, when she reached the climax of a musical phrase, her arms relaxed and flowed into the next gesture until she reached a new musical peak. There was a continuous line to her singing and movements which were really very simple. Everything about her struck me as natural and instinctive, never intellectual. She was extremely stylised and classic, yet at the same time human – but a humanity on a higher plane of existence, almost sublime.'[1] Both Cynthia Jolly in *Opera News* [USA] and Peter Dragadze in *Opera* [UK] were captivated: 'The fabulous reception accorded her in this aristocratic theatre

moved Maria Callas to tears. After the sextet – even before the great scene – she was called to the curtain a dozen times, and flowers rained down on the stage. She picked them up one by one in a graceful allusion to the coming Mad Scene, in which she outdid many a stage Ophelia. She remains more strongly herself with every performance she gives, yet penetrates always more perceptively into the role at hand. It will for instance be difficult to hear 'Spargi d'amaro pianto' from another singer [however finished] without finding it pallid. Callas' supremacy among present-day sopranos lies in no mechanical perfection but in a magnificently tempered artistic courage, breathtaking security and agility, phrasing and stage-poise; and in a heart-rending poignancy of timbre which is quite unforgettable.'[2] 'Callas again had a great personal triumph, holding the public in suspense with the breathtaking clarity and agility of her coloratura, when contrasted with the almost contralto quality of her voice in the recitatives and first act arias. Her Mad Scene produced an emotional thrill that few other living singers are capable of, and the unusual combination of a dramatic voice, with a soprano leggiero 'top', gave a completely new aspect of this role.'[3]

For di Stefano, the evening was successful for completely different reasons because, unlike Callas, it was, the EMI recording apart, completely unexpected. Only in his second season at La Scala, di Stefano's phenomenal early triumphs had, as we shall see, become too much things of the past. The reactionary attitudes at the Met had not sustained his interest and he had returned to La Scala in 1952 where he sang ten successful performances of *La Bohème* opposite Rosanna Carteri and a similar number as Enzo in *La Gioconda*, a new role, six of which were opposite Callas, at least a year therefore before they became an operatic item. His next Scala appearance, only a few days before *Lucia*, was in *Rigoletto* which by all accounts was an abject failure. According to Peter Dragadze, 'the conductor, Nino Sanzogno frequently appeared to lose control of the orchestra which threw both the stage and pit out of balance, both in tempo and volume. He had little conception of the Verdian style and conse-quently completely lost the intensity of the drama. Leonard Warren, making his Scala debut in the name part, sang extremely well but at times his interpretation of the role seemed to lack strength and force. Rosanna Carteri was quite miscast as Gilda; her voice was too heavy for the role and she had to leave out the *fioritura* in 'Caro nome'. By the time she reached Act Three, her voice was so tired she began to sing flat. Even her superb musicianship could not save her from public disapproval which reached its climax after the Quartet. Finally, little can be said in favour of di Stefano as the Duke [in which role he

OPERA

Vol 5 No 5   MAY 1954   2s 6d

Callas and di Stefano

The toast of the operatic world.

had taken the Met by storm at his debut in 1948]. He is passing through a very bad patch and has lost much of the beautiful timbre for which he was known.'[4] By his own admission, di Stefano was taking his voice to the point where 'every lingering shadow of technique would disappear',[5] the aim of which was naturalness and spontaneity; others would claim it led to monotony.

It might not therefore be too much to say that *Lucia* on 18th January 1954 saved di Stefano's career. As Peter Dragadze wrote in *Opera*: 'The tenor won back the laurels he lost in *Rigoletto*; his performance as Edgardo was of a first-class standard and it was most moving to see how the rest of the cast, as well as the public, gave him every encouragement.'[6] Callas and di Stefano took the Karajan production to Berlin and Vienna, and they sang the opera together in Chicago. Lucia was certainly one of Callas' greatest roles; she sang it 45 times. But it is, after all, one of the great 'soprano' operas and if ever there was an Edgardo of the century it was surely di Stefano. It suited his voice and temperament to perfection; like Callas, he recorded the role twice and sang it a total of 33 times, 20 of which were with Callas. A critic once observed that the great thing about di Stefano is that he always sounds as if he's 'dying with his voice' – here, accompanied by that plaintive cello in 'Tu che a Dio', never more so.

From this moment, then, in 1954 until early 1959, we were to have the age of Callas and di Stefano. If they weren't actually singing together on the Scala stage, it was likely that one or other would be. But before we look forward to those heady days on that and other stages, and in the EMI studio, let us turn the clock back and discover how it all began.

Chapter Two

1944–1946

Ten years before, in 1944, very few people had heard of either singer. In the fifth year of the war, Maria Callas, not yet 21 years old, was a leading member of the Greek National Opera in Athens and Giuseppe di Stefano, just over two years older, was a prisoner of war in Switzerland. She was about to assume two important roles, Martha in D'Albert's *Tiefland* and Leonore in *Fidelio* and then seek international recognition by returning to New York. He, the possessor of a most glorious voice, was still trying to make up his mind if he wanted to sing in opera at all, and was doing what he liked best, singing Italian songs. The next few years would see startling developments in both careers of a highly erratic and unexpected nature.

Mrs Kalogeropulos decided that Maria Callas would be a singer long

'FIDELIO' 14th August 1944
HERODES ATTICUS, ATHENS
Maria Callas is Beethoven's heroine
at only 20

before her daughter did. So we cannot be too surprised that at the tender age of eighteen the future diva was singing professionally one of the great operatic roles – Floria Tosca. This precocious start to her career was a product of a daring, dedicated determination that would quite soon sweep her to unrivalled heights in the operatic firmament. She learned her art in the isolation of war-torn Athens which was probably no bad thing when she came to take up the mantle again in post-war Italy. But, as an American-born Greek, it would not be easy in that country and so it proved.

Di Stefano was also marooned. He had yet to appear on the operatic stage and confined his vocal efforts to the recording studio with Radio Lausanne thanks to the devoted influence of a beautiful young Russian painter and writer, Wala Dauwalder. Unlike Maria, he had had no conservatoire training;

Mussolini's ambitions had seen to that. But early lessons with Adriano Tocchio, a Milanese tenor and later with the celebrated baritone Luigi Montesanto enabled him to freelance as a madrigal singer [alongside Cesare Siepi] and he enjoyed warming up cinema audiences in Milan before the main feature. Many of his favourite songs found their way onto disc, the best being ten items recorded in HMV's Zurich studios in 1944, with Edoardo Moser the piano accompanist. The French song 'Si vous l'aviez compris' by Luigi Denza is a particular delight. His first recorded operatic aria was probably Werther's 'Pourquoi me reveiller' in June 1945, though with Luigi Marchio he had three months previously cut the Pearl Fishers duet. The very first notes of the recitative are sung with that exquisite, plangent tone, a promise of so much to follow. Sadly, the reprise of the great melody is omitted. For Radio Lausanne, he had already recorded editions of *L'Elisir* [September 1944] and *Il Tabarro* [February 1945], both conducted by Otto Ackermann. Arias were recorded between June 1945 and 1946 from *Manon*, *L'elisir d'amore*, *L'Amico Fritz*, *I Pescatori di Perle*, *Tosca*, *Bohème*, *L'Arlesiana*, all with piano. When those from the first three were released on an LP anthology in 1981, J.B. Steane wrote in *Gramophone*: 'They might indeed make the angels weep. Youthful promise for

'MANON' 20th April 1946
TEATRO MUNICIPAL, REGGIO EMILIA
Di Stefano's debut at 24
a Des Grieux to remember

some reason moistens the eye. The young man, with subtlety, sensitivity, a golden voice and all the world before him. Piano accompaniments and a certain amount of swish and grit in the surfaces should not deter anybody who cares for good singing from listening to them.'[1]

Activity of this kind proved a useful springboard for the young di Stefano to make his operatic debut at a time when Callas' unproductive return to America was beginning to look like a big mistake. Her teacher in Athens, Elvira de Hidalgo, had warned her as much and it was di Stefano, in fact, who first made the Italian headlines with a sensational debut on 20th April 1946 as Des Grieux in Massenet's *Manon* only ten days after a second recording session in the HMV Milan studios under his popular name Nino Florio. The conductor was Umberto Berrettoni who would soon be conducting Maria in *Aida* and *Norma*. Di Stefano's success at the Teatro Municipal in Reggio Emilia was immediate: within a fortnight he was singing Nadir at the Fenice; his Zurga was Giuseppe Valdengo. On 3rd August, he took his third new role, the Duke of Mantua, to Lugo under Rainaldo Zamboni, singing opposite Lina Pagliughi. And the very next day, he sang another new role [his fourth], Alfredo in *La traviata* opposite Margherita Carosio, a feat surely rare in the annals of opera, and unequalled in that respect even by the prodigious achievements to come of Maria Callas.

Born on 24th July 1921, recently 80, Giuseppe di Stefano was, and is, clearly a man of prodigious Sicilian energy and charm. His first season is ample proof of this for he was preparing his debut in yet another two operas – first *L'Amico Fritz* at Lugo under Sanzogno, with the mezzo Ebe Ticozzi [who would be Mama Lucia in the 1953 Callas/di Stefano EMI recording of *Cavalleria rusticana*], with two further performances at the scene of his April debut under Argeo Quadri. Then at Bologna on 26th October, he sang Elvino ['his lovely timbre and expressive phrasing were quite admirable'][2] in *La sonnambula* opposite Margherita Carosio, whose withdrawal from another Bellini opera [*I puritani*] in 1949 was to have a sensational effect on Callas' career. Further performances of *Manon* were given at Piacenza, Ravenna and Cesena under Quadri and Giuseppe Podesta, opposite Dolores Ottani. Di Stefano's career was 'racing ahead, with his attractive, well-placed voice, taste, energy, variety in his delivery, and good looks.'[3] As Giorgio Gualerzi stated at the time, his personality, too, is special: 'daring, instinctive, generous, calculating, spontaneous and contradictory, imaginative and insolent.'[4] His first year ended spectacularly at the Liceo, Barcelona, opening the season with *Manon* [opposite Victoria de los Angeles who eight years later would be his Butterfly on the EMI recording], *La sonnambula,* and *Rigoletto* with Carlo Tagliabue in the name part, a total of 28 performances. He also continued his recordings for Radio Lausanne with an abridged version of Lehar's *Paganini* in French, the celebrated 'Girls were meant to love and kiss' sung with all the grace, tonal beauty and that special ardent tug which informed all his best performances. In the new year, 1947, one more *Rigoletto* performance remained at the Liceo before moving back to Rome for five performances of *La sonnambula* under Antonino Votto [a celebrated conductor in the Callas/di Stefano canon] and *Manon* under Vincenzo Bellezza whose gifts di Stefano cited in his recent *Gramophone* interview [September 2001]. Three performances of *The Pearl Fishers* under

Votto with Onelia Fineschi, who at the other end of his career would be Maddalena to his Andrea Chenier in Florence, completed his stay in Rome before moving to Trieste for another five under Berretoni. With 42 performances behind him in eleven cities in just ten months, he now prepared himself for the most important of them all.

Chapter Three

1947

Di Stefano's debut at La Scala as Massenet's Des Grieux on 15th March and Callas' Italian debut at Verona as La Gioconda on 2nd August constitute two of the most celebrated and significant operatic events of that year, 1947, indeed of the last century. Di Stefano's stunning appearance opposite a Scala favourite, Mafalda Favero, eighteen years his senior and with a cast under Antonio Guarnieri which included Siepi, immediately confirmed him as the natural successor to Gigli and led to an important record contract and international acclaim. To Eugenio Gara, a vocal authority: 'He had only to come on stage for the Chevalier des Grieux to leap from the pages of Abbe Prevost's novel. I have never seen this happen before, in any *Manon*, and I can't imagine it easily happening again. He is a fine-looking young man, he moves well, has a bright, penetrating gaze, his gestures are spontaneous and his diction crystal-clear. If ever anyone was born for the theatre, this man was. His voice is gentle and ingratiating, with a refined, well-blended sound as long as he stays in the middle register, his top notes real and supported, not thinned-down ones bordering on falsetto.'

Callas' appearance at Verona turned out rather differently: artistically 'excellent and much applauded',[1] it ended two barren years in New York and then, once again, appeared to lead nowhere. *Musical America* noted Richard Tucker's encores of 'Cielo e mar'; that Tullio Serafin conducted a 140-strong orchestra to a 25,000-strong audience. But of the soprano who sang Gioconda there was no mention. Nevertheless, it had two enormous consequences: she met her future mentor, Serafin, and her future husband, Battista Meneghini, a rich Veronese businessman. Neither singer, however, for the time being was to play any part in events at the all-important Scala, as di Stefano found himself shipped off to the New York Metropolitan Opera and Callas floundered in the Italian provinces.

Meanwhile, unlike Maria had been in New York, di Stefano was busy. He gave further performances of *Manon, Rigoletto* and *The Pearl Fishers* in Parma, Rome, Perugia, Pisa and Venice to which he added the role of Wilhelm Meister in Thomas' *Mignon* in Rome in May under Angelo Questa with a cast that included Italo Tajo, the celebrated bass and the mezzo Anna Maria Canali who would later appear in many of the EMI Scala sets. Di Stefano's recording of the two tenor arias from Mignon would be widely admired and already

cuts had been made in the HMV Milan studios, later superseded in London.
Di Stefano took his Wilhelm Meister opposite Giulietta Simionato on to La
Scala in October, the very month that the Greek-American soprano, in the
wake of Verona and after a humiliating audition, was told that the theatre
which had opened its arms to the Sicilian tenor had absolutely nothing for
her. Who said the war was over?

By now it was known that di Stefano was bound for the Met in the new
year and of course the publicity machine required recordings. But sessions in
London pencilled in for the end of 1947 were dogged by difficulties which
were a foretaste of troubles ahead, as correspondence between HMV in London
and La Voce del Padrone in Milan makes clear. The Italian subsidiary
enthusiastically promoted the 'good-looking boy with a beautifully lyrical
voice and a brilliant future' but they also warned that he was 'immature,
becoming difficult'.[2] After di Stefano cancelled the arrangements for a second
time, HMV made clear their 'great disappointment and annoyance. To obtain
hotel accommodation, an orchestra and the services of Erede [the conductor]
on precisely the dates which di Stefano approved has proved a major
undertaking and a last minute cancellation without any reasonable excuse or
apology, as far as we know, is an outrageous piece of bad manners. We are
constantly dealing with artists of international reputation and never in the
20-years experience of the writer of this letter have we been treated with
such indifference and lack of appreciation by an artist as by this young tenor.'[3]
On his arrival in London three weeks later, HMV in a further letter notes that
he 'raised difficulties over his hotel and moved himself to the Savoy, from
which he has been ejected as he was only able to obtain rooms for a few days.
He cancelled his first recording session which fortunately we foresaw as likely
and we had another singer standing by. In other words, he has been most
difficult like most tenors.' However the letter also states that he did 'two
recording sessions of four arias and two Sicilian songs. He sang magnificently
and we have the highest expectations of the results. Our impression is that this
young man is very intelligent, and if he continues with his studies he should
have an international career.'[4]

HMV's expectations were indeed realised and the results were obviously
worth their trouble and maybe all the better for it. The first record was released
only two months later, prior to his debut at the Met and reviewed in *Gramophone*
in February 1948: 'Di Stefano is a discovery and a thrilling one. This young
tenor seems to carry all the guns. He can open out his tone to the fore without
assaulting our ears and without losing quality and he can sing softly as well. It

is abundantly evident not only that he has temperament, all Italians have that, but that he can get right to the heart of what he is singing. The well-worn aria from *Tosca* throbs with sincerely felt emotion which is passionate but never out of control. The aria on the reverse, from an opera few of us are likely to know, is an unusual choice and shows off this artist's softer tones very well. Cilea's *L'Arlesiana*, produced in 1896, was his first well-known opera. This excerpt is more in the nature of an *arioso*, simple and expressive music beautifully sung.'[5] The two Sicilian songs *A la Barcillunisa* and *Cantu a timuni* followed next in April. Alec Robertson wrote: 'I am not an authority on Sicilian songs but the two chosen by di Stefano appeal to me as being the real thing and lacking all trace of the commercialised article of which one heard too much in the Neapolitan songs of the Piedigrotta festivals. There is a perceptible oriental strain in these songs and much of the sweet languorous melancholy that assaults the heart of the sensitive foreigner. I cannot imagine that the songs could be sung with greater sympathy and understanding than is shown by di Stefano. His lovely singing lingers in the memory and I hope he will do more in this rich field.'[6] – which indeed he did, though nothing better than his thrilling *A la Barcillunisa,* with its glorious rise from G to top B. It is full of that joy and pride which is so characteristic of di Stefano's singing. The two Mignon arias came in October the same year, prior to his December reappearance at the Met: 'Both these arias are sung with unfailing beauty of tone by this exceptionally gifted young artist. Of all the present generation of tenors whom I have heard, he seems marked out for the highest place; for his most beautiful voice is allied to such an innate feeling for the musical phrase that from such a performance as this we receive the maximum of pleasure. No one who loves fine singing will regret the purchase of this record.'[7] Finally, May 1949, our critic raved about two arias from *La Traviata* and *Manon* recorded at the same time ['Una furtiva lagrima', 'La donna e mobile' and *Manon's* Dream had been rejected]: 'I cannot understand all the fuss about Tagliavini, in spite of the fact that his American recordings do not do him justice, while young di Stefano is on the map. Here is a voice of thrilling quality, forward and free; here are excellent diction and passionate feeling. The singing is not impeccable, for di Stefano scoops up to his 'Ah! dispar ' each time except in the final climax but this is a fault that can easily be remedied. This is altogether a thrilling record for tenor addicts.'[8]

Alec Robertson, a critic raised primarily on church music, did not succumb easily to the blandishments of opera. All the more significant therefore is his admiration for these early recordings on 78 which passed the mantle of Gigli on to di Stefano. As Mr Robertson said, he seemed to carry all the guns, and, as a friend of mine [a Covent Garden habitué] once said, he had that extra virility, a masculinity, which Gigli's tone sometimes lacked. Of the six arias, the cream is probably 'E la solita storia'.perhaps because it is less well known; it is beautifully written and di Stefano's voice caresses the phrases at half and full volume magnificently. Both *Tosca* and *Traviata* arias are indeed very good though probably fall short of later interpretations, in the complete recordings of 1953 and 1955 respectively, with markedly greater *rubato* under more distinguished conductors. The three French arias worthily remind us of di Stefano's achievements in that area before he gave himself more fully to the Italian repertoire at the Scala and elsewhere.

Chapter Four

1948

With news of his stunning new recordings before him, di Stefano duly arrived in New York to make his debut in *Rigoletto* at the Met on the 25th February 1948, having completed his commitments in Italy [*L'Amico Fritz* in Parma and Ravenna and performances of *Rigoletto* and *Manon* at the San Carlo, Naples.] Callas meanwhile, through a chance meeting with a colleague of Serafin was singing her first role since the Verona debut – Isolde at the Fenice. On the strength of her 'brilliant and lyrical'[1] performances, she was engaged to sing five performances of Turandot, a role she was to sing many times [too many times?] in the next eighteen months alongside other heavy parts: Leonora in *Forza*, Aida, Brunnhilde and Kundry. She also began to sing Norma and Elvira in *I Puritani*.

But a closer look at these crucial roles must wait because di Stefano was making his debut at the Met where, according to *Musical America*, the 'walls were bulging and the ceiling resounding. Rejoicing behind the rails was at fever heat and although it was not exactly prejudicial to the success of the newcomer, it still was enough of an irritant to disturb many. In other words, what seemed to be a claque was a real nuisance, and in view of the disposition of the majority to like the tenor, an unnecessary one. The outbursts which greeted his tentative beginning grew wilder and wilder until there were bravos even in the midst of arias and one shout, 'Boy, you're a natural' which nearly upset the lad, already in an agony of nervousness. His recovery was swift however and his assurance grew as the evening waned. Some of this generous applause spilled over for the new Gilda [Carmen Gracia] and Rigoletto [Leonard Warren] but it was natural that the darling of the mob was the young hero.

'Soberer customers had reasons to approve him as well. Mr di Stefano's voice is clear, manly and fluent. It has some sweetness in the middle range and in moderate or soft passages and if he does not yield an inclination to force on attacking higher notes, his top voice should be open up and really ring. He is free from too much *portamento* and turns a phrase neatly, so that there is hope for musicality, although he was tempted into holding final high notes too long. His rhythmic sense improved after some false starts and stumbling in 'Questa o quella' from which Pietro Cimara saved him by adroit conducting. His best singing came in the third act when 'Parmi veder' was movingly and ringingly delivered. He also showed a feeling for florid style in 'La donna e mobile' and was secure in the quartet. Almost painful shyness made for stiff and decidedly amateurish acting but a feeling for the stage is obviously present and it is to be hoped that he can learn. With any sort of artistic humility, so that he is not spoiled by too much adulation too early and not led astray by the antics of the claque, the youth should be a fine lyric tenor–actor and a distinct addition to the American stage.'[2]

Four weeks later, di Stefano repeated his earliest success in Manon to similar acclaim: 'His tone was unfailingly beautiful and usually expressive and had the rich velvety sound we have seldom heard since the days of Gigli and Lauri-Volpi. His light volume was not equal to the exertions of the B flats in 'Ah! fuyez' to be sure; the exquisite pianissimos in the dream were more than adequate recompense.'[3] After both productions went on the usual Met tour to Baltimore, Boston, Dallas, Los Angeles and Cleveland, di Stefano joined the international summer festival at Mexico City for the first time in June 1948 to give further performances of *Rigoletto,* 'with extraordinary success'[4] and *Manon,* plus *La Traviata,* all with Valdengo in the baritone roles. The recorded tapes of *Manon* amply show the perfect condition of di Stefano's voice – an easy, lustrous quality with no hint of strain, delivered with all the exquisite ardour at the singer's command. In October he repeated these three roles in Rio de Janeiro where he added a new one to his repertoire: Rodolfo, in *La Bohème* opposite Toschiko Hagasawa, conducted by Questa. His Met debut in this and other new roles followed quickly in 1949.

Callas' progress in Italy had been less spectacular, so much so that after singing in the Italian provinces and winning excellent notices in Udine, Trieste, Genoa, Verona, Caracalla, Turin, Rovigo, for Leonora in *Forza* ['a first-rate actress, thoroughly prepared and secure in her top register'[5]], Isolde ['noble, almost solemn, superb queen and passionate lover'[6]], Aida, but mainly Turandot ['a large, penetrating voice, well-schooled and expressive'[7]], she seriously considered returning to America. Once again Serafin came to her rescue and, when di Stefano was breaking new ground in *Bohème,* she made her debut as Norma in two impressive performances at the important Comunale in Florence: 'Maria Callas was new to us, but after her entrance in the first act, we were immediately aware of finding ourselves in the presence of a soprano of truly significant ability. Her voice has an unusual colour, and her schooling – although rather different from what we are accustomed to hearing – has undeniable merits. Callas has created an interpretation rich in subtle and touching accents of femininity. She offers in *Norma,* besides the implacable priestess of the last act, the woman in love and then betrayed, the mother, and the friend.'[8] Much more significant still was the consummate ease with which, at five days notice, she assumed the role of Elvira in *I Puritani* at the Fenice again under Serafin, even while she was singing ['splendidly ... perfectly ... superbly'[9]] another new, very different role, Brunnhilde: 'Even the most sceptical – aware from the first notes that she was not the standard light soprano of tradition – had to acknowledge the miracle that Maria Callas accomplished, the flexibility of her limpid, beautifully poised voice, and her splendid high notes Her interpretation also has a humanity, warmth and expressiveness that one would search for in vain in the fragile, pellucid coldness of other Elviras.'[10] Yet another debut followed quickly – a 'magnificent'[11] Kundry in Rome, which she repeated the following year in the RAI Studios, the recorded tapes constituting her first complete operatic recording. It was soon necessary therefore to decide where her future lay – to continue with the heavier roles or take up the *bel canto* mantle. In choosing the latter, her career wisely followed the opposite route to di Stefano as he later began to shed the lighter roles for which his voice was especially suited, feeling obliged perhaps to assume meatier, more prestigious parts. However, at least one commentator, Stefano Riccardi, has taken the view that di Stefano's change from *lirico* to *lirico spinto* was due rather to his generosity of voice and interpretation where he felt restrained in a repertoire made of weak characters, and pale and languid leading parts.

Chapter Five

1949

Di Stefano introduced his Wilhelm Meister at his first appearance in the new season at the Met on 23rd December 1948 opposite Rise Stevens. He would not have been too pleased with the review in *Musical America*: 'The young artist was only half effective most of the time. He may never have sung the role before, and he almost certainly had not sung it in French. The second act aria 'Adieu, Mignon!' had scarcely more than occasional agreeable moments. By the time his third act opportunity 'Elle ne croyait pas' came along he was more sure of himself and gave some indication of the caressing vocalisation his audiences hope he may be able to achieve in another year or two. It will probably take him longer to learn to act, for he displayed hardly more than the barest rudiments of the craft.'[1] His Met debut on 21st January as Alfredo, although under rather difficult circumstances when Eleanor Steber took over from an indisposed Bidu Sayao at very short notice, was much better: 'Mr di Stefano sang with the lovely, velvety tone of which he is capable, and with great conviction. The opening phrases of 'Un di, felice' could hardly have sounded better and to Alfredo's denunciation of Violetta he brought an edge of passionate reality that the passage often lacks. 'De mei bollent spiriti' was only slightly less well sung.'[2] For his debut as Rodolfo opposite Licia Albanese, a role in which di Stefano was to excel, he was 'ill-at-ease in the first act but overcame first-night nerves after that and rediscovered the usual warmth and vibrancy of his voice'.[3] On another occasion when he substituted for an indisposed Jussi Bjorling, another great Rodolfo: 'Di Stefano and Albanese sang persuasively and provided vocal lustre in a performance which, despite its high spirits, showed a lack of precision in ensemble'.[4] And with Lawrence Tibbett and Patrice Munsel, 'Di Stefano returned to the role of the Duke for the first time since his Met debut. Any tentativeness which may have been apparent at that time has now completely vanished and he sang the role with the utmost confidence and finesse. Apart from his habit of pushing up to high notes which may become a bothersome mannerism if he does not correct it, di Stefano's performance warranted only the highest praise. His voice sounded remarkably free and beautiful at all times; his phrasing was constantly musical; and he delivered Verdi's melodies with a model legato, yet with the requisite pungency of accentuation. Though his acting did not penetrate far below the surface of the character, he looked well and demonstrated that his stage

demeanour is rapidly attaining a polish it has sometimes lacked before now.'[5]
At a later performance on 28th January: 'di Stefano sang with the richness of
tone and the stylish superiority that have come to be expected of him in the
part. His 'Parmi veder' was especially beautiful.'[6] Di Stefano's 43 career performances as the Duke from his debut in Lugo on 3rd August 1946 to his final
performance on 15th September 1958 carried an especial charisma. The role
was perfect for the confident sex-appeal of a handsome Sicilian. He may have
overdone it from time to time, but even at the end, witnessed by the writer in
the Vienna Staatsoper, he was full of insolent charm and unquenchable cheek.

   That season, he added three new roles: Nemorino, with Marilyn Cotlow,
Valdengo and Tajo: 'By the time he reached 'Una furtiva lagrima' di Stefano
was singing with luscious tone quality and smoothness of phrasing. His acting
was, to put it kindly, abecedarian.'[7] When he sang the role later on tour in Los
Angeles, 'after a stiff beginning, di Stefano warmed up to an amusing comic
characterisation of the love-sick swain and he sang with an ease, facility and
tonal beauty that he had previously demonstrated here in *Manon*. His beautifully
sung 'Una furtive lagrima' won a prolonged ovation.'[8] In *Gianni Schicchi* with
Tajo in the name part, di Stefano sang Rinuccio's arias 'very pleasingly, with
the exception of a forcing in climaxes which makes one tremble for the future
of his fresh, appealing young voice. If he begins shouting high notes now, for
easy applause, he will not have them in his voice later in his career when he
needs them for more serious artistic purposes.'[9] This kind of critical comment
is easy to make, but given di Stefano's relatively early decline, it should not be
overlooked. His final new role that season which he never sang again was
Fenton, opposite Albanese with Warren as Falstaff, Valdengo as Ford and
Regina Resnick as Alice, conducted by Fritz Reiner.

   It had been a busy season: for Callas in Italy, 20 performances including
four new roles. And for di Stefano at the Met, 14 performances [plus 12 on
tour], where he had also sung a similar number of new roles. Callas and di
Stefano both had relatively short international careers, a fact somewhat
concealed by their fame. They lasted barely twenty years. There are a number
of reasons for this and one often cited is the intensity of their work. Certainly,
four new roles in one season would seem too many in addition to other
performances, and there are not infrequent references to over-singing and
over-performing in the earlier years which would militate later against
maintaining a pre-eminent position on the world's stages.

   The 1948/49 seasons in America and Italy now over, both singers repaired
to Latin America during the summer months: Maria to Argentina singing her

final Turandots with del Monaco in Buenos Aires, only her second appearance as Norma [four performances] and one Aida, all under Serafin; di Stefano back in Mexico City, singing five roles, two of which were new. By a curious coincidence, both singers were married at this time. Maria was distinctly unhappy to have to set sail from Genoa on her wedding night and counted the long days before being reunited with her Italian husband. And di Stefano's operatic performances during his honeymoon with his American bride were obviously not models of concentration. Maria opened the season at the Colon: 'The Greek soprano Maria Callas was new to our public, who as an actress made an expressive Turandot and sang her part, one of extreme difficulty, with a voice we shall evaluate on another occasion because the nervousness of a performance and a slight vocal indisposition did not permit one to hear her in the fullness of her means, although one could appreciate her middle voice and the facility of her upper register.'[10] Her Norma was indeed 'much more in accordance with her vocal endowment. As an actress she achieved a vigorous and human dramatic interpretation, and from the point of view of her voice she stood out in 'Casta Diva', which she sang with a delicacy and fine musical sense and had skilful moments in the rest of her part.'[11] Her solitary Aida was a concession to the local diva's interest in that role.

Di Stefano opened his Mexico appearances with *La bohème* and *Mignon* opposite Fineschi and Simionato respectively which were 'well done',[12] and a concert of his beloved Italian songs which the broadcast tapes show were ecstatically received. But by all accounts he was ill-prepared for three new roles. As Fernando in Donizetti's *La Favorita*, he was in such difficulty that Simionato turned her back on the audience to try to feed him the right words. Yet he had 'such a pronounced musical sense that, his scant knowledge of the libretto notwithstanding, he was able to reconcile words and music perfectly.'[13] *Musical America* described his Fernando as 'splendid'![12] Certainly on the evidence of the recorded tapes, very little appears amiss. His Act I aria 'Una vergine, un angiol di Dio' is most beautifully sung, and the famous 'Spirto gentil' from Act IV is sensational enough to demand an encore. Count Almaviva in the *Barber* was surely one new part too many, even in di Stefano's early career, though 'Se il mio nome saper voi bramate' stopped the show. As for Werther, a role which fitted him like a glove and which he was still singing 15 years later, the conscientious Simionato suffered, by di Stefano's own admission, 'the torments of hell. "You are irresponsible," she said. "It is not possible to sing with someone who changes the text constantly and makes up the notes, and the music as well."'[14] But the audiences were delirious, as the live recordings of all four operas, with casts including Enzo Mascherini and Siepi, show. *Musical America,* obviously indifferent to hearing a French opera in grotesque Italian, even said *Werther* 'was, above all, a triumph for Mr di Stefano.'[12]

As we shall see, Mexico City was to welcome Maria Callas for the first time the following year. Di Stefano went instead to Italy. They repeated this summer schedule in 1951 and thus with two Mexico seasons each behind them, everything was perfectly in place for their joint arrival in 1952 when their five appearances together made an unforgettable impression and forged an unprecedented partnership.

Chapter Six

1950

The sensational success of Callas' unexpected performances as Elvira in *Puritani* in January 1949 at the Fenice had prompted her first RAI broadcast recital which in turn [November 1949] led to studio recordings of arias from *Norma*, *Puritani* and *Tristan*, on the local Cetra label as opposed to the international HMV label which di Stefano, as a Scala artist, enjoyed. The *Puritani* Mad Scene in particular created a huge impression when it was released in the UK rather later [March 1952] on the EMI Parlophone label. Lord Harewood, who had heard Maria's 1947 Gioconda in Verona, welcomed it profusely in his recently founded *Opera* magazine: 'This is the most exciting soprano singing to have come out of Italy on records since the war. The voice itself is magnificent; there is a certainty and rare command of style about the singing, and a real and affecting pathos in the treatment of the whole scene. Callas' *legato* in the slow section of the aria seems to open a whole realm of musical possibilities to her, and the mighty E flat with which she ends the *cabaletta* reminds one of her extraordinary range and power.'[1] An earlier BBC transmission of the Cetra disc had transfixed Walter Legge of EMI who immediately set out in pursuit of a permanent contract for Callas which was to become such a feature of the dawning LP era.

Meanwhile there were further new roles for both singers as the new season loomed. The Met opened on 21st November 1949 with a televised 'Rosenkavalier' with Steber, Stevens and Erna Berger. Di Stefano, of course, was the Italian singer, and not judged a success: 'He seemed ill-at-ease musically and failed to achieve the sumptuous effect the aria pre-supposes.'[2] In a second performance he still sang the aria 'shakily'.[3] His Faust three weeks later, on 23rd December, was rather better: 'Mr di Stefano used his naturally beautiful tenor voice to good effect, especially in 'Salut demeure' but he lacked both style and the conviction that he was portraying a love-sick, doomed mortal.'[4] This somehow is true. His heart was not really into Gounod's hero, certainly on the evidence of the performance on recorded tapes from 31st December conducted by Wilfred Pelletier. Later we read 'di Stefano, in beautiful voice, sang with a real sense of vocal character in the first act.'[5] and in Dallas was 'excellent'.[6] Altogether that season at the Met or on tour, he sang six roles including the Duke: on 6th January 'in one of his best roles, di Stefano sang with lovely smooth tone and commendably smooth line.'[7] As Nemorino, on 23rd January, 'di Stefano gave one of his most gratifying performances at the Met so far, singing with ease, freedom, attractive phrasing and colour, and he found ways of making his characterisation of the naïve hero more amusing than it had been last season.'[8] As Rinuccio, on 26th January, 'di Stefano made the basic points of his grateful music'.[9] And as Rodolfo, on 7th February, 'di Stefano has never sounded better in his three seasons at the Met: his high C [a real one, untransposed] was free, secure and beautiful and his entire vocal performance was technically expert and stylistically satisfying'.[10] Thus, after a troubled start, di Stefano's third season at the Met picked up well. Two more followed but he began to show signs of impatience with an entrenched system which could never accommodate the outgoing Sicilian personality. Soon the call of home would prove too strong and this the Scala would quickly take up.

Another Callas sensation was created in Naples on 20th December 49 with her assumption of Abigaille in Verdi's *Nabucco*, a magnificent performance on an evening of high emotion when the public went wild with enthusiasm, shouting "Viva l'Italia, Viva Napoli, Viva Trieste". The war had ended only four years before. The whole nation had suffered the same adversities. It was an historic moment, full of idealistic longings for the reconstruction of an Italy then on its knees. "Oh my country, so beautiful and lost…" Students were marching through the streets of the cities, skipping school with the approval of their teachers and demanding that at the least Trieste remain part of Italy. It was a time when no one could even contemplate that Italy might again be divided. The generous-hearted Neapolitan public were in this respect very similar to those who had applauded young Verdi at La Scala when his name signified the struggle for the unification of Italy. As for Callas herself, the critics were unequivocal: 'Callas displayed an uncommon dramatic flair. She astonished with both the size and range of her voice which combines the power of a dramatic soprano and the high notes of a light soprano.'[11] 'The dramatic situation, besides offering a display of vocal fireworks, was also revealed through the force and incisiveness of her temperament. Her splendid voice, smoothly produced throughout its wide range, was equal to all of the requirements of the part including the most difficult florid passages.'[12] She never sang Abigaille again, an unsympathetic role which she disliked, and continued with her increasingly familiar Norma [in the Fenice with 'extraordinary musical abandon'[13]], Aida [in Brescia] and Isolde [in Rome, where 'she makes us feel the enchantment of the memorable parts of the opera.'][14] A month later came an opportunity to which she responded and then regretted. On 12th February, Renata Tebaldi had embarked on a run of ten Aidas at La

Scala. Before the seventh on 12th April, she became indisposed and Maria agreed to take over: after all, she had waited nearly three years to be invited. From day one at the post-war Scala, Renata Tebaldi had been the preferred soprano. She enjoyed the patronage of Toscanini, no less, as, for example, did Elisabeth Schwarzkopf of Herbert von Karajan. Of course, Maria Callas had Tullio Serafin but, strange to relate, that was less a help than a hindrance because, even before Maria arrived in Italy, he was *persona non grata* at the famous Milan house. We may note that he looked after Maria in Verona, Venice, Genoa, Turin, Florence, Rome, Buenos Aires, Naples and São Paulo, but during the entire Callas era [1947-1965], he never once conducted her or anybody else at La Scala. Fortunately [and again strangely], this did not apply to the EMI Scala series of 1953 onwards when he was in charge of no fewer than eighteen recordings.

At the Scala on 12th April 1950, neither the audience nor the critics were friendly towards Callas' Aida: 'I did not care for Maria Callas, who, although

PALACIO DE BELLAS ARTES, MEXICO CITY 1950-1952
The Soprano of the Century

9th August 2001. The author's pilgrimage fifty years later

she has been singing for a while, is new to La Scala. She obviously possesses temperament and a fine musicality but her scale is uneven. She seems to improvise differently, from note to note, the method and technique of her vocal production. She does not have clear diction and she also forces her high notes, thereby jeopardising the security of her intonation.'[15] Nor was the management courteous and she vowed never to return without a proper contract which Ghiringhelli withheld for as long as he could. His favoured Italian diva duly recovered for the 10th and last performance.

The lingering pangs of unease felt by the Greek-American soprano in post-war Italy were now similarly visiting the Sicilian tenor in the United States. For while she headed west towards America – albeit Latin América – he, ironically, for the first time returned to the land of his fathers to give them four of his most celebrated roles: Nadir and Rodolfo at Verona, Nemorino in Naples and Des Grieux in Trieste. What was to be one of his last performances in *I Pescatori di perle* drew the first comment on his career from the newly founded *Opera* magazine. J.J. Jarvis wrote: 'Di Stefano was in excellent form, a thrilling voice used with intelligence and a rare sense of style. His performance was only marred by a tendency on two occasions to sing flat.'[16] No such support came from little-known Mexico where Maria also sang four roles to such spectacular effect that she was soon advertised on the front of the Palacio de Bellas Artes, – a magnificent domed theatre built entirely in marble in 1925, so heavy that the entire building has already sunk three feet - as "LA SOPRANO ABSOLUTA DEL SIGLO" – still, in 1950, only midway through the century! First to be heard was her now usual calling-card, Norma. The reaction was a trifle mixed. Three critics: 'She is without a doubt a good actress, she has an imposing presence and her school of singing is one that can easily cope with the greatest difficulties. But the timbre of her voice is very uneven and does not always fulfil to the requirements of profound delight.'[17] 'Maria Callas is undoubtedly an extraordinary singer. The public has not even had time to evaluate her, and nonetheless, the feeling of being confronted with such an exceptional voice was in the air. It has been a long time since a soprano in such a class has been heard in Mexico; and in Maria Callas we meet not only her remarkable extended range, but also the special colour, the perfect agility, and the volume necessary for enabling us to say that in the Greek soprano there exists the quality of pure gold.'[18] 'Maria Meneghini Callas is a supreme soprano who sings the very high notes, and even staccatos, of a coloratura, as well as very low notes appropriate not even to a mezzo, but to an authentic contralto. What an admirable extension of the voice. We were enchanted, and if anything saddened us at the conclusion of such a glorious performance, it was that we would never again hear another such Norma in our life.'[19]

But it was the famous E flat at the conclusion of the Act 2 of *Aida* that aroused the city's unquenchable passion for the soprano, as Mariano Paes wrote in *Excelsior*: 'Don Antonio Caraza Campos, who has been directing the National Opera with such success for five years, tells us that while he was examining the score with Maria Callas, he told her that the high E flat had not been heard here since the distant times of the great Angela Peralta ... and, according to him, he heard Maestro Guichenne suggest to Callas that she perform the heroic deed. She resisted doing it, but finally agreed during Saturday's performance. In the heat of the moment, at the conclusion of the great scene, this woman's vocal organ rose to the most glorious heights, leaving us literally 'knocked out.'[20] It also knocked out the vocal bad manners of the tenor. *Tosca* followed which she had not sung since her performances in Athens in 1943. The supreme artistic achievement, however, was her assumption for the first time of Leonora in *Il Trovatore,* where her command of line and phrase, as heard on the broadcast tapes, was total. She was to sing the great Act IV aria many times, always to breathtaking effect, and never more so than on 20th July 1950.

Chapter Seven

1951

The summer over, both singers once again prepared themselves for important debuts. First came di Stefano on 28th September 1950 at San Francisco: Edgardo in *Lucia*, 'producing some unusually fine vocalism'[1] Three days later he took part in the first of three concerts, singing two arias – Flotow's 'M'appari' and 'O Souverain' from *Le Cid* which curiously he never repeated. Of the two, Massenet's glorious aria is exceptional, sung with all the warmth, poise and ardour at di Stefano's command. In the Donizetti opera, he appeared opposite Lily Pons, with whose very experienced Lucia a six-year Maria Callas had long before found fault. "I could do much better," she said, as di Stefano found to his delight when he next sang the role two years later at Callas' debut performance in Mexico City. Before that, of course, she had achieved much: a taste in comedy with Fiorilla in Rossini's *Turco*, the first Callas performance to be reviewed in *Opera*: 'Maria Callas was the surprise of the evening in that she sang a soprano leggiera role with the utmost ease, making it difficult to believe that she can be the perfect interpreter of both Turandot and Isolde. In Act I she astounded everyone in the theatre by emitting a perfectly pitched high and soft E flat at the end of an extremely attractive and vocally difficult aria.'[2] A single performance of Aida on October 2nd in Rome caught on tape gives us our first taste of Callas in the title role. Her incomparable Violetta was born in Florence on 14th January 1951, and, most blazingly significant of all, she sang Elena in *I vespri siciliani* as part of the Verdi anniversary celebrations at the Maggio Musicale Fiorentino: 'There was an assurance and a tragic bravura about her singing that was frequently thrilling…her dramatic flair was very much in evidence in the smooth cavatina and exhortary cabaletta with which she roused the Sicilians against the French in Act I and the smouldering fury of 'Il vostro fato e in vostro mani' was extraordinary.'[3] So wrote Giuseppe Pugliese in *Opera*, a view shared by the magazine's founder, Lord Harewood and its future editor, Harold Rosenthal. It was an event which always attracted the sort of international attention which Callas had hitherto been denied. It was a further irony of their story that, just when Callas secured a contract with the mighty Scala from a hounded Ghiringhelli at this Florence festival, di Stefano should soon be relinquishing his at the Met, one of the world's other great opera houses. Maria had never come by the early success which di Stefano had rightly enjoyed and he would soon find he needed the sort of support at the Scala that her new status could in the course of time provide.

Meanwhile, he appeared in four of his roles at the Met: first Alfredo on 19th November when 'the tenor sang melodiously and true to pitch.'[4] His next role Count Almaviva in the *Barber* on 6th December was, predictably, a big mistake: 'di Stefano trying his hand at a florid role was many fathoms beyond his depth. He did not sing the ornamental passages badly; much of the time, instead, he did not sing them at all. Scales emerged as smears; three-note turns were simplified into staccato-accented single notes. He should not have been willing to sing the role in public – the management should not have been willing to let him do so.'[5] A further performance [22nd December] 'fared no better'.[6] By the end of the following month, however, we read that 'di Stefano had patently been working at his music, for he now sang most of the *coloratura* accurately and completely, and in general used his beautiful voice in the interests of tastefulness and expression.'[7] In *Faust* on 24th January 'he accomplished a fabulous diminuendo on a beautifully produced high C in 'Salut demeure''[8] which Rudolf Bing later described as his greatest single moment as manager of the Met. Of two performances of *La bohème* we read: 'di Stefano sang [opposite Sayao] with strong line, when he was not taking liberties and had considerable velvet in his tones'[9] and 'he was in spectacularly fine voice and sang Rodolfo's music [opposite Albanese] with as continuous an outpouring of beautiful tenor tone as the Met can offer nowadays.'[10]

He also took part in the famous Toscanini performance of Verdi's Requiem on 27th January 1951 in Carnegie Hall. He had recently recorded a couple of Sicilian songs, 'Abballati' and 'Muttetti di lu Paliu', in the RCA studios which the veteran conductor admired as did the *Gramophone* critic, Oliver King: 'I have seldom encountered a more thoroughly satisfactory vocal record. Of course, in the nature things, it is of limited appeal, and I confess that my Italian does not extend to being able to follow the Sicilian dialect in which it is sung. But I do earnestly recommend all readers to listen to this little gem. It is *the* vocal record of the month, and probably of the year. What a superb artist di Stefano is!'[11] At 29, perhaps di Stefano was not a perfect choice for the Requiem, but 'his naturally warm, limpid voice and his innate musical enthusiasm made up in large measure technical shortcomings.'[12] Harold Rosenthal in *Opera* reviewing the issue on LP in 1957 said that 'in 1951 di Stefano was still able to produce a beautiful covered tone when needed and in the *Hostias* sounds like a young Gigli',[13] and Alec Robertson in *Gramophone* likewise 'found him in fine voice and singing in better style and with more consideration for his colleagues than he [would do] in the de Sabata recording.'[14] Probably Toscanini's brisker tempo would account for this. Under the conductor's watchful eye, di Stefano's launching of the Kyrie in one breath is as thrilling as the composer would have surely intended.

Di Stefano also at this time recorded a number of items from *La bohème* which enjoyed much success despite Alec Robertson's quibbles in *Gramophone*, 'It must be very difficult to sing 'Che gelida manina' as if for the first time and I must confess that I found di Stefano's rendering rather mannered and smudgy in outline. His voice, which I have not heard for some time, sounds as fine as ever in itself, but he approaches his top C with much circumspection. It is a good and true note but he does not open out on it; it's an interesting bit of vocal adjustment. In the duet with Leonard Warren, di Stefano sings more sensitively and uses more variety of tone; indeed it is well sung by both of the artists, in as excellent an ensemble as one could wish. The quartet is also well sung, with plenty of Italian fervour, but with less beauty of tone and refinement of detail than in the Decca complete recording. Di Stefano, whose voice, as such, is finer than that of Prandelli, is moving in his emotional outburst.'[15] Harold Rosenthal in *Opera* is even more enthusiastic: 'Di Stefano, after a promising start to his career, has disappointed, but here, with authentic gold in the voice, he is back to his old form; he sings the 'racconto' with a welcome sweetness of tone; there is much to admire here though he obviously modelled himself on Gigli.'[16] In a later release [November 1954] he opines that 'di Stefano is probably the best Rodolfo on records' and that 'he and Leonard Warren are excellent in the last act duet',[17] a view supported by Philip Hope-Wallace in *Gramophone*. When these items were issued on an LP compilation in 1973, Alan Blyth, of the new generation of critics, even more favourably and accurately observed that 'the young di Stefano banishes memories of his self-indulgent, downward transposed 'Che gelida' at his recent [1973] recital in London with his glorious performance here, impassioned, 'straight' and in the right key, with a really thrilling, open top C, and the final phrase in one breath. He and Albanese partner each finely in 'O soave fanciulla', and, with Warren, di Stefano begins their duet with just the right creamy half-voice, only opening up at the reprise. A Met *Bohème* with these three artists must have been worth going a long way to hear.'[18] Di Stefano's Rodolfo was indeed worth going a long way to hear, or so the writer and three teacher colleagues thought in 1963 when they absented themselves from a games afternoon to reach London from Wakefield, 200 miles away, in time for curtain up. It was not one of the happiest of decisions as the report on pages 143-144 makes clear, though it was a thrill to hear him sing opposite my favourite Covent Garden Mimi, Joan Carlyle. Di Stefano's 104 performances of the role from 3rd March 1948 in Rio de Janeiro to 22nd July 1972 in Benevento gave countless pleasure, as did his glorious recording in 1956 with Callas.

Once again, the summer arrangements echoed the previous year; Callas was bound for Mexico City and di Stefano for Verona, thus keeping the Atlantic crossings business in good shape. But 1951 was to be different in one very important respect. After both artists repeated their triumphs of 1950 [another *Aida* E flat, much to del Monaco's fury; a lovely *Traviata* with Cesare Valletti from Callas, and five 'memorable' performances of *Manon* with 'some beautiful singing from di Stefano and Magda Olivero'],[19] they joined a host of other great names for much excitement in Brazil, the plaything of Barreto Pinto, a local millionaire businessman and impresario. Nothing he liked better than to arrange a programme which would maximise rivalries, and 1951 was one of his best. The mythical feud between Callas and Tebaldi probably began here and their fans milked it to death once Callas arrived at La Scala. Previously, they had hardly met; Callas, however, as we have seen, was well aware of Ghiringhelli's preference for Tebaldi. Into this operatic cauldron, with his Des Grieux in tow, was plunged di Stefano, who, having hitherto never sung on stage with either soprano, within a week had partnered both; and both in *Traviata*, of all operas, the supreme test. Tebaldi had earlier failed in it at La Scala, less than a month after Callas' triumphant debut in the role in Florence; she, Callas, was insisting on its inclusion in her Scala contract to seal her supremacy. Di Stefano witnessed the opening shots with Tebaldi's arrival in Rio de Janeiro on 28th August for *La bohème* opposite his Rodolfo. Then they all met up in São Paulo for three *Traviatas* where Callas had had to cancel an *Aida* before making her debut in *Norma*. Audience reaction was, of course, divided between the rivals' Violettas and later Toscas, Tebaldi's Mimi and Callas' Norma and tempers flew over encores at a Gala concert in Rio. Callas left in high dudgeon with both singer and impresario. But the performance of *La Traviata* on 9th September 1951 in the Theatro Municipal, São Paulo, built in 1904 in the style of Charles Garnier's monumental Paris Opéra where seven years later Callas would give the 'Gala of the Century', was an historic occasion because it proved to be the first, last and only time that what a critic was later to describe as EMI's unbeatable line-up – Callas, di Stefano, Gobbi, under Serafin – were ever on stage together. Tito Gobbi in his autobiography remembered it well: 'I cannot believe that anyone else in the whole history of the work ever sang that first act as she sang it then. Later perhaps she looked the part more convincingly, later she may have added certain refinements to her characterisation of the role, but I find it impossible to describe the electrifying brilliance of the coloratura, the beauty, the sheer magic of that sound which she poured out then. And with it – perfect diction, colour, inflection and, above all, feeling. It was something one hears only once in a lifetime. Indeed, one was fortunate to hear it at all!'[20] The local newspaper, *O Estado de São Paulo* was of the same mind: the soprano got two columns, the tenor and baritone hardly two lines between them!

Amidst the hurly-burly of this Brazilian season, it is likely that both Callas and di Stefano were too busy singing other operas opposite other singers to consider the significance of their first meeting in São Paulo. Mexico a year

A uniquely historic performance

later was much more important when Callas declared that "this was the tenor we need for the [EMI] recordings," and di Stefano was impressed by her power: "She sang like a man". Peter Hutchinson's assertion that Callas was brought to real greatness by having worked with di Stefano in Mexico, and lost it again when he stopped working with her, is surely an over-simplification. But certainly the ensuing recordings especially point to a joint inspiration – noted for example by Philip Hope-Wallace in *Rigoletto,*and by others in *Tosca, Bohème, Ballo, Cavalleria, Lucia,* and above all, *Manon Lescaut.* And their last Scala collaboration on stage – *Ballo* in 1957 – was a *tour de force.* The 1951 *Traviata* at São Paulo, being a 'soprano' opera, would not have engaged very much interest on the tenor's part, especially a tenor of four years' standing at the Met when Callas had yet to justify her new contract at La Scala. *Puritani* in Mexico in 1952 would prove a much sterner test. Nevertheless, whilst São Paulo is but one stop on the Brazilian circuit and Mexico City had its own festival by which time Callas was an established star and di Stefano had left the Met, the great Brazilian city had proved an admirable mid-wife for the Callas/ di Stefano phenomenon.

Chapter Eight

1952

In the relative calm of the new seasons back, respectively, at the Met and in Italy, di Stefano repeated his familiar roles in what was to be his last and probably least successful season at the Met. Reviews in *Musical America* point to an air of boredom and indifference which suggest a much-needed change of scene. This was indeed provided with his impending move to Italy where he would soon become the leading tenor at La Scala when Maria Callas had suddenly become its prima donna.

Meanwhile, we read in *Musical America* that when, at the beginning of the 1951/52 season, di Stefano replaced an indisposed Bjorling as Rodolfo: 'Someone should at least teach him to time his movement at the very end so as not to spoil Puccini's climax. Di Stefano made a good deal more use of expressive devices than Victoria de los Angeles but did not communicate very much ardour. His acting was vestigal'.[1] Rather worse, given the fame of di Stefano's success as Des Grieux was the report in *Opera* of Massenet's *Manon* on 7th December [the same night, incidentally, which set in motion Callas' monumental Scala career with Verdi's *I vespri siciliani*]: 'It was not a happy idea to bring back *Manon* to the Met: the house is too large for this fragile work, Cleva did not seem to have the flair for this French score and the cast, including di Stefano, did not seem happy in their roles.'[2] Two critics in *Musical America*, respectively James Hinton Jnr and Cecil Smith, confirmed this view: 'Di Stefano, whose voice is in some ways almost ideally suited to Des Grieux's music, spent the evening subverting this natural advantage. He had some stirring moments from the purely tonal standpoint, but there was little Byronism, little line, and almost no special feeling for Massenet's music about his performance. He scooped up to notes, pushed his voice until the tone became ugly and often squeezed it sharp on the top notes. He did his best singing in the first ten seconds of 'La rêve' but spoiled it at that point with a great tasteless *portamento* and blast of tone. He looked plebian and acted without conviction.'[3] Two weeks later [December 26th] 'di Stefano provided many moments of tonal beauty but he continued to show few signs of any effort to find out what the role is about either musically or stylistically.'[4] At another performance [1st January 1952]: 'di Stefano did not understand the character of Des Grieux but his voice sounded disarmingly warm and vital during much of the time. Nothing could be said in defence of the style of his performance. Yet there is real excitement in his singing, not merely the loud passages but in the diaphanous pianissimos that he was able to spin out.'[5] Finally by 6th March, 'he is stylistically somewhat improved'[6] but a trifle late!

On 11th December, he was in good voice for Alfredo, though 'his command of the score seemed insecure.' On the 22nd, as the Duke, 'di Stefano looked a little on the lump side in his Renaissance costume and did not act with much point and snap. His voice sounded extremely well except when he squeezed it over the pitch but he didn't seem entirely sure of the notes.'[7] Worst of all, however, was his debut as Pinkerton in *Madama Butterfly* which was not yet nearly the success it was later to be: 'Di Stefano's Pinkerton was lifeless in action and utterly routine in song. Many tenors sound better in this Puccini score than in almost any other music. Di Stefano, perhaps because he seemed to be still thinking hard about the notes, sounded less well than usual. His gestures would have scarcely alarmed a mosquito.'[8] Cecil Smith reviewing the season in *Opera* [May '52] observed that di Stefano 'had tended to push his lyric voice until some of the velvet it once had seemed to be permanently rubbed off'.[9] Even before the end of that season, he had taken a brief Italian break in Trieste to sing Werther and in Modena to sing in *Manon* opposite Magda Olivero where he had a bad cold: 'By the end of the third act he had completely lost his voice. After stopping the orchestra, he addressed the audience, telling them it was useless for him to go on as he could barely even speak let alone sing. The audience were most sympathetic and he continued, recovering by the end of the last act which was sung with his usual style. The audience cheered him at the close of the opera for about twenty-five minutes.'[10] He was also back in Sicily to give performances of *Rigoletto, L'Amico Fritz* and *Tosca*, in readiness for his return to the Scala in December 1952.

Callas, for her part, went from strength to strength: first, a magnificent opening to the 1951 Scala season when she repeated her Florence triumph as the Duchess Elena, which at a stroke wiped out four years in the operatic wilderness. Within a fortnight, she at last sang her renowned Norma in the operatic holy of holies to ecstatic reviews: 'The importance of this performance lay in the consummate artistry of Miss Callas who is not only Italy's finest dramatic-lyric soprano but also an actress of exceptional gifts and stage presence. She electrified the audience by her very presence even before singing a note. Once she began to sing, each phrase came out effortlessly and the listeners knew from the first tone of a phrase that she felt instinctively as well as consciously just where and how that phrase would end. She never rushed and she never dragged. Her tones came out round and full, with a legato like that of a stringed instrument. Her agility was breathtaking. Hers is not a light voice but she negotiated the most difficult coloratura without batting an eye, and her downward glissandi made cold shivers run up and down the hearer's spine. There was occasionally a slight tendency to shrillness and hardness on the high notes, although her pitch was faultless. It is to be hoped that this defect resulted from fatigue, for it would be sad to hear so superb an instrument lose any of its sheen.'[11] After her Elena and Norma, Callas appeared as an even less familiar heroine, Constanza in *Il Ratto dal Seraglio*, the singer's only sortie into Mozart, a splendid coloratura role which had critics gasping: 'In Maria Meneghini Callas, La Scala found a secure, exceptionally agile and vibrant interpreter of this tremendously difficult role because of the *tessitura* and perilous acrobatism of the running passages which she attacked and conquered with a vocal virtuosity that earned her unanimous admiration and clamorous ovations. Even though it was completely different from the heavier *spinto* parts she had been singing at La Scala lately, she sang with delicacy and feeling, reaching a climax in the difficult aria during the second act.'[12] Her concert performance of 'Tutte le torture' in San Remo nearly three years later on 27th December 1954 gives us a very good idea of just how startling it had been.

Immediately afterwards, Tebaldi took over the Scala schedules as Margherita in Boito's *Mefistofele* and as Adriana Lecouvreur in Cilea's opera, a practice which Ghiringhelli was careful to adopt to keep the 'rivals' apart until Tebaldi withdrew three years later. One further triumph remained before the arrival of summer excitements. Callas' success the previous year in Florence had secured her return to the Rossini 150th anniversary celebrations in his rarely performed *Armida* in which Callas, if anything, created an even more sensational impression. The broadcast recording gives some idea of the reckless, breathtaking bravado with which she sang the powerful lines and passionate high notes: 'Where are such roulades, such trills, leaps, such speed and fireworks demanded of the singer? One can readily believe that no one today save Maria Callas, undisputedly the finest woman singer on the Italian stage, could possibly negotiate the incredibly difficult part and make it sound like music.'[13] 'It is possible to feel that phrases beneath the florid passages are far too much overlaid with ornament; but it is impossible to regret it when Maria Callas is singing them. This American-born Greek soprano deserves fully the considerable reputation she has won, for she must be one of the most exciting singers on the stage today. Her presence is imperious, her coloratura not piping and pretty, but powerful and dramatic. It must be noted that a nasty edge crept into the tone from time to time; but when she sailed up a two-octave chromatic scale and cascaded down again the effect was electrifying. Her brilliance continually startled and delighted throughout the opera. But whenever tenderness and sensuous charm were required, she was less moving. This seems to be her present limitation; it may well disappear quite soon.'[14] And so indeed it did as her singing of Bellini roles would testify.

★   ★   ★

Di Stefano has always said that it was his destiny to sing with Callas. At this point in the narrative, one has to feel that this must be true because so many factors are engaged. La Scala itself is probably the key. With five seasons at the Met behind him, di Stefano was set fair to return to the great Italian house. Likewise having rejected Callas for four years, La Scala's future lay with her. Their collaboration therefore seemed inevitable and it was sealed for ever, first on stage and then in the studio, as we shall now see.

At the conclusion of the *Armida* run in Florence and the Met tour in America, both singers respectively packed their bags and made for Mexico City where expectation was at fever pitch. Di Stefano was back to revive memories of his exploits in 1948 and 1949, and Callas was to cap her huge successes of 1950 and 1951. 1952 therefore marked what a Thomas Hardy poem once called 'The Convergence of the Twain'. They were to sing five operas, two [*Lucia* and *Rigoletto*] new to the soprano, and two [*I Puritani* and *Tosca*] new to the tenor. As Saloman Kahan outlined in *Musical America*: 'The two outstanding elements of the 10th anniversary season were the first production of an opera dealing with the Spanish invasion of Mexico by a Mexican composer, Ricardo Castro Atzimba, and the brilliant work of two singers, Maria Meneghini Callas and Giuseppe di Stefano. The season began auspiciously with *I Puritani*. It proved an excellent vehicle for the magnificent vocal and histrionic art of Callas whose Elvira was impressive from every angle. She is undoubtedly one of the greatest sopranos of our time. Di Stefano sang and acted beautifully in the difficult part of Lord Arthur Talbot. The rest of the cast was adequate in a score that abounds in taxing pages. Picco conducted expertly. Mugnai conducted a *Traviata* in which Callas' portrayal of Violetta will not be soon forgotten. Di Stefano's Alfredo was memorable too but Campolonghi's Germont was less satisfactory. In the title role of *Lucia* which she had never sung before, Callas again excelled. The ovation after the Mad Scene, which had to be repeated, lasted twenty minutes. Local critics expressed the opinion that Callas' vocal achievement as Lucia was greater than that of

Luisa Tetrazzini whose singing is still vividly remembered here. Di Stefano was a worthy Edgardo. Picco had the orchestra and singers well under control. As an anti-climax, came a pedestrian performance of *Rigoletto*, Campolonghi was neither vocally nor histrionically up to Verdi's demands, di Stefano's Duke far from outstanding, and Callas' Gilda, not an ideal role for her, did not improve the situation. The best singing of the evening was contributed by Ruffino as Sparfucile and Garcia as Maddelena. Mugnai conducted. Callas and di Stefano were once more up to expectations in *Tosca* conducted with spirit by Picco.'[15]

Inevitably, these performances in Mexico City have been superseded by what was to follow. But the broadcast tapes show that they are certainly not unworthy of scrutiny. *Traviata* is probably the best; *Rigoletto* certainly the worst. News of Callas' spell-binding Elvira in *Puritani* ensured an arresting start to the season. It was her thirteenth performance of the role, having, after Venice, revived it in Catania, Florence and Rome. It is an impressive performance but she had to contend, *pace* Kahan, with some very poor direction in the pit. Her 'Son vergine' is exquisite, rising passionately to a high E flat. In 'Vieni al tempio', singing an octave above the line, her high C's and D are magnificent, quite outclassing what we later hear on the EMI recording. Conversely, the Mad Scene is much worse, far too slow with a tempo that cripples that climactic E flat. Perhaps the real surprise of the evening is di Stefano's debut as Arturo, who makes a huge impression in his famous entrance 'A te o caro', much more tender, assured, and unstrained than in the studio recording, though the ensemble is less good. The final 'Credea misera' gives only a verse each to the tenor and soprano but enables di Stefano to proceed again to a really secure D flat and the finale is less perfunctory than Serafin's.

Callas' debut as Lucia followed and that was equally assured. The Act I aria is topped by a superb E flat. Her duet with di Stefano's more experienced Edgardo was boldly sung, so much so that both singers marched ahead of the beat as the conclusion beckoned. Lucia's duet with her brother ended with another fearless E flat but was out-lasted by the baritone, as Sordello was later to do to his cost four years later at the Met. The sextet went quite well, especially when di Stefano joined the B flats, but the baritone is heard growling too obtrusively throughout. The Mad Scene, despite one failed E flat, created such a sensation that the whole thing was encored. Di Stefano, nerves not withstanding, then delivered his two arias, just a trifle too speedily on this occasion; in the EMI recording the following year under Serafin, they go perfectly.

'LA TRAVIATA' 3rd June 1952 MEXICO CITY
'Uno duetto del siglo' [de los Reyes] – a duo of the century

Callas was in magnificent voice for her Violetta and was broadly matched by di Stefano's ardent Alfredo who, for once took the high top B in 'Amor e palpito dell'universo intero' before his partner launched her concluding E flat. Her 'Amami, Alfredo, quant'io t'amo' was monumental but strangely it aroused no applause. At a perfect pace, she rode the wonderful finale to Act II scene 2 beautifully, following di Stefano's manic outburst, making an unexpected rise from E flat, G, B flat to E flat in alt seem completely natural, though it's seldom, if ever, done. This was the season when neither singer would duck an optional high note if it were on offer! Under Giulini, the Scala performance three years later [eventually issued by EMI] would be different.

Neither singer excelled themselves in the travesty which followed. The broadcast tape of *Rigoletto* is dominated by the prompter who did his loudest to keep all and sundry on board. A plethora of optional high notes [mostly good ones] was again much in evidence and di Stefano's 'La donna e mobile' was, as usual in these parts, encored. But altogether it is a relief to turn to their final offering that summer – *Tosca*. Callas, of course, had first sung the role at 18 in Athens [in 1942] and had revived it two years previously in Mexico City and on four subsequent occasions. And it marked di Stefano's debut as Cavaradossi, a role in which he would become famous. What is remarkable about this performance is that it so closely resembles what each singer offered de Sabata just over a year later when they made the now legendary recording for EMI. Callas' raillery may be less subtle in the love duet and she jumps ahead of the beat for her climactic B flat in 'Vissi d'arte', but it is nevertheless the real, ripe thing. Di Stefano's two arias are as to the manner born; an ovation of over two minutes forced an encore of 'E lucevan'. This was the stuff of history.

Never one to stint, di Stefano then gave the Mexicans his 'splendid' Des Grieux', his 'deeply touching' Werther, and 'one of the best' Rodolfos. Di Stefano was to return many times to Mexico City; Callas never did, despite a tearful farewell on the part of the artist, chorus and audience which rather put out the tenor – a short-lived upset like all their squabbles except the last [*Ballo* in 1957], by which time their stage collaboration had run its course, which meant inevitably that their studio recordings, the chief glory many would say of the partnership, would also be at an end. Of course, the miracle is that they ever started, one of the great achievements of the gramophone. When they met in Mexico City in 1952, neither artist had recorded a complete opera in the studio and the time was now ripe technologically, very ripe indeed, because the LP era, ideal for opera, was just dawning. Indeed, on the

Decca label, it had already begun in the shape of Tebaldi, partnered variously by Prandelli, Campora and del Monaco, in popular Puccini and Verdi. Perhaps it could be argued that Callas' 'late' arrival at La Scala and di Stefano's 'absence' in New York had wasted several 'recording years' when their voices were at their most resplendent. But fortunately EMI [ie. the HMV and Columbia labels] were initially nervous about LP strategy and their eventual decision to go ahead coincided exactly with Callas' contract. Di Stefano, already an EMI artist on the HMV label, fell perfectly into place, especially after Mexico. The Decca artists [lusty Scala singers] may have stolen a march on EMI, but the latter felt rightly that the future lay with the extraordinary Maria Callas and the Scala-bound di Stefano. The magnificent Columbia Scala series on record was thus born at precisely the time when these two great artists first appeared on the Scala stage, the one event clearly reflecting the other. Of the first thirty performances given in the new Scala 1952/53 season, over half had either Callas or di Stefano, or both, on the stage.

Chapter Nine

1953

Prior to the eagerly awaited excitements of the forthcoming Scala season, Callas sang two roles at Verona. Peter Dragadze in *Opera* found her less at home as Gioconda than in her usual roles. But her Violetta was 'the greatest thrill of the season; hearing Callas sing Violetta was an unforgettable experience. Her acting technique is of the simplest and she appears to make no effort to dramatise the situation physically, as the colour of her voice clearly depicts every emotion and sensation she is experiencing. The difficult 'E strano' was sung with such amazing ease and lack of effort that one had the impression that she could go on singing indefinitely without losing strength and the perfect line of her voice.'[1]

Verdi's *Macbeth* provided a memorable Scala opening on 7th December 1952. Peter Dragadze was impressed: 'Poor lighting and static staging were amply compensated by some really beautiful singing from Maria Callas as Lady Macbeth and Enzo Mascherini as Macbeth. Callas gave her part the depth and feeling that only she now can give to such a dramatic role, with the truly heart-rending climax to the sleepwalking scene, after which she had seven enthusiastic calls which for the Scala is a lot. Callas' voice, even since last season has improved a great deal, and the second passagio on high B natural and C that she formerly had in her voice has now completely cleared giving her an equally coloured vocal line from top to bottom. The biggest surprise was Mascherini's Macbeth, in which part he gave a great performance of high artistic and vocal standards, balanced and sustained throughout the whole opera.'[2] A 'disappointing' *L'Amore di Danae* by Richard Strauss, given its first performance in Italy, intervened before di Stefano appeared as Rodolfo in *Bohème*, 'conducted and interpreted with extreme finesse by Victor de Sabata. Although his voice certainly is not as perfect as it was three years ago, he sang his role with a rich warm vocal colour.'[3] Before the month was out, both artists appeared in *La Gioconda,* Callas for the last time; di Stefano for the first. 'Callas was not up to her usual standard in this role as her voice sounded tired, especially in the heavy spinto passges. Di Stefano sang cleanly, acted intelligently and won the immediate sympathy of the public on his first entrance by the warmth and security of his voice.'[4] The local critic praised the new partnership: 'No less dazzling in glories and merits than di Stefano, but slightly diminished by the too much that she is bestowing upon operatic audiences, was Maria

'LA GIOCONDA' 26th December 1952 LA SCALA
Giuseppe di Stefano and Maria Callas [with Ebe Stignani] are applauded for the first time
together by the Scala audience

Callas a Gioconda equally passionate and delicate.'[5] So much then for their Scala debut together. Within a month they would be in the studio recording their first complete opera together *Lucia di Lammermoor*. *La Gioconda* played a significant part in Callas' career: the Verona debut, of course, but it was also her first complete recording [on Cetra 1952] and one of her last for EMI – one of her very greatest, recorded in September 1959 in the wake of her new passion for Onassis. Her singing of the role, in Act IV particularly has a special distinction; her ultimately magnanimous deference to the mezzo is heart-breaking and puts the tenor in a very bad light. Di Stefano took his wonderful Enzo to Naples, Rome, Verona and Chicago. When he recorded it with Zinka Milanov [just too late in her career], captured in the rich glow of the new stereo era, his Enzo was certainly good enough to win our forgiveness. The Scala performances above were not broadcast so we can only imagine their Gioconda and Enzo together from their respective performances on disc.

Maria's third and final appearance at La Scala that season was her magnificent Leonora in *Il Trovatore*. But before that and after five performances of *La traviata* at the Fenice and in Rome where Cynthia Jolly in *Opera* reports: 'Traviata drew a storm of disapproval from the local press which found in Maria Callas an unsuitable Violetta; the public undaunted went to see her in large numbers and quarrelled over her loudly in the foyers. Even the ushers took sides; one would be enchanted by her sheer expertise and the other shocked by her lack of feeling in the part and *la voce troppo forte*. Even the most unprejudiced were startled by the unusual things she put in and the customary things she left out. An exciting, questionable performance, in fact, from a magnificent and highly capricious singer. The first act succeeded admirably if untraditionally, when one remembers the bird-like coloratura Violetta is used to receiving. This, clear-cut and sturdy, belonged to the Callas of *Armida*; and never have I heard the descending couples of semiquavers [when she hears Alfredo outside] so beautifully handled. She seems to have acquired a new beauty of tone in the high register and the whole voice is better blended. In the second act, however, more than dramatic brilliance and vocal relaxation is required and here she failed to find true tenderness or penetrate the pain of renunciation. 'Amami Alfredo' was disappointing and she disagreed violently with the conductor at the difficult rhythmical transition to 'Morr, la mia memoria' The third act was a scene after her own heart, but in the fourth, she did not fully exploit the tragedy, using histrionic means instead of the infinite variety of subtle changes which Verdi presents to the singer in this scene.'[6] This, of course, was the production to be recorded on Cetra the following September. She then gave her first performances of *Lucia* since Mexico City during the Florence Maggio Musicale, first with Lauri-Volpi and then with di Stefano. The older tenor had partnered her Naples Leonora in January 1951 [and had been booed for his efforts], and in May the following year in three performances of *Puritani* in Rome immediately prior to her departure for Mexico City, by way of preparation perhaps, as *Opera* reported: 'This all-purpose soprano, a prototype of the legendary singers of old, makes a buxom Elvira who is vaguely disconcerted when she has no virtuoso flights in view. Her tone is not uniformly beautiful but the general impression is overpowering. Her *bel canto* style is liable to sudden bursts and protuberances which disappear entirely in passages of agility, so that her descending scales are like rippling water. Add to that her proudly confident sense of the stage and you have one of the singing heroines of the 20th century'.[5] The previous February, they had shared her second Martini and Rossi concert at the RAI studios, very narrowly missing di Stefano's first with Lina Pagliughi before he returned to complete his last season at the Met. The day after di Stefano replaced Lauri-Volpi on the Comunale stage, he joined Callas there to record the work for EMI. Serafin remained at the helm; Ettore Bastianini, the Maggio Musicale baritone and a Polygram artist, was replaced by Tito Gobbi. The 'unbeatable EMI line-up' was therefore now in place for the first time; it was to reassembled that year on three further occasions with only minor adjustments. The release of the *Lucia* recording which was to make a huge impact on the operatic world, being a non-Scala affair, was in fact delayed to allow two subsequent works [*Puritani* and *Tosca*] recorded with Scala forces, to lead the way under the Scala imprimateur.

In March two further performances of *Lucia* with Callas and di Stefano in Genoa followed the recording, this time under Ghione, who would later conduct Callas' celebrated Lisbon performances of *Traviata*. Before the first of the Scala series was recorded, Callas returned to the theatre itself to sing her glorious Leonora in five delayed performances of *Il Trovatore*. which according to the *Opera* critic were 'worth waiting for and had the success it truly merited. This was not due to the usually dominating figure of Manrico, but to the almost unforgettable singing of Leonora and Azucena taken by Maria Callas and Ebe Stignani. Callas again passed the difficult test and showed once more her remarkable artistic intelligence, her exceptional gifts as a singer, and the fact that she possesses a vocal technique second to none. Her handling of the dramatic content of her part was a masterpiece of artistry.'[8]

Even before these performances were completed, EMI began their recording of *I Puritani,* on this occasion in the Basilica di Santa Eufemia to avoid the

Scala schedules. Released in November, the critical response of the scholarly Alec Robertson in *Gramophone* was on the whole very encouraging. He begins by deploring the plot, due it would seem to the regrettable absence of the great Romani, but quickly agrees that this is wholly compensated for by Bellini's 'lavish outpouring of melody'. He was not too happy with either Panerai ['adequate, but not stylish'] or Rossi-Lemeni ['impressive, but, lacking consonants, becoming tiresome']. He continues: 'The opera, however, belongs to Elvira, Arturo, and the many big ensembles, and its success relies on them. At the start of the opera, Madame Callas sings exquisitely in the 'prayer', with the chorus off stage; but it is a little time before she settles down to her part in the duet with her uncle. There are some ugly sounds in this duet, and the first authentic thrill comes at her cry 'Ah padre mio'. She dominates the big ensembles magnificently and sings the 'Polacca' in great style, shooting out a high D [as also at the end of the opera] with thrilling effect. I enjoyed her most in the appealing pathos of 'Qui la voce', though she is a little uneven here, and the few phrases that introduce it, 'O rendetemi la speime', which are quite exquisite. The many florid passages do not of course, daunt this great Norma but, I feel, are more effective sung by a voice of lighter calibre. It was exciting to hear di Stefano in a full-length opera, and in a cruelly demanding part. No tenor sings the F in alt Bellini wrote into the finale of the opera for Rubini, but di Stefano takes the C sharp in 'A te o cara', and sings the same note [D flat] in the finale with fine ringing tone, to say nothing of a D in the duet with Elvira in the last Act! His voice seems to have developed greatly in power and to have an added brightness of tone: if he can keep its lyric qualities unimpaired there will be no need to look further for a successor to Gigli.'[9] He concludes that it is an extremely interesting issue – as well he might after the usual diet of Verdi and Puccini – the first 'complete' recording of the opera and the first official post-war Scala recording. Harold Rosenthal in *Opera* makes his own highly pertinent comments: 'Who would have thought a year or two back that a complete recording of *Puritani* was within the realms of possibility?' He cites the advent of Callas, the revolution brought about by LP and the importance of the full co-operation of La Scala. 'As Elvira, Callas is heard to excellent advatage, especially in the quasi-recitative passages to which she alone of present-day singers can give such expression. In 'Vieni al tempio' her voice is at its most beautiful; the 'Mad Scene' is not quite as convincing as it shoud be, partly because she sings it with the concert ending.' Rosenthal blames Serafin for this but that is how it was in the theatre. Di Stefano? 'He is no 'bel canto' singer, but he is at times very exciting; he is far better in the last act than in the 'A te o cara' ensemble in which one has the feeling of strain.'[10] [In fact, what the critics had to say about Di Stefano's performance was the subject of a nine-letter correspondence in *Opera* over a five month period – March, May, July 1954. It is aired in Chapter 10, pages 65-68]

As the *Puritani* set was the first of their recordings to be released, it aroused perhaps more than usual interest, not all of it complimentary. Dynley Hussey in *Musical Times*, for example, applauded EMI's enterprise but, despite its many beautiful pages, he found rather too much of the opera humdrum. Of course, he wasn't alone in those far off dark ages. He was just as grudging about the recording: 'Poorly reproduced, ensembles lacking definition; Callas gives us some beautiful singing, but one is always conscious of an over-careful articulation of the vocal tone, which never flows freely or spontaneously. Di Stefano has the unfortunate habit of attacking his notes well below the belt.'[11] So it is some considerable relief to turn to *Musical America* where we read:'The phenomenal Maria Meneghini Callas is the Elvira in the cast of the excellent recording of Bellini's *I Puritani*. If the half-forgotten [or at least neglected] operas of an era of prodigious vocalism are to be revived on records, it is essential that they should be sung as much as possible in the style and spirit of their time. Miss Callas has the technical virtuosity and the musical intelligence needed for this task of realistic re-creation. Her singing is exciting, both in its surety and in its felicities of phrasing and dramatic colouring. The voice itself is not memorably beautiful in natural quality, but she sings so well that it seems warm and rich in timbre when she wishes it to sound that way. Miss Callas belongs to the lofty company of Ponselle and Milanov. As Lord Arthur Talbot, Di Stefano has the role to make any tenor of today tremble in his boots. He sings it very creditably, apart from some overstrained high notes and one or two questionable breaks for breath in those endless phrases Bellini loved to write. The quality of his voice is caressing and he atones in ardour for a certain lack of polish.'[12]

Before their next recordings in August, *Cavalleria rusticana* and *Tosca,* both artists were busy, notably Maria whose Medea at the Maggio Musicale Fiorentino astonished all who saw it. Medea was to become a very particular speciality, suited not only to her vocal skills but to her acute dramatic instincts. As Cynthia Jolly in *Opera* pointed out, 'with Callas in one role after another, the time was evidently opportune to feed the public's omnivorous taste for strong meat. And Medea is very strong. Callas had learned the strenuous part in a few weeks, and yet she has never to my mind given a more even or sung-in interpretation. Deeply immersed in the role in its duel aspect of frenzied threats and convulsive pleading, she played no tricks either of voice or mannerism.'[13] All the critics went overboard. Teodoro Celli, a distinguished authority wrote: 'The viability of *Medea* depends on the singer who has the tremendous burden of the title role. Maria Meneghini Callas was Medea. She was astonishing. A great singer and a tragic actress of remarkable power, she brought to the sorceress a sinister quality of voice that was ferociously intense in the lower register, and terribly penetrating in the higher register. But she also had tones that were heart-rending for Medea the lover, and touching for Medea the mother. In short, she went beyond the notes, directly to the monumental character of the legend, and she handed it back with devotion and humble fidelity to the composer.'[14] This was a role Callas made entirely her own; she took it to the Scala, then the Fenice, to Rome, Dallas and Covent Garden. It was also the last role she sang at the Scala [3rd June 1962] where she had recorded it five years earlier.

The coronation of Elizabeth II was celebrated at Covent Garden in June 1953 with performances of three of Maria's greatest roles: Aida, Norma and Leonora in *Il Trovatore*. She had had an ecstatic welcome in the Bellini the previous November, her debut and her first appearance abroad in a world ranking opera house. *Opera* devoted eight pages, including six photographs, and a cover photograph to the occasion. Here is what Cecil Smith, a noted American critic had to say: 'The first somewhat delayed appearance in Britain of Maria Callas, as Norma, proved to be as supercharged an event as everyone had hoped. To be sure, Miss Callas is not – as some suppose – the only soprano alive who can encompass all the notes in the part. In 1951 I heard Herva Nelli sing Norma [in Philadelphia] with complete technical fidelity and great beauty of tone; I daresay a few others I have not heard could also make a satisfactory stab at the music. But Miss Callas is a singer of grand format. She understands the epic scale of the music that depicts Norma's function as prophetess, almost demi-goddess, to her people; and she senses the pathos and special intimacy of Norma's "sub rosa" private life with Pollione, her servant, Clotilde, and her two children. I did not always feel that her voice completely bore out her intentions in the moments of most imperious dramatic accent, as Ponselle's and Cigna's did. And I sometimes felt that she saw her part as a series of differently characterised separate numbers, and did not achieve the effect of inevitability with which Cigna swept through the score as if it were the second act of *Tosca*. But these are really my only serious qualifications about one of the finest performances to be heard in any operatic role today. Essentially,

Miss Callas sings with two voices. Her chest voice and her upper voice are open and clean, with a splendid cutting edge that makes for exactness of pitch. In the middle register her tone is heavily covered. Each of the four times I heard her, the Casta Diva disappointed me a bit, for she sounded rather as if she were singing into a bottle – until she moved above the passagio to F and the notes beyond. By some mystifying alchemy, however, these two voices coalesced into one as the evening progressed. In the scene with Adalgisa at the beginning of the second act, her middle-register production suddenly ceased to be mannered at all; and she proved herself capable of a dozen wonderfully expressive colorations, none of which ever threw her singing out of joint. Her *fioriture* were fabulous. The chromatic *glissandi* held no terrors for her in the cadenza at the end of "Casta diva" and in the second act duet previously referred to. One of her most stunning moments came at the end of the stretto concluding the first act when she held for twelve beats a stupendous, free high D. From this point onward, Miss Callas held her audience in abject slavery. She rewarded them by never letting them down, and by reaching a peak of eloquence in the infinitely moving closing scene of the opera.'[15]

Some, including Andrew Porter, thought the four 1953 performances, with a similar cast except for Simionato instead of Stignani, even more brilliant. *Aida* was conducted by Sir John Barbirolli, whose sensitive and electric conducting by turns supported Callas' singing to the full. *The Times* spoke of 'never-to-be-forgotten moments of beauty, power and subtlety, but also one or two off-setting features due to an excess of emotion which was allowed to disfigure Miss Callas' actual singing. In "Ritorna vincitor", for example, her sense of conflict was so acute that her line [particularly in the beautiful soft ending] was often spoilt by gulps and bulges of tone. Yet "La, tra foreste vergini" in the third act was done with lovely intimate tone and seductive phrasing such as this theatre has not heard for many a long day.'[16] But those days were now numbered, for the role had run its course by the end of the following month in Verona. The same was soon true of Leonora in *Trovatore*, a thousand pities because Callas' spell-binding readings of the glorious role almost defy description. Cecil Smith felt exactly the same about her three Covent Garden performances as his *Opera* colleague, Peter Dragadze, had done the previous February at La Scala after he had dealt with the 'abysmally crude' staging and Erede's 'dreadful' conducting: 'Against these irritants, Miss Callas more than held her own. Without resorting to old-fashioned Delsartian plastique she was more fortunate in carriage and gesture than I feel she was, on the whole, in *Norma*; and in some way I cannot define, she embodied both Leonora's passionate humanness and the formality with which the score and libretto universalise her emotions. Her voice – or, rather her use of it – was a source of unending amazement. For once we heard the trills fully executed, the scales and arpeggios tonally full-bodied but rhythmically bouncing and alert, the portamentos and long-breathed phrases fully supported and exquisitely inflected. The spectacular ovation after 'D'amor sull'ali rosee' was still less than the soprano deserved, for she had truly evoked for us the grand manner of the golden age. To my mind this *Trovatore* was a finer achievement than her *Norma*, more unflawed, and more perfectly settled into her voice.'[17]

Previously from Rome, Cynthia Jolly in *Opera* reported that Callas' Norma performances there had 'proved as great a draw as they had at her debut in London. She last sang the role in Rome with Stignani in 1950. She sang 'Casta diva' in the original G major but in spite of this *tour de force* she did not fully come into her own until the admirably concerted first duet with Barbieri, when the marvellous pathos of some of her notes and boldly-handled triplets and *ritenuti* began to send shivers of delight down one's spine.'[18] *Lucia* which closed the Rome season was 'memorable for Guelfi's massive vocal resources as Enrico and Callas' touching simplicity in the title role. To hear all the lower notes of the part was a rare, unforgettable experience. She phrased beautifully, with the sweetness of her piano tone very much in evidence, and a whiteness at the beginning to fix the innocence of her characterisation. She played it with a languid willowness almost unbelievable to those who had seen her a couple of days previously as Medea. In the Mad Scene, she allowed no hint of exhibitionism to interfere and concentrated on the Opheliaesque changes of mood, taking infinite care to round off every roulade and cadence.'[19]

It cannot be said that di Stefano's stage appearances at this time in a variety of Italian opera houses in any way rivalled Callas' in London, Florence, Rome and elsewhere. He delivered, however, a magnificent set of Neapolitan Songs in the HMV Milan studios which quite soon found their way on to ten inch 78s and then an LP. In *Gramophone*, first Malcolm Macdonald reviewed four of them in August and October 1953: 'The blue Mediterranean shimmering in a heat-haze; fishing boats drawn up on the beach, the view of old Vesuv' across the bay, shrouded in pink: peace, contentment and ease: the distant strain of the café orchestra, the leader extemporising his little bits of obligato, the harp rippling away. It is all here for considerably less than the train fare; the singer's obvious relish in it seems only too understandable. And anyway he didn't, at the time, know that the engineers weren't perhaps in quite such a sun-drenched frame of mind.' The facetious critic continues: ' "Operatic and

Song" the column-heading says [I hope!]; this one is both at once. Di Stefano continues his translantic evocations of the Mediterranean; the material is always a waterfront song, the style that of full-bloodied opera, with all its airs and most of its graces. The Tosti seems a little less of a hotch-potch of all the songs that ever went like this before than the other; and it is spared the infliction that Falvo receives of a score loaded with muted brass in the most inappropriate fashion. I suppose it *is* an American arrangement; it doesn't, to these ears, sound like it.' W.A. Chislett reviewing in *Gramophone* the eight-song LP the following year [July 1954] kept his bile to himself: 'As di Stefano's stature has increased in other directions, he has lost a little of that meltingly lovely tone which distinguished his singing five or six years ago; but it has by no means gone altogether as this record amply demonstrates and I can think of no other tenor today who would be more uniformly successful in such a programme.'

Soon both their voices were to be heard to glorious effect in two recordings, one of which, *Tosca*, would go down in history. The first was *Cavalleria rusticana*, issued on three LP sides, an odd number as Philip Hope-Wallace noted in *Gramophone*: 'If you bought the second record on its own you would still hear a sizeable portion of an opera which is, so to say, a late starter. Side two starts with the Easter Hymn and side three with Santuzza, after the row at the Church door, turning to Alfio and in vulgar parlance 'spilling the beans'; followed by Alfio's vow of vengeance, intermezzo, chorus, men's quarrel and di Stefano's powerful 'Addio'. But what I think instantly strikes you is that in the rather conventional opening passage of Santuzza's distress you seem to be hearing the music sung for the first time. Callas is an exceptional artist in this creative artistry if in nothing else. Whether Callas' interpretation strikes you as 'beautiful' or not, it is arresting. In page after page of this durable favourite, the music comes at you characterised, experienced and weighted with an artistry wholly out of the ordinary. Against this you must reckon that quite a number of the notes, in an uneven scale, are overloaded, ill-placed or pinched, with an unpredictable or hooty

---

Cavalleria Rusticana

MASCAGNI

**MARIA
MENEGHINI CALLAS**

as Santuzza

Turiddu ‒ ‒ ‒ **Giuseppe di Stefano**

Lucia ‒ ‒ ‒ ‒ ‒ ‒ ‒ **Ebe Ticozzi**

Alfio ‒ ‒ ‒ ‒ ‒ **Rolando Panerai**

Lola ‒ ‒ ‒ ‒ ‒ **Anna Maria Canali**

Orchestra & Chorus of
La Scala, Milan

conducted by **Tullio Serafin**

*(Recorded in co-operation with the
" E. A. Teatro alla Scala", Milan)*

33CXS1182 (single-sided)

33CX1183 (double-sided)

Complete on 3 sides

quality. To ignore these may be easier for some people than others but to deny them in their wish to canonise a superlative artist and to raise her above all criticism seems to me impossible. Enough that she makes her solo 'Voi lo sapete' deeply affecting, and the quarrel hair-raising and with the superb amplitude of Serafin's conception, she makes the Easter Hymn sound as one had forgotten it could sound. The tempi are on the slow side by some reckonings, but there is nothing scamped or slapdash about the performance, no suggestion of a bawling match. The chorus are not perfect and the baritone [Panerai] is rather a crude singer. Otherwise the only matter in question is whether di Stefano is superior to Bjorling. He has a natural advantage over the Swede in his ringing and clear enunciation of the Italian text. And though he is not always so stylish or so musical a singer, he scores several times; eg. right at the start, the Siciliana is more poetically sung, and the Italian's pathos is more elemental. It is finally a matter of personal taste whether you prefer this new version to the HMV. It is way ahead of Decca [with Nicolai and del Monaco].'[20] Harold Rosenthal in *Opera* thought it 'certainly the best of the three available: Callas' was a real flesh and blood creation, full of passion and feeling. The short scene with Alfio before the internezzo is one of the most exciting things I have heard on records; and her singing of the hackneyed Easter Hymn and 'Voi lo sapete' sounds spontaneous.' He thought di Stefano 'miscast, without the style of Bjorling, but he does not shout like del Monaco and his 'Addio' is an exciting moment.'[21] Indeed it is, and it is somewhat ironic that this critic finds a red-bloodied Sicilian miscast as a red-bloodied Sicilian! *Musical America* also preferred the sound of di Stefano's 'more lyrical tenor to del Monaco's robust ringing voice, even though di Stefano pushes it too hard in this performance.'[22] Callas' performance was found 'superb, electrifying in dramatic intensity, white-hot in vocal incandescence. She does not have one of the warmest, most naturally luscious voices of the contemporary operatic stage; her top notes are not infrequently strident in quality and her voice is sometimes hard. But I know very few artists today who can sing so excitingly and brilliantly or on such a grand scale of virtuosity. Her Santuzza is not to be forgotten even on discs. In the opera house in must have been hair-raising.'[22] It was: in Athens, as a 15-year-old student, and as a 20-year-old member of the National Opera company.

Tosca was the first of the Scala series to be recorded in La Scala itself and conducted by the music director, Victor de Sabata. The producer, Walter Legge, whose first Scala recording this also was, captured the voices to perfection in his mono series where, as Richard Osborne recently observed, the soloists

and orchestra were more vividly and atmospherically 'placed' than in any later
stereo versions. Infinite pains were taken to make this the classic it became.
There were stories of twenty-eight takes for the Te Deum alone. Alec Robertson
in *Gramophone* was generally impressed, though incredible as it may seen today
almost fifty years later, less so with Callas: 'The recording of the orchestra is
sharper and clearer and fuller than it was in the excellent Decca set and de
Sabata makes the music sound even more dramatic than Erede did. The balance
in the Cantata in act two is again poor [Is it not possible for Tosca's voice to
dominate the ensemble here?] but the engineering of the big choral finale in
Act I is better done than in the Decca set, and as good as can be hoped for.
I thought also that the imaginative Prelude to Act III came out rather better
than before and once again the part of the shepherd is well sung by a boy.
Comparing the casts, di Stefano has, of course, a more resonant voice than
Campora and makes the most of his many opportunities to display it. If he
does so sometimes to excess in the Italian manner, the result is undeniably
thrilling, while in 'O dolci mani' in the last act, his soft singing is both tender
and beautiful. He could have characterised the part I think more clearly and

THE EMI 'TOSCA' August 1953 LA SCALA
Floria Tosca Mario Cavaradossi Baron Scarpia

in this respect Campora has the better of him. Tito Gobbi is easily the best of three Scarpias available and in spite of a lack of power at the top of his voice which is an undeniable handicap in the Te Deum and the final moment of his advances to Tosca in the second act, he does make one feel the evil nature and the slimy piety of the man. Callas, strangely enough, shows little of the dramatic force of Tebaldi's vocal acting which made one's blood run cold at the moment she stabbed Scarpia and her 'Vissi d'arte' does not compare well with Tebaldi's in beauty of tone and perfection of control. At the same time she gives us some lovely singing in the first act and has her moments of drama in the other two, but it is not somehow the great performance I expected. It is more than possible that Madame Callas' Tosca is more effective on the stage than on discs but whatever the reason her performance recorded this not equal to that of Tebaldi.'[23] Harold Rosenthal in *Opera* put his finger on the difficulty: 'Callas is a different sort of Tosca than those to which we are accustomed.' Callas herself said from the start that people weren't sure what she was about. The refinement and musicality she brought to heavier parts like Tosca was the reverse side of the coin which brought weight and feeling to lighter parts like Lucia. Critics of the old school, like Robertson and to a lesser extent Rosenthal, were slow

'THE UNBEATABLE EMI TEAM' *Left:* conductor [Victor de Sabata] *Centre:* producer [Walter Legge] *Right:* singers [Maria Callas, Giuseppe di Stefano, Tito Gobbi]

to understand. Now, fifty years on, it is crystal clear. But even then, the greatness of the recording was largely apparent. *Opera:* 'This ranks as one of the finest recordings of a complete opera ever made. Not the least reason is the superlative reading of the score by Victor de Sabata, whose natural theatrical sense and loving care make the opera sound as never before. After him, honours go to Gobbi's Scarpia of immense power. Callas is highly dramatic, smouldering with passion, authoritative to the highest degree. Di Stefano is never less than good, and at times first-rate. His voice often sounds more beautiful than it has done for many a month.'[24] *Musical America* thought the tenor 'more impressive than I have ever heard him; Gobbi makes a chilling reality of the dark character of Scarpia; and Callas achieved great vocal and dramatic effectiveness';[25] all quite different from Britain's *Musical Times,* while praising both di Stefano and Gobbi thought 'Callas makes Tosca sound too much of a shrew, and her singing is often unrhythmical, though she makes some of the dramatic points well enough.'[26] Time would make amends for such scurrilous assessments of Callas' reading of Puccini's great heroine; J.B. Steane in 1997 spoke of the 'lasting value of Callas' portrayal in which vehemence and delicacy were wonderfully mixed, 'Vissi d'arte' the centrepiece with the fine detail of everything around it.'[27]

Both *I Puritani* and *Tosca* recordings were released before the start of the 1953/54 season at La Scala, and gave an enormous boost to what was soon to occur on that famous stage. Prior to that and immediately following his recorded Cavaradossi, di Stefano took part in a performance in Lucerne of Verdi's Requiem with Schwarzkopf, Dominguez and Siepi under Votto. This gives some idea of di Stefano's pre-eminence among Italian tenors at that time and the following June [1954] exactly the same cast, but this time under Victor de Sabata, was assembled by EMI to record the work in their Scala series. It has never captured the justifiable following for the Toscanini or Giulini recordings: Alec Robertson in *Gramophone* found many weaknesses in both the [slow] interpretation and [uneven] recording. Schwarzkopf, he said, lacked sufficient tone [though not art], the mezzo and bass were respectively 'splendid' and 'excellent', and di Stefano 'in very good voice, avoids any sobs in 'Ingemisco' but is inclined to sing too loudly in the trio 'Quid sum miser' and in the 'Offertory'.[28]

Callas preceded her return to the Scala in 1953 with four performances as Norma at Trieste with Boris Christoff and opposite, for the first time, Franco Corelli. The broadcast recording indicates huge excitement throughout, with an especially fine D flat to conclude the first act. Similar presence was sadly lacking in the studio recording of *La Traviata* she made for Cetra shortly after the charismatic *Tosca* for EMI. Her impetuous need to record her stunning Violetta made it contractually impossible for her to record the role two years later in much superior conditions with di Stefano/Gobbi/Serafin for EMI, a circumstance which has been regretted ever since. As it is we have the promised recapitulation of performances she gave at the beginning of the year in Rome with Franco Albanese and Ugo Savarese under Santini which does not begin to rival what was to follow at and after Visconti's magnificent production at La Scala in 1955. For once, the timing was all wrong. The critics were in fact remarkably tolerant. Desmond Shawe-Taylor preferred the set to HMV [Carteri] and Decca [Tebaldi], as did Philip Hope-Wallace; Harold Rosenthal thought it 'as good as you're likely to get'.[29] Even into the next century [March 2000], though lamenting the 'plodding' conductor and 'insensitive' male singers, Alan Blyth, in *Gramophone,* concluded 'All is not lost, for in Act III Callas, relatively uninspired till then, rises above her surroundings to give us a death scene of poignancy…in better voice than either of her later renderings on CD [Lisbon and 1955 Scala]. With this new transfer on Warner Fonit Cetra, in excellent sound at mid-price, it's worth hearing, even if the shattering Violetta of 1955 and 1958 is not yet present elsewhere.'[30]

Chapter Ten

1954

As the Cetra recording of *La Traviata* was not released in Italy until April 1954 and in the UK much later in January 1958, its reception had no bearing on what was to follow in the new Scala season. That was left to the release of the first EMI recording of *Lucia* in Florence which in the New Year took the operatic world by storm. Just three weeks before it was transmogrified on to the Scala stage itself, Alec Robertson in *Gramophone*, a trifle cautious over both *Puritani* and *Tosca* recordings, was beside himself: 'When Lucia makes her first appearance, there is that rather naive business with the harp, by way of establishing 'atmosphere' and then comes her solo 'Regnava nel silenzio,' sung with a lovely legato by Callas who has already, one need hardly say, established Lucia in the recitative as a person of character. She ends the aria with a beautifully executed cadenza, displaying those wonderful rich high notes of hers but preceded by some rather bumpily recorded trills, the only place one can say this of them. 'Quando rapito' with its exquisitely done decorations and finely moulded sequences completes one's utter enjoyment of what is clearly going to be a great performance of the part. Di Stefano, who now appears, uses his fine voice more circumspectly than in *I Puritani,* and the ensuing year duet, with a thrilling entry by Callas at 'Deh, ti placa', is most enjoyable. Both artists excel in the singing of 'Veranno a te', which it is silly to write-off as a commonplace waltz. The sextet may seem small beer compared to the *Rigoletto* quartet, or the *Meistersinger* quintet, but it is undeniably effective sung with such an excellent ensemble – how cunningly the orchestral part, pizzicato, fixes one's attention – and the contract episode is most dramatically presented. Callas' interpretation of the Mad Scene is filled with the deepest pathos and it has an impulsive, excitable note in it that conveys the derangement of the poor girl's mind. With all this goes the most superb vocalisation. In the cadenza before 'Spargi d'amaro', Callas knocks the little flute out and we hear him only as a little timid tootle in the background. Here is certainly some of the finest singing of our time, and there is one moment in the repeat of 'Spargi d'amaro' when the voice is recorded with all the actuality of three dimensional sound. It is startling. After the final thrilling E flat in alt, I had to take a turn in the garden. It is rough luck on Edgardo to have to follow on such an achievement: but without any straining after effect, di Stefano sings his celebrated aria 'Fra poco' very well and in the later scene, when he stabs himself, his singing, to a beautifully played cello obligato, is very moving. Much credit is due to Serafin for his admirable direction of the opera and the engineers for a most excellent recording.'[1]

And again, Harold Rosenthal was enormously impressed: '*Lucia di Lammermoor* has in its one hundred and fifty years of life become more and more a prima donna opera, a work revived for the star personality. Yet it has far more in it than one would think, an ensemble opera; one gathers that Karajan's production of the work at the Scala is also the kind that treated the opera as worthy of consideration for its own sake. One gets the impression too that Serafin in this recording looks on the work as something more than a show piece for his prima donna, though as that prima donna happens to be Callas, he might be forgiven had he so chosen to do! Under his direction, the opera has dramatic pace, excitement and moments of great beauty; the orchestra and chorus play and sing in the best Italian tradition.' He reminds us though, *vis à vis* a more complete Nixa release of the work at the same time, that he makes some regrettable cuts in the score. A background to Lucia's role is then considered: 'The role of Lucia was originally one that could be tackled by any lyric soprano with a coloratura technique; then in the process of time it has come to be regarded more and more as the personal property of the 'soprano leggiera'. As coloratura soprano voices became less and less voluminous and more and more fragile, so more and more ornaments were added. Lily Pons in New York generally transposes the Mad Scene up a whole tone, while Mado Robin reaches the dizzy heights of a high B flat above high C, a whole octave above what Donizetti originally wrote! Now Callas can do wonderful things in the upper register, but her voice has far more weight to it than the usual type of Lucia; indeed this Lucia is a dramatic soprano, who can sing coloratura music with the best of them. Desmond Shawe-Taylor thought her voice had become too dark and heavy and therefore missed the simplicity of the character. But could Pagliughi, Carosio, dal Monte et al, even begin to invest their Lucias with the tragic overtones that Callas is capable of? Did such intelligence ever colour the interpretations of Patti and Melba? – I doubt it. No, with Callas, Lucia becomes a tragic heroine of the kind generally associated with the great classic operas. Her vocalism is not one hundred per cent perfect, but what gifts this artist possesses. Di Stefano sings well for the most part and the voice often sounds quite beautiful. Gobbi's Enrico is, as one would expect, extremely dramatic and the letter duet with Lucia is most exciting, but I would prefer a smoother tone.' Arie was the weak link, he said [he of the Florence performances]. The recording, 1953 vintage, was subject to too much pre-echo but he added 'that of course makes no difference to one's final judgement that the Callas-Serafin *Lucia* is one of the most exciting operatic experiences of our time.'[2] And *Musical Times* for the first time was unequivocal about the performance if not the edition: 'Maria Callas gives the title-part special distinction. Without the brilliant technique of a Tetrazzini, she endues Lucy Ashton with genuine pathos and a surprising degree of dramatic power. It is a pity that the exigencies of space necessitated a cut in the Mad Scene which ruins its admirable dramatic construction and turns it into a long soprano solo. This is a prima donna's opera but both Gobbi as Ashton and di Stefano as Edgar Ravenswood sing splendidly.'[3] Finally from *Musical America*: 'First of interest is the Lucia of Miss Callas, American-born soprano, who has spent most of her professional life so far in Europe. The listener may be surprised by a quite different performance from what he has been accustomed to. Miss Callas is no shrinking violet and she brings to the role a robustness of voice and a sanguinity not associated with Lucia in this country for many years. The bigness of her tone, however, does not prevent her from negotiating the delicate coloratura with ease. Di Stefano, frequently heard here at the Met and elsewhere, shows himself at his very best. The voice is remarkably voluminous, it is clear and ringing, and the singing style frequently bears witness to the best traditions of *bel canto* in the bravura manner.'[4]

Thus against this glowing avalanche of publicity the new heroes of La Scala on disc appeared at La Scala on stage. Audiences could see as well as hear the splendour of an opera as never before with an intensity and musical passion unknown within the Donizetti canon. The Scala *Lucia* of January 1954 was the first instance of the new *bel canto* era when the traditional light soprano role of meaningless vocal thrills would give way to a flesh and blood creature of tragic dimensions, with production values to match. After this would follow the lesser known triumphs at La Scala of Gluck's *Alceste*, Spontini's *La Vestale*, Bellini's *La sonnamula* and *Pirata* as well as Callas' consummate assumption as Norma, and two Donizetti resurrections, *Anna Bolena* and *Poliuto*. All this in addition to great Verdi roles, Elisabetta de Valois, Violetta and Amelia. Di Stefano, Verdi apart, took no part in this. He had turned to meatier roles: Don Jose, Alvaro, Puccini's Des Grieux, Canio, Radames, Osaka, Maurizio, Calaf, all at La Scala. In any case he was not a *bel canto* singer in the usual sense of the term, as an extended correspondence in *Opera* made clear on the subject of his recorded Arturo in *Puritani*:

SITTINGBOURNE, KENT.

[a] I know it is generally fruitless to disagree with critics but I would be interested to find out if any of your other readers agree with me that your review of *I Puritani* was undeservedly charitable towards di Stefano's singing. Many people certainly seem to admire exceptionally high tenor notes for their own sake, whether they are pleasant to listen to or not, but surely Bellini is the one composer who must be treated with the easy phrasing which only comes from a true 'bel canto' technique. To say that di Stefano 'showed signs of strain' in 'A te o cara' was meiosis of a very charitable kind; he gathered himself for his high notes and hurled himself at them [generally from slightly below] with a violence most alien to the style of this gentle composer. It is true that not many tenors can produce a high D of any sort, but a tenor who devoted polished and elegant phrasing to the rest of the role and transposed the occasional D, would surely be nearer to Bellini's Arturo than di Stefano.

It may well be that no other tenor could sing the role better than di Stefano, but even if that is so, it is always dangerous to accept low standards 'faute de mieux'. I am told that di Stefano and del Monaco are two of the most highly paid tenors of today, but if their standard of singing is to be accepted as a fair criterion for younger singers, there seems to be little chance of hearing Bellini, Donizetti and the earlier Verdi roles really worthily performed.[5]

LONDON SW2

[b] While agreeing with you entirely on di Stefano's singing being better in the last act of *I Puritani* than in the first, I cannot agree that this top-ranking tenor can possibly be excluded from the list of 'bel canto' singers. Furthermore, I am prepared to back my opinion against you, that di Stefano will, in the ensuing years, established himself as the foremost lyric tenor of the day.[6]

[NO ADDRESS]

[c] We are in absolute agreement with the views expressed (in letter [a] above). Anyone familiar with the way that Bonci, de Lucia and in later years Tito Schipa used to sing Bellini's music must surely find di Stefano's singing, with its over-emphasis and complete lack of finesse, vulgar to say the least. The essence of Bellini is in that elegant, languorous melancholy which can be sometimes heard in the performances of the great singers of the past, and it is rendering

him less of a disservice to leave his operas unperformed than to reduce them to mere shouting matches.[7]

LONDON SW11

[d] Di Stefano and del Monaco may lack style, but they possess voices. All too often modern tenors are accepted merely on the score of elegant style, or because they showed musical intelligence to some degree, but the most important requisite for an operatic tenor is surely a strong, free, natural voice and that is what is often lacking. After the weakened colourless performances given by many of our local tenors, one longs for a full-blooded Italian voice capable of riding the orchestral climaxes.[8]

RAF DONCASTER, YORKS.

[e] I entirely agree with (letter [a]). The singing di Stefano in *I Puritani* is tasteless in the extreme. Perhaps his method of production makes it essential for him to push up to his high notes. For those not equipped with superhuman Caruso voices, the method of broadening the tone, when in possession of the note, *having commenced on* the note cannot be too highly recommended as a means of making a beautiful sound, and preserving the voice. While agreeing with (letter [b]) that di Stefano may become the leading lyric [Puccini?] tenor, when regrettably Gigli and Bjorling pass from the scene, I cannot place him among any list of 'bel canto' singers. To convince the writer of the justice of this, I must advise him to hear the acoustic record of Bonci singing 'A te o cara' with piano accompaniment and allow him to draw his own conclusions.[9]

COLUMBUS EVENING REPUBLICAN, USA

[f] In defence of my favourite tenor, and in exception to (letter [a]), I am writing to defend di Stefano's performance in the recently released *I Puritani* recording. At the time I read your review, I was nearly moved to the point of writing to take issue with the statement that 'di Stefano is no *bel canto* singer' which is on the face of it the most ridiculous statement in the entire magazine. Who has a beautiful voice if he has not? Strain at singing a high D? Well, *rather!* But what about the rest of the recording? If the opera is a 'tour de force' for the soprano, what is it then for the tenor, who has excruciatingly difficult tessitura to contend with – pages and pages of it. His performance in *I Puritani*,

Tosca [in the current review of which he is brushed off with two sentences] and *Lucia* are breathtakingly lovely. And I wonder if the reviewer has heard Signor di Stefano's performances on records of the two Mignon arias or the record of two Sicilian folks songs which he made. I can recommend them highly to all those who are so absurd to say he is not a 'bel canto' singer. To one who has heard di Stefano spin out a shimmering diminuendo from the high C in 'Salut! Demeure' to a whispered sigh, such criticism for the singer seems high-blown indeed. I agree with (letter [b]) that di Stefano is one of the very best in the world today. Our own Eugene Conley, who also sang *Puritani*, cannot even be compared with him. Who do you have in mind who could sing Arturo better?[10]

FROM THE EDITOR

[g] *I have heard the recordings mentioned but they were made at the beginning of di Stefano's career when his voice was undoubtedly one of the most beautiful ever to have come out of Italy. Overworking during his initial seasons in America would appear to have affected the voice, and it is not yet fully recovered.*[11]

US ARMY, ORLEANS, FRANCE

[h] I find the di Stefano controversy an interesting one. I first heard him in Los Angeles in 1948 during his first season in United States. His voice was then that beautifully lyric instrument recorded in the *Mignon* excerpts. Afterwards, I heard him in concert and opera several times, and in numerous Met broadcasts, in such roles as the Italian Singer in *Rosenkavalier,* Alfredo, Fenton, and Des Grieux. I do not think that his schedule of singing dates was particularly strenuous, and the roles he undertook were not especially heavy. I was quite surprised then when I heard him last autumn after a lapse of well over a year. On the Martini-Rossi programme from Italy he sang things he never would have attempted in the States, such as 'O tu che in seno' from *Forza*. The evidence of the arias he chose for that broadcast and his singing of such operas as *Puritani* and *Lucia* can only lead me to believe that it was his own ambition that led him away from the lighter roles of the Italian and French repertory. I cannot say that I deplore the change. Some of the original sensual beauty is now lacking in his voice, but there is an added dramatic excitement he now projects that I would never have suspected before. Indeed, the only disappointing thing I have heard the 'new' di Stefano do was the

Rigoletto from the Scala this year; in that performance he showed no sense of nuance or shadings.[12]

LIVERPOOL

[i] Recent correspondence regarding di Stefano prompts me to race to the support of (letters [c] and [e]) as it would any student of the theory of the vocal art. Space limitations, however, prevent the controversy being thrashed out thoroughly in the correspondence columns of your magazine. I will therefore confine myself to the observation that support for di Stefano seems to vary inversely with the writer's knowledge of 'bel canto'.(Letter [h]) does not appear to have progressed in this latter direction beyond translating the expression from the Italian! It must be pointed out that even if di Stefano is one of the best in the world today, this fact does nothing to establish him as a 'bel canto' tenor. Further, any tenor who finds the tessitura of the role of Arturo excruciatingly difficult, would do well to leave it alone. On the other hand, Bonci, for all his grace and technical ability, and aptitude for Bellini singing, was not a 'bel canto' tenor either.[13]

BRIGHTON

[j] Playing side four of *Lucia* four or five times to hear Callas, I found I became tired of di Stefano's singing of 'Tombe degl'avi miei' and it was a relief to play Gigli's old disc of the same aria.[14]

When Opera North performed *I Puritani* in 1985, their General Director, Nicholas Payne, assessing current versions of the opera on CD, wrote of di Stefano's 'wonderful sense of anticipation' in 'A te o caro', a sentiment with which this writer wholeheartedly agrees. But it would not have pleased those attacking di Stefano above. For them, there is no room for personality, let alone the animal excitement of a tenor of di Stefano's make-up. They want the notes the composer wrote; anything more gets between them and the truth. Interpretation, feeling, passion is not desirable. But for Callas and di Stefano it was: absolutely.

The eighteen roles referred to above on page 64 sung by Callas and di Stefano at La Scala between 1954 and 1958, either individually or together, constituted nearly half of the entire opera schedules, a residency of unprecedented richness, density and excitement. In 1954 alone, after Karajan's *Lucia,* we find twenty performances altogether between 4th April and 13th June, with Callas singing four of *Alceste* and five of *Don Carlo,* and di Stefano singing seven of *Tosca* and four of *Eugene Onegin,* both with Tebaldi. Rome was also having its share, with Callas 'distinguishing herself in *Trovatore* in a movingly sung 'D'amor sull'ali rosee' with beautifully timed trills'[15] and di Stefano in a 'splendid' *Bohème* and a 'vigorous and bouncy Duke. But he knows little about singing softly and takes all the top notes at a run. The material is there but he insists on over singing which may well be disastrous.'[16] In Milan too, the critics were having a field-day. 'Alceste might be a part less suited to Callas than others of which she has been a supreme interpreter.'[17] Earlier, *Opera* [January 1954] had even announced that the role would be sung by Tebaldi instead of Callas. Clearly, third thoughts prevailed because Riccardo Malipiero found Callas 'touched most moving heights, sang with exquisite line and with most moving tone and telling expression.'[18] The local critic, Mario Quaglio, agreed: 'She excelled in personifying the protagonist in a stupendous fashion, artfully interpreting the role with remarkable skill and with exquisite adaptability of voice – deeply moving in the dramatic passages, soft and persuasive in sentimental expression.'[19] As Elisabetta de Valois, the reviews were less ecstatic; two, *Opera* and *Corriere della Sera* respectively, were somewhat at odds: 'Perhaps Callas' voice is not quite suited to Verdi's music; for this wonderful singer, so confident in difficult passages and powerful in dramatic passages, lacks the sweetness and softness necessary in moments of abandon…'[20] '…the new Elisabetta, Maria Meneghini Callas, whose singing was effective, as always, and more sweet than usual…'[21] Martin Meyer in *High Fidelity* reports a story which would have chilled Renata Tebaldi, about to sing with di Stefano in *Eugene Onegin*: 'It was Callas' last performance of the season which had seen the greatest triumphs of her career. In the row behind me, a man broke off his applauding to say to his companion, '*La Regina della Scala*' – The Queen of La Scala. And at the end of the last curtain call, a straggler turned to the stage and called, *con amore,* '*Arrivederci, Maria!*'[22]

It was at this point that the Italian diva decided to leave the great Italian house until Callas was no more. Ghiringhelli had continued to try to keep them apart in the Scala schedules but was only partially successful and there is, after all, only room for one queen in any kingdom. *Tosca* was nonetheless well received: 'Tebaldi, di Stefano and Silveri made a well balanced trio. The soprano possesses a voice whose exquisitely suave timbre is enough to console one for the sadness of life, and her artistry numbers among its many qualities perfect placing and rare modulations of tone. Di Stefano is a generous tenor, perhaps

occasionally too generous, but whose vocal powers are consistently reliable.'
Also from *Opera, Eugene Onegin* had a glowing report: 'Artur Rodzinski
conducted with great authority...Tebaldi [Tatiana] sang and acted with great
feeling and dignity...di Stefano sang the part of Lenski with a nobility and
control rare for an artist who is normally carried away by enthusiasm.'[24]

Earlier in the season on 26th March at the Teatro Massimo in Palermo, di
Stefano appeared in *Werther* which was much enjoyed by Cecil Smith: 'The
extortionate seat prices presumably reflected the size of the fees di Stefano
and Clara Petrella asked in return for their services at the Sicilian opera house.
If I am wrong in this guess, I do not know what the money *did* go for, since
the scenery was of the bargain-counter variety. The new production of *Werther,*
if it is typical, left the impression that Palermo is lagging far behind Naples
and Rome in the practices of up-to-date stagecraft. The scenes were skimpy
and characterless efforts to create a romantic aura; and the stage direction was
as spineless as the stage picture. When di Stefano and Petrella were on the
stage, however, the surrounding shortcomings seemed unimportant, as such
shortcomings frequently do when first-class singers lift their voices on an
Italian stage. The tenor's recent recordings have made his present vocal condition
a subject of much speculation. On this particular evening his singing was of a
quality to confound the prophets of doom who fear that his best days are
numbered. I have heard di Stefano repeatedly ever since his salad days at the
Met. I have never heard his voice sound as warmly beautiful [though the top
notes are not as light and lilting as they once were], and I have never heard
him accomplish an entire part with such exceptional artistry. In response to a
merited ovation, he repeated the second half of 'Ah, non mi ridestar' [clearly
by pre-arrangement], despite the no-encore rule; and I confess that I was as
delighted as everyone else to hear it again.'[25] Immediately prior to this impressive
display, di Stefano's profile was further raised by his film *Canto per te*, a slight
but charming piece in the Hollywood mould, built around his feeling for
Italian songs. His recordings on HMV 78s are seen to be admired by pedestrians
in the street as well as fans indoors. He also sang three numbers within the
screenplay, one of which 'Piu bella del' sole' has an elegiac rise to top C.

After the end of the Scala season, both Callas and di Stefano appeared at
Verona in Boito's *Mefistofele* and, according to Magda Olivero, in rather fraught
circumstances. She had been engaged to sing the opera with di Stefano: Callas
then insisted on some performances [her only essay in the role], including the
prima on 15th July. This she sang with Tagliavini, only to be rained off after
the second act. She then sang the role with di Stefano on 20th July and

Tagliavini was back for 25th. Di Stefano sang three performances with Olivero between times. Absolutely no comment, other than that as neither Callas nor di Stefano sang the opera again, it would seem unduly enterprising of them to learn their parts just for this outdoor summer festival. Given the attendant traumas, they must have wondered if it had all been worth it. It is, of course, a grand piece, much in favour in Italy where it was composed, superior in my view to Gounod's once ubiquitous but now dated work. Shortly after Verona, Maria included the great Act II aria in her magnificent EMI recital of lyric and coloratura arias. Poor health prevented di Stefano from finishing a complete recording of the opera for Decca, but a single CD shows how good it was.

Before and after the Verona roundabout, EMI recorded four complete operas in the Scala series: first *Norma*, in April. Opinions vary very considerably over the relative merits of this and Callas' later recording of Bellini's masterpiece. Many opt for the stronger-voiced priestess of 1954 but they undeniably lose the better sound, and support [Corelli in particular], and above all the greater art of the diva by 1960. Hilary Finch chose the 1954 recording for Radio 3's *Building a Library* in 1999, enlisting Filippeschi and that 'personification of youthfulness' Ebe Stignani in support. However, the latest critical survey [John Steane in *Gramophone* January 2002] rightly, in my opinion, backs the second recording.

Callas then undertook to record a role she never sang on stage: Nedda in *I Pagliacci*. It was two years yet before di Stefano essayed his debut in the part [at La Scala]; Gobbi had been singing Tonio since 1941. Three reviews make interesting reading because each of these EMI champions have their moment of glory. From *Gramophone*: 'Di Stefano is perhaps a somewhat less dignified or subtle Canio than either Tucker or Bjorling but perhaps the role is not one where subtlety counts for much, nor style either. Di Stefano is in the best sense 'Italian' in his singing of the part and at the same time less ruthless than del Monaco. His words are beautifully clear, far more so than the non-Italians', and the menace he puts into such episodes as 'Un tal giocco' and the yell of rage with which he springs on his spouse and her lover near the end of Act I are most exciting. Heartbreak and passion are not sparingly suggested in the great solo 'Vesti la giubba' and the terrible climax to the play within a play. I find di Stefano a realistic and exciting Canio. Other advantages of the set are not so clear. Mme Callas is surely not very suitably cast as Nedda, often more effectively taken by a contrastingly light, womanly and sensuously pleasing type of voice. Madame Callas – it goes without saying – *acts* the role excitingly enough. Her taunting of Tonio is tigerish. She, in a rough way of speaking,

'MEFISTOFELE' 20th July, 1954 ARENA DI VERONA
A unique appearance together in the Arena…

'spits out' her words with tremendous effect. In the love duet, she is one of the few Neddas I can recall who actually sings clearly the third syllable of 'Non mi tentar' which Victoria de Los Angeles, for instance, lets slip, and in the play scene she admirably suggests the mounting horror behind Columbine's playful repostes. But though the ballatella is sung with a proud swing, I think it is conceived on far too robust a scale. Too many of Madame Callas' high notes turn into perilous and wobbly shrieks. Tonio gives Tito Gobbi some chances for vivid vocal acting which he takes very well [i.e. just before leaving the stage to Canio for 'Vesti la giubba', Tonio's word of advice could hardly be better or more sinister. In the prologue he is a little less opulent than one would have expected, but he sings with meaning and sincerity and fine style, taking the lower version where it is suggested at the climax but finishing on a 'Ring up the curtain' which is all that the most exigent top note fan could ask for.'[26] From *Opera:* 'I think that Serafin has made this set into the definitive

... Margherita under Faust's spell

Pagliacci. The freshness of the music, which after all has become very hackneyed, is one of the joys of this set; another is the Nedda of Callas which is a most convincing characterisation. Her scene with Tonio is one of the most vivid pieces of operatic acting I can recall and the way she reserves a different voice for Columbine is another sign of her fine theatrical sense. Di Stefano has not the weight of voice for much of Canio's music but he is nowhere less than

satisfying and often, as at the end of the first act, very exciting. Gobbi's Tonio is stylishly sung, and he is another of those singers who acts with the voice.'[27] From *Musical America*: 'With her exceptional vocal technique, musicianship and dramatic understanding, Callas gives a particularly perceptive, securely sung performance as Nedda, although more sumptuous voices have been heard in the part. Gobbi is outstanding, Panerai and Monti satisfactory. Di Stefano is perhaps miscast as Canio. Even with the help of the microphone, his voice seems to lack the force to make the role's climactic moments sufficiently powerful. However, he sings with considerable accent and verve, and his inadequacies are almost lost in a recording so beautifully conducted.'[28]

So much for the critical response to the EMI recording. The opera, of course, favours the tenor and baritone, and both di Stefano and Tito Gobbi made a big impression in it during their careers. Di Stefano at La Scala and later in Chicago where he 'achieved a personal triumph, not only after his stirring singing of 'Vesti la giubba', but throughout his performance'.[29] He performed the aria for the TV cameras which is featured in the Warner Art of Singing video. Gobbi's Tonio, too, is immortalised on film; he always loved singing the Prologue, a glorious outpouring of verismo opera at its best.

THE EMI 'PAGLIACCI' June 1954 LA SCALA
Canio and Nedda take a break during recording sessions

Un Turco in Italia demonstrated Callas' little-known gift for comedy in EMI's recorded version of a production that had enchanted audiences in Rome in 1950 and would do again at the Scala in 1955. The final recording that summer was *La Forza del Destino*, with a 'blazingly exciting'[30] Callas opposite Richard Tucker with whom she also recorded *Aida* the following year. Tucker was a tenor after di Stefano's heart – open, virile – and Alvaro a part in which he later had much success. In his 1958 recording with Milanov [again, like *Gioconda*, too late in her career], di Stefano was outstanding. Harold Rosenthal in *Opera* 'enjoyed di Stefano's singing more than in any complete recording he has done for a very long time. There is more than a hint of beauty in the voice, and he sings with great authority.'[31] *Musical America* felt that 'Di Stefano did not have the right voice for Alvaro but in a recording this mattered less than in an opera house. In any case, he has the natural vocal beauty and warmth of style to make a highly satisfactory contribution. He starts with ambiguities of pitch but by the end of the recording his singing takes on an impassioned beauty that is very exciting,'[32] Di Stefano first sang Alvaro at the Scala opposite Tebaldi in 1955, her last appearance in that theatre for four and a half years, and then at Palermo and Florence, also with Tebaldi, La Scala and the Vienna Staatsoper with Antonietta Stella, and in Cologne at the new opera house with Leyla Gencer, a total of twenty-seven performances. If the above may suggest some disappointment on the part of the writer that di Stefano did not record *Forza* with Callas, it does not take into account the all-important question of timing. Di Stefano did not first sing Alvaro until eight months later and in any case he was recording Pinkerton at the time on the HMV label in the Teatro dell'Opera, Rome. This was with Victoria de los Angeles at her special request and one can easily see why as a correspondent in June 1958 in *Gramophone* made abundantly clear:

LUSAKA, NORTHERN RHODESIA

The singer I think is not touted highly enough is Giuseppe di Stefano. To my ear he has the richest and most glorious voice of all contemporary tenors. I even think he is better than most of the highly touted tenors of yesterday. The singer who springs to my mind is Gigli. In my humble opinion he could not hold a candle to di Stefano and if Gigli's voice was pure gold then I do not know what can be said of di Stefano's splendid organ. I have never heard a rendering of the popular Neapolitan songs to compare with di Stefano's, not even Caruso's, and as far as opera performances are concerned, neither

Bjorling nor Tagliavini or even Tucker can give as thrilling a performance as this tenor.[33]

This correspondent's observations were borne out by Harold Rosenthal's review in *Opera* where 'in the love duet there is more than an echo of Gigli in di Stefano's excellent Pinkerton.'[34] Alec Robertson in *Gramophone* found the tenor's Pinkerton 'a hard-boiled one, but his open-throated singing gives one many vocal thrills that lie outside Campora's range [in the earlier Decca set]; and he is in splendid voice. Gobbi is a somewhat severe Consul, but with moments of feeling and his fine youthful voice tips the scales in his favour [*vis à vis* Decca's Inghilleri'].[35] Their Pinkerton/Sharpless partnership is probably the finest on record.

Pippo entertains Maria in his mother's Milan shop [Summer 1954]

As if four complete recordings were not enough that year, Callas found time to visit Watford Town Hall near London to record two superb recitals. First came eleven arias from Puccini operas in which, given the singer's much publicised distaste for the composer's music, her brilliant differentiation between the seven roles is all the more remarkable. For once these famous arias are sung in character and not, as so often, mere show pieces for the voice. I do not believe Callas disliked what Puccini wrote; there is far too much love in her work. But with her career now heading towards *bel canto*, she simply regretted its absence in his and other *verismo* operas. She probably preferred the coloratura challenges of her second recital though you would never guess it, so exquisitely beautiful is her Adriana Lecouvreur, her Maddalena, her Margherita and, above all, her La Wally. Did she do anything better than Catalani's 'Ebben, ne andro lontano'?

Before the new glories of the 1954/55 season burst upon the operatic world, it had the pleasure of an unusually enjoyable Indian summer in Chicago where the new company had certainly stolen a march on the more hidebound New York Met. As *Musical America* reported: 'Maria Callas was the true glory of the season and it was doubly good to have Giuseppe di Stefano in our midst.'[36] Opening with her Norma which was, as Claudia Cassidy wrote in the *Chicago Tribune* 'something to tell your grandchildren about,' she continued, 'I wouldn't have recognised Callas without the advance pictures. She was wand slim, beautiful as a tragic mask – with a glint of gaiety. She has presence and style, and she sings magnificently. In the shift toward coloratura roles there is a slight unsteadiness in some sustained upper tones. But to me her voice is more beautiful in colour, more even through the range, than it used to be. Her range is formidable, and her technique dazzling. She sang the 'Casta diva' in a kind of mystic dream, like a goddess of the moon briefly descended. When it came to pyrotechnics, the glitter of her attack, the feather drift of a falling scale – it adds up to formidable, beautiful song.'[37] Seymour Raven in the same newspaper took up a similar vein for *La Traviata*: 'After last week's Norma, Maria Callas revealed further the depth with which she has studied her roles. Her acting reinforced last week's impression that she is a brilliant stage personality. The impact of other singers lines is noticeable in her reactions. She elevates Alfredo and Giorgio Germont so that they 'take it from there'. It is small wonder that her singing is red with the blood of dramatic music, pumped by the pulse of Giuseppe Verdi.'[38] For her final role as Lucia, Claudia Cassidy went overboard: 'Maria Meneghini Callas has the town's opera-goers bewitched. An innocent bystander wandering into last night's *Lucia* in

the Civic opera house might have
thought Donizetti had scored the
Mad Scene for the audience. Near
pandemonium broke out. There was
an avalanche of applause, a roar of
cheers growing steadily hoarser, a
standing ovation, and the aisles were
full of men pushing as close to the
stage as possible. I am sure they
wished for bouquets to throw, and a
carriage to pull in the streets. Myself,
I wish they had both. For this creature
called Callas is something special, and
with all courtesy and justice to the

33CXII31-32

'LUCIA DI LAMMERMOOR' 15th November 1954 LYRIC THEATRE, CHICAGO
Lucia, with Edgardo, in the slimmed down Florence '53 costume

many artists who have worked to put the Lyric Theatre of Chicago in the big time, she has sparked it. She is a superb singer in the grand style, a lyric actress of enormous talent, an artist whose presence on the stage is a guarantee of her best possible performance. Call this pride in herself, or in the art she serves – it makes no difference. To an artist of quality, the two are inseparable. Remember that Callas, however slender, blond, and lovely to see, is a dramatic soprano who sings Turandot, Aida, Norma, and not so long ago, La Gioconda. Remember that she just sang a glittering *La traviata*. Then listen to Lucia's first act, spun like warm silk, sometimes with an edge of steel. It can tell you how she would sound in *Trovatore*. But none of this is fair warning for the Mad Scene, sung with a beauty and purity of coloratura and *fioriture* that can set susceptible folk roaring for joy. To use a voice of that size with such superb technical command, and to subordinate that technique to the mood of music – that is singing in the grand manner. Di Stefano did some fine singing of his own in a dark, ardent tenor, wearing a handsome tartan the while, and proof of his quality came in 'Fra poco a me ricovero.' Even after the Mad Scene, it was no anti-climax. True, his ardour almost dynamited the sextet, but you know how the kilted gentry can be crossed.'[39] *Musical America* added that di Stefano's Edgardo 'cut a remarkable figure; his voice has come to full flower in the years since he left the Met.'[40] James Hinton Jnr in *Opera* went further: 'Di Stefano has improved artistically out of all recognition since his last tour of duty at the Metropolitan, two years back. Although the voice no longer had quite the purely lyrical sheen it had when he first appeared, it had gained somewhat in weight and a great deal in capacity for making strong dramatic accents, and it did not seem to have suffered materially from having been used in roles verging on the dramatic. More, where he had once seemed simply a careless boy with a lovely voice, he now seemed a grown man and a serious, purposeful, responsible artist, capable of realising his gifts. He sang, all told, better than I ever heard him sing at the Met, acted convincingly, and made a real tour de force of the final scene.'[41] He also gave two performances of *Tosca* with Eleanor Steber and Tito Gobbi under Nicola Rescigno who had conducted throughout. He again 'sang well, spinning out phrases in the last act with almost Gigli-like finesse.'[42] Meanwhile, Maria had returned to Milan to prepare her monumental opening of the new season.

Chapter Eleven

1955

Maria Callas had persuaded the Scala to open the 1954/55 season with Spontini's little-known opera *La Vestale* on the strength of recorded arias she had heard Ponselle sing. She had also persuaded the Scala to engage Luchino Visconti to direct the production, upon which no expense was spared. The first point indicates how important Callas had grown to the fortunes of La Scala. But that a singer should also actively seek a world-class theatre and film director is extraordinary. Most would go to considerable lengths to avoid them. But Callas was an artist through and through. Of course music and singing was pre-eminently important but it was not enough, just as she said a beautiful voice was not enough. A great performance needed to be seen as perfectly as it was heard; not for nothing had she willed a transformation from her large, ungainly self into a slim, dramatically convincing beauty. As Peter Hoffer wrote in *Music and Musicians*: 'The role of Giulia is the perfect one for her, covering the entire vocal range and allowing much freedom for acting. She also looked superb. It is a pleasure to watch her, and one begins to believe at last in the action on the stage.'[1] The local *Corriere della Sera* was equally impressed: 'Among the performers, Callas sparkled, an artist who without making us forget the Medea of last winter was able to bring the figure of the heroine to life with the powerful breath of her energetic modulations.'[2] Riccardo Malipiero in *Opera* on the other hand did not agree; nor did he understand that Visconti's stage conception was a tribute to the Second Empire style of the composer rather than the Roman style of the librettist. He found Callas 'not quite so brilliant: perhaps the part did not suit her, perhaps she was a little tired, perhaps as many maintain, she has sung too much. She is always the supreme artist, but those tiny faults which had already been detected in her vocalism and had been submerged by her other great qualities, now seemed greater and more apparent.'[3]

Malipiero was in the same grudging mood when he saw *L'elisir d'amore* four days later with Rosanna Carteri and di Stefano under Giulini, who 'is not at all suited to this kind of opera; he lacks the lightness of touch and the buoyancy demanded by the music'. 'Di Stefano,' he thought, 'tends to be more a dramatic tenor than formerly and his Nemorino seemed dark and heavy.'[4] In the new year, audiences should have heard *Il Trovatore* with Callas and del Monaco but the tenor pleaded an indispositon and took on Andrea Chenier instead, being no vocally dramatic slouch himself. If he thought this would dish his soprano, he should have known better. She was quickly note-perfect as always though still our critic thought she was 'rather wasted as Maddelena whom she nevertheless sustained with dignity'.[5] This was Tebaldi territory, after all, and the *Corriere del Teatro* thought she certainly passed the test: 'Maria Meneghini Callas, in silken gowns, imparted amorous rapture and delicate abandon, projecting with admirable talent the rich and plentiful sounds of her extended range.'[6] Ten days after *Andrea Chenier* came a new production of *Carmen*, directed and conducted by Karajan. But Malipiero was as unimpressed with his efforts as he had been with Visconti's in *Vestale* though he loved di Stefano's Don Jose, making his debut in the role: 'He was brilliant, creating a lively character and singing with heroic tones.'[7] Thus in the first two months of the Scala season, audiences were able to see either Callas or di Stefano in three out of every five evenings, with a choice of ballet or operas by Milhaud [*David*] or Weber [*Il Franco Cacciatore*]. Both singers then repaired to Rome with, first, Callas again as Medea: 'Her portrayal of the part has changed considerably since her 1953 affirmation. It is less feminine than before; dramatic power is sharpened rather than deepened with a whole new range of significant gestures and striking poses. The upper part of the voice [apart from the highest notes] is slightly more acid, but in compensation Callas has acquired the lower spoken tones of a great actress.'[8] Then di Stefano's 'splendidly vigorous'[9] Werther before he sang Riccardo for the first time, later to become one of his finest parts: 'Although he has a way of disregarding the orchestral beat and ploughing his own furrow in ensembles, he made a good Riccardo; his sense of style was sure.'[10] Afterwards, he moved on to the land of his fathers, Sicily's capital Palermo, for over a dozen performances of Rodolfo and Des Grieux before returning to La Scala.

Callas meanwhile was back there to prepare her second of three productions that season with Visconti – Amina in Bellini's *La sonnambula*. The *Opera* Scala critic was, as usual, looking for faults but found very few: 'Bernstein lingered dangerously over certain parts of the work, and pushed on rather too impetuously in others, risking a disintegration of stage and pit – but nevertheless succeeded in revealing the beauty of a score which normally receives but scant attention. Callas' Amina had something of the same quality; she is, as we all know, a great artist and a perfect actress, and despite the strange lapses from her astounding vocal best, it was impossible not to yield to her Amina.'[11] So it melted this critic, and everybody else if reports are correct. For the Scala revival two years later, we read [Bruno Slawitz in *Musica e dischi*]: 'Callas made of Amina a pathetic and at times sad character, perfect in every phrase, in every expression. She sang Amina with Bellini's music in her heart, and words of ineffable longing on her lips, such as Bellini certainly conceived. She has become a mistress of interpretation and of *bel canto*.'[12] Claudia Cassidy was there for *Chicago Tribune:* 'Callas approaches the front of the stage and begins the great aria 'Ah! non giunge' which concludes the opera; very gradually the lights in all the tiers of boxes come on, and afterwards, the lights of the house itself. Soon the whole of La Scala is brilliantly lit and the opera ends a few minutes later in full light. Most extraordinary and exciting effect. As you can imagine the entire audience rose to its feet to applaud and one could hear neither orchestra nor singers at the end of the opera.'[13] By the time she reached the Edinburgh Festival that year, exhausted and against doctors' orders, she bewitched her audiences still as the performance on 29th August, heard by Harold Rosenthal, [the editor of *Opera,* writing for *Musical America*] testifies: 'The voice was not always perfectly produced or all the sounds fell pleasantly on the ear; but the musicianship, the intelligence and intensity with which she invests her roles were in evidence throughout the evening. Dramatically her interpretation was a *tour de force;* by very nature Miss Callas is an imperious figure more suited to great tragic roles of the lyric stage, and yet, although Anima is a Giselle-like figure, the soprano was able by her personality to make us believe in the figure she created.'[14] Little did he, or anyone else at the time, suspect what the dreadful consequences would be of that particular festival visit.

But, first, back to 1955 with its special glories. Even before Callas completed her ten performances of *Sonnambula,* she reincarnated her 1950 Fiorilla, much liked by Peter Hoffer in *Music and Musicians:* 'Maria Callas was brilliant – looking delightful, singing and acting magnificently with the finesse and subtlety and artistic ability that usually one only dreams of.'[15] Predictably, Malipiero in *Opera* was less happy: 'Maria Meneghini Callas was not altogether successful'[16] was all he could manage which was still more than he wrote in his review of *Cavalleria rusticana* which ignored di Stefano's Scala debut as Turiddu altogether. He had then nothing whatever to say about two new Scala productions: *Forza* and *La traviata.* The former marked di Stefano's debut as Alvaro, sung with 'considerable distinction'[17] according to *Musical America,* and Tebaldi's 1955 farewell from the Scala; the latter, of course, was Visconti's legendary production which made Callas the Violetta of the century and drove di Stefano's Alfredo to distraction: he left after the *prima. Opera* reviewed the release of the performance on CD over thirty years later: 'The story of

how Callas and Visconti rehearsed this production for months on end – much
to di Stefano's chagrin – is well-known, its truthfulness borne out here by the
astonishing unanimity with which every detail of the conception has been
realised. Perhaps Callas' Lisbon performance of the opera catches her fine-
tuning of the role of Violetta to an extra degree; but that production did not
have the soprano working in a team of anything like the same calibre. The
difference wrought by Giulini really does show, in the pacing of scenes, in the
heart-rending climaxes that well up at the close of 'Dite alla giovine' or
'Amami, Alfredo', and ultimately in the final ensemble, where colour and
phrasing in voice and orchestra fuse into a single musical line. This is what
turning music into drama is all about. Di Stefano, despite the impatience he
may have felt with his colleagues or even possibly because of it, makes an
ardent Alfredo, who explodes into a fit of near manic rage during the showdown
at Flora's party. Bastianini is a strong Germont pere. No other *Traviata* on disc
can touch this as a thrilling occasion.'[18] As for reports at the time, at least in
the July 1955 issue, Violetta, and Turiddu, warranted an *Opera* photograph
each – but for *Forza*, nothing. The same issue also [rather pointedly?] put a
photograph of Tebaldi's Violetta on the cover. All this being as it may, Scala
audiences no doubt enjoyed having the pleasure once again of seeing one or
other of their heroes in the last two months of the season as frequently as they
had in the first.

And now with summer on hand, the EMI recording studios were almost
ready and waiting, but for an RAI recording of *Norma* in Rome, captured in
part on film which was used by malicious media bodies to invalidate her vocal
difficulties three years later in the same role and in the same city. Apart from
Tosca, Cav and *Pag,* it cannot be said that Callas had recorded much familiar
fare. She was now to commit one Puccini and two Verdi operas to disc and set
new standards on works which everybody thought they knew everything
about. According to an interview she was to give in New York the following
year at the time of her Met debut, *Tosca* and Puccini in general occupied the
least place in her scale of preferences. But anyone hearing her searing Butterfly
on disc would certainly never guess it; J.B. Steane, doyen of vocal critics, has
made no secret of the fact that in his opinion it is her greatest recording, that
she is the greatest Butterfly and that Butterfly is the greatest opera! With
Karajan at the helm, one can readily agree. Gedda sang a gentlemanly Pinkerton
when it would almost certainly have been di Stefano but for his recording
with Victoria de los Angeles the year before. With *Aida,* Richard Tucker returned
to join Callas, Barbieri and Gobbi who under Serafin projected the drama

'LA TRAVIATA' 28th May 1955 LA SCALA
High drama on the stage ...

... rapturously received in the auditorium

and beauty, as opposed to the mere spectacle, of this exotic work. Callas had sung her last of thirty-three Aidas two years before at the Verona Arena where the opera is usually most at home. But certainly not on this recording where Aida's agonising choices are laid bare.

A very different Verdi work – *Rigoletto* – was the final choice that year and maybe after the debacle over three months before, nobody would have expected di Stefano to join the cast. But his Duca was world-famous, and rightly so. Gobbi was a natural Rigoletto; Callas, on the other hand, had had no luck with Gilda at all and quickly dropped the part after two performances in 1952 Mexico City best forgotten. More the wonder, then, at her ravishing performance on disc, which despite reservations, as Philip Hope-Wallace said at the time, once heard is never likely to be forgotten. The set as a whole has had over the years a mixed reception and has become something of a classic after initial doubts, as expressed, for example, by Hope-Wallace in *Gramophone*: 'The three soloists, on which all depends, do not serve us up just another *Rigoletto*. All seem bent on extracting the last drop from the famous score. Yet the result is not in some ways quite what I believe is wanted. It seems monstrous to blame singers for taking too *much* trouble, but one cannot resist saying that Mme Callas' Gilda and Signor Gobbi as her father make rather heavy weather of that marvellous second scene. She misses the virginal, blithe insouciance of the girl, he breaks up music which is nothing if not spontaneous. Left alone with Giovanna, Gilda then has that wonderful foretaste of Violetta and even suggests the great lady Leonora of *Trovatore* with a marvellously calculated *arch* of sound. When di Stefano bounces in, the temperature goes up sharply. If this duke is not anything like as sweet-singing as Tagliavini at his wooing, he outclasses both Peerce on HMV and del Monaco, and would get very high marks save that, when he does bring off a fine drawn decrescendo, his tone clouds right over. Such little flaws just keep this ardent duke out of the first flight: one climatic note in the first verse of 'La donna e mobile', for example, is not so perfectly in tune that we do not wince at the idea of it coming round again [the second verse is quite sure however]. Probably the quartet and his 'Parmi veder' are his best moments; and the brutal little laugh in the first scene certainly gives us the character even if 'Questa o quella' is rather coarse. However in the first duet with Callas, the team Callas-di Stefano, about which so much has been written [!], are well up to form and the 'Addio, addio' is highly exciting, if less naively charming than some versions, with both singers indulging in high-powered 'tops' at the end. Generally Callas' lightening and fining of her voice and also keeping it much steadier than usual, though not

THE EMI 'RIGOLETTO' September 1955 LA SCALA
Gilda e il Duca di Mantova: 'Io t'amo.'

always eliminating that cupped up hooty tone, seems bent on showing restraint. But her 'Caro nome' is all the same a much more elaborate and prima donna-ish affair than Erna Berger's [on HMV]. Not that she ever sounds bored or perfunctory; quite the contrary, a world of significance invests every syllable of the wonderful old aria. But where the others opt for simplicity, Callas embroiders with extra trills and also that cadenza with the 'bird tweetings' at the top which always seems to me to hold up the dreamy flow of the aria and so to spoil it. Nevertheless, as usual, some features of the agility of Callas' 'Caro nome', the glissandi and the span of some phrases on a single breath where an ordinary canary leggiero would merely peck are very striking. Judging by his best, which is a very high standard indeed, I have to confess to finding Gobbi's Rigoletto a shade less impressive than imagination had led me to expect. He acts with his voice beautifully especially in the 'Piangi' duet where he and Callas show for finer artists than the conductor, but something elemental is only 'suggested' tentatively and by artifice which fails to conceal the art used to convey it. The scene with the courtiers from 'Lara, lara' onwards and the 'sack duet' of the death scene exhibit a few dense patches in his compass where the tone sounds less young and generous than Warren on HMV and there is a tendency to labour phrases which, with a perfect cantabile, should 'sing themselves'. Nevertheless, the total effect of Gobbi's performance is very noble; perhaps with a subtler conductor, the 'cardinal' flow which is so important an element in a really *great* Rigoletto would have come forth more strongly. But these are hypercriticisms.'[19] They were not shared by the editor of *Opera* as far as Gobbi's performance was concerned: 'The overall impression is something of a disappointment, mainly due to the conducting of Serafin which is rather slow and dull, and to moments of vocal ugliness from Callas and di Stefano. Gobbi's Rigoletto is one of the most moving and powerful I have ever heard. Like Callas he acts with his voice, approaching the text with an intelligence rare among Italian singers. Callas' Gilda is likewise intelligent, moving and musicianly. She lightens her tone and generally produces a girl-like quality of voice. The 'Caro nome' is done as a show-piece, but the 'Tutte le feste' and ensuing scene with Rigoletto is Callas at her best, while the death scene is hardly less good. Di Stefano is enormously exciting; his voice is a trifle heavy now for this role, or rather he does not sing with as much elegance as does Tagliavini for example. What a pity that Serafin still sanctions the cut between the Courtiers' Chorus and 'Povero Rigoletto': di Stefano would surely have been most exciting there.'[20] It was, in fact, the omission of 'Possente amor' which caused J.B. Steane to knock this recording off its best recommendation pedestal in his Radio 3 'Building a Library' review in 1996. Forty years previously, it was Serafin who fared worst: 'slow and dull' was echoed everywhere before his real qualities were properly recognised. Nor did di Stefano escape: his Duke was 'quite dreadfully bad,'[21] according to *Musical Times*.

He was most certainly not that in three major events to follow: two recordings – *Traviata* on EMI with Antonietta Stella and *L'elisir d'amore* on Decca with Hilde Gueden, and two performances of *Lucia* with Callas and Karajan in Berlin. He had earlier that summer recorded a number of Puccini and Verdi arias [*Fanciulla, Turandot, Gianni Schicchi* and *Forza*] which were released in various formats, and 'Celeste Aida' which never was. The EMI *Traviata* debacle has already been considered on Page 61; it was re-issued on CD for the first time to celebrate the tenor's 80th birthday on 24th July 2001. Even on this occasion, J. B. Steane in *Gramophone* found his Alfredo uneven: 'at times vivid, powerful and even graceful, but the voice had lost much of its youthful glow and too often the uncovered high notes call aloud for protection.'[21] Harold Rosenthal in *Opera* [November 1956] thought him 'on the whole a good Alfredo; but the voice has not now the velvety quality it had some years ago.'[22] There can have been few critics however who did not capitulate to his Nemorino which between January 1949 and December 1974 gave an enormous amount of pleasure in theatres throughout the world. One such was the King's Theatre in Edinburgh, where he made his British debut during the same Festival as Callas' *Sonnambula*. Harold Rosenthal on that occasion was not uncritical: 'A wholly delightful performance of a work that is now rivalling the same composer's *Don Pasquale* in popularity. The 'star' of the evening was Giuseppe di Stefano who really overdid the comic acting, and turned Nemorino into a typical village idiot – he surely had more brains than that. The tenor was also apt to try and steal the limelight when any other artist was within an ace of doing the same thing. He sang beautifully however, but spoiled 'Una furtiva lagrima' with an excess of emotion. I do hope we can see him in some of his more dramatic roles in London though.'[24] This was a nice thought but a slightly forlorn one since Covent Garden had to wait four further years for three performances of *Tosca* and until 1963 for three promised *Bohèmes* from which he withdrew after the first with increasingly recurrent vocal problems. The 1955 recording of *L'elisir* however was a gem as *Opera* readily agreed and much liked both the tenor and the object of his desire: 'Hilde Gueden offers her most enchanting performance on disc since her Rosalinde of some years back. Her Adina is not over coy, it is charming, it is well sung, and does not have the shrillness and shrewishness that characterised Carosio. Di Stefano having apparently transferred his allegiance from Columbia to Decca is well served by his new masters. [The Decca connection was in the family and he continued, in fact, with Columbia until July 1957 and HMV until 1961]. The voice, often Gigli-like in habits and quality, is faithfully captured. There is much charm in his Nemorino, and his singing is never less than adequate and often a great deal more than that.'[25] Philip Hope-Wallace in *Gramophone* found di Stefano 'at the very top of his form. This is satisfying. Sometimes recently I seemed to be in danger of forgetting the di Stefano of that 1947 *Arlesiana* winner. He seemed bent on sheer size and on out-doing Callas in some of his complete Columbia recordings. Now here for Decca he sounds relaxed, elegant and happy and he sings the role fully and gracefully making much more of it than Nicola Monti. The two solos are fine, as are the duets.'[26] Mr Hope-Wallace was surely right to recall di Stefano's recording of 'E la solita storia'. Has there been a finer recording of a tenor aria?

Reunited with his usual studio partner, who incidentally would never have considered recording the role of Adina, the Scala company made for Berlin for two performances of their celebrated production of Donizetti's much darker opera, *Lucia di Lammermoor*. Desmond Shawe-Taylor, doyen of opera analysts at the time was deeply impressed; 'It was more than the glamour of Maria Callas that amazed the Berlin public; it was the deeply romantic and not in the least absurd effect made by the opera as a whole. Karajan treated the work with the utmost seriousness as a romantic masterpiece. From the RIAS orchestra he drew playing of great refinement; and his production was not only free from the usual modern eccentricities but continuously impressive. There was a fine effect when the chorus, at the appearance of the demented Lucia, transformed themselves by a sudden movement of their cloaks from revellers into a sombre host of mourners, fading gradually into obscurity as the light increasingly fell upon the doomed heroine. Thus an awkward problem – that of the presence throughout the long Mad Scene of a shocked and sympathetic chorus – was by a single stroke converted into dramatic gain. Maria Callas I must say was tremendous. No more than on other occasions was she a flawless vocalist; but when singing at her best she diffused a kind of rapturous pleasure now virtually inaccessible from any other source; and even when she jolted us with one of those rough changes of register, or emitted one of her cavernous wails, or sang above pitch on a final E flat in alt, she was always the noble, forlorn, infinitely pathetic 'Miss Lucy' of nineteenth century tradition. Nor did her performance end with the Mad Scene; through ten minutes of solo curtain calls she remained with consummate art half within the stage character, with her air of wondering simplicity, her flawless miming of unworthiness, her subtle variation in the tempo of successive appearances and in depth of successive curtseys, and her elaborate byplay with the roses which fell from the gallery – one of which, with such a gesture and such capital aim, she flung at the delighted flautist! Oh yes, an artist to her fingertips: the real royal thing. I dare say she will never sing any better than she does now; there is Greek resin in her voice which will never be quite strained away; she will never charm us with the full round ductile tone of Muzio or Raisa or Ponselle. But she has sudden flights, dramatic outbursts of rocketing virtuosity, of which even those more richly endowed singers were hardly capable. Certainly at the present time she is unparalleled. She was excellently supported by Rolando Panerai, one of the best of the younger Italian baritones, and by Giuseppe di Stefano, though the latter on the second night was declared unable to complete the opera owing to an indisposition which had not been previously perceptible; he was very creditably replaced in the final scene by the Lord Arthur Bucklaw of the evening, Giuseppe Zampieri.'[27] If Mr Shawe-Taylor is being mischievous here, could he be suggesting that di Stefano found the ten minutes of solo curtain calls as intolerable as the hullabaloo four months earlier over *Traviata* which caused him to quit?

In any event they were certainly together for their next engagement which was another season in Chicago where they were welcomed back with open arms. *The New York Times* had wheeled in the all-American Howard Taubman to do the honours for *I Puritani* which opened the season, the 'principal ingredients of which were Maria Meneghini Callas and Bellini. Miss Callas is the 31-year-old soprano who is credited with having restored ancient lustre to the title of prima donna. Her voice is so wide in range and so flexible that she is coloratura, lyric and dramatic soprano. She has the equipment for roles like Elvira that a more prudent generation of singers today rarely dares to undertake. Miss Callas, who was born in New York, and went to Europe to make her career, came here last year trailing clouds of prima donna glory. She had a reputation of being temperamental. She insisted on getting paid more than any other singer. She was billed as a personality, and evidently she lived up to her billing. When she stepped out on the stage, there was such an ecstatic greeting that the show was stopped dead in its tracks. Thereafter, she could do no wrong. Chicago is that way about her. And you can't blame Chicago. Not that Miss Callas is the perfect singer. She reminded one who had heard her in Italy four years before that she was capable of uneven work, that she could be strident and off-pitch. But she has gained in authority. And when she is in the vein, she is an extraordinary vocalist and technician. At the end of the first act, her soaring top notes cut through the large ensemble with sovereign power. In the Mad Scene where the prima donna goes mellifluously mad, Miss Callas handled with restraint when she could have hammed all over the place. She tore no passion to tatters on this occasion. She let her voice do the job. She places reliance on the right thing. *I Puritani*, of course, is an opera for voices. Its story is no great shakes dramatically but Bellini expressed everything through song. And he had the singers. One can only guess from the music the extent of their vocal gifts, but such singers are rare today as is the art of bel canto. Monday night's *Puritani* quartet made a brave effort, but nowhere did one have the exquisite polished lyricism that Bellini demands. Di Stefano sang the tenor with reasonable effectiveness.'[28] Stewart Manville was equally star-struck in *Opera* and rather more generous towards di Stefano who 'won his share of the ovations that continued throughout the evening. His beautiful voice was secure in high places and wonderfully fresh.'[29] His heaped superlatives for Callas' performances need not be repeated. He added that the cast generally was the 'kind opera devotees like to think up with friends at intermission time, never for a moment believing these will actually take shape. Somehow Chicago managed it for *I Puritani*: Callas, di Stefano, Bastianini, Rossi-Lemeni.' On the other hand, *Musical America* felt that the opera had been revived expressly for her; for the opening night at the Lyric theatre, it was a dead weight. There were two long intervals in the first act alone. But nonetheless, 'make no mistake about it: Miss Callas is the premiere singing actress of today. The most sustained and rewarding music was heard in Act III between Callas and di Stefano. This gifted tenor had a way of vaulting up to a high C or D [he had plenty of both] that was thrilling to hear.'[30]

Il Trovatore with Bjorling followed within a week, unrivalled for many a long year, wrote Claudia Cassidy in *Opera*: 'If you were to insist that the two *Puritanis* earlier in the week stole some of the lustre from Callas' 'Tacea la notte', that could be true. But she sang it superbly in line and style and her fourth act was a wonder. Her aria was so breathtakingly beautiful it stopped the show, yet so much a part of the vocal splendours of this exquisitely Spanish Leonora that it was the poignant climax of the whole. No one will claim that Bjorling's is the robust tenor to pierce the operatic din. It just plain gets lost. But his love song in gentle mood was matchless in sheer beauty, and his 'Di quella pira' glittered like his flashing sword.'[31] Next on the menu of this veritable feast was *La bohème,* the 'finest tribute to which came not in the ovations,

though they were many and usually deserved, but in the little flutter of protest
that silenced applause after the last act duet for tenor and baritone until Serafin's
orchestra had sung the postlude. This meant that the audience was caught up
in the spell of the opera, a spell recreated by skill, damaged by rudeness, but in
the end made indestructible by Tebaldi and di Stefano, who touched the gentle
heart of Puccini's melting score. As the only opera repeated from the Lyric's
opening season, *Bohème* was in most ways a highly reassuring improvement.'[32]
Musical America added: 'It was a pleasure to see and hear in di Stefano a tenor
who was ardent and youthful in looks and voice. When the duet got under
way, he and Tebaldi poured out glorious floods of sound that reminded one of
the Rethberg/Gigli team at the Met in the Twenties.'[33]

'MADAMA BUTTERLY' 11th November 1955 LYRIC THEATRE, CHICAGO
Butterfly: 'B. F. Pinkerton. Down.'

Callas and di Stefano were brought together again in *Madama Butterfly,* the soprano's only performances on stage, 'fascinating both to the collector of Cio-Cio-Sans and of Callas lore, exquisitely displayed in some of the old Chicago Opera's loveliest settings, with di Stefano its perfect Pinkerton, and with Nicola Rescigno's orchestra firing the whole ardent Puccini from the pit. For that full throated, soaring ardour was seldom heard from the stage. This was an intimate *Butterfly,* brushed almost from the start by the shadow of tragedy to come. Not even its love duet was the flood of melody to send pulses pounding. Rather it set the mounting ardour of the man against the muted ecstasy of the woman. This was not the only way to sing such Puccini – in memory of magnificent love duets I do not say it is even the best way. But with Callas and di Stefano on stage, it was a way of warm Puccini persuasion. Many an experienced opera-goer felt that way about the entire performance, feeling [with a touch of awe] that Callas had worked out the complicated and taxing role to its geisha fingertips. My own regard for her talents goes higher than that. As a decoration she was exquisite, with the aid of another Butterfly beauty of older days, Hizi Koyke, who staged the performance. As a tragic actress, she had the unerring simplicity, the poignant power that thrust to the heart of the score. But in the first scene she missed the diminutive mood, which is that of Butterfly's essence. This was charming make believe, but was not Cio-Cio-San, nor was it the ultimate Callas. Di Stefano's Pinkerton was handsome, young, romantic to a degree, and with a beautiful voice; he had precisely the ardour for what he wanted, the indifference, even the contempt, for what he did not value. He was authentic.'[34]

From here Callas returned to the Milan where she was due to open the season in *Norma,* revive her triumphs in *Traviata* and joust with Gobbi in the *Barber.* Di Stefano remained in the United States where he was welcomed back to the Met after a three-year absence, having won the 1955 Orfeo d'Oro as the outstanding tenor.

Chapter Twelve

1956

When di Stefano returned to the Met on 30th November 1955 as Don Jose in *Carmen,* Wolfgang Nolter in *Musical America* observed that 'it was good to hear his beautiful voice again and to observe that he has improved in stage deportment and dramatic ability in the meantime.' He was heard in four roles in the course of seven weeks, the most successful being once again the Duke, and Cavaradossi opposite Zinka Milanov for the only time in their careers. *Opera* observed that he did not appear to be singing too well on the first night of *Carmen. Musical America* explained: 'Although his voice was a bit dry and whittled down in the first act, it gained in volume and lustre as the evening progressed and at all times it had the caress, the plasticity and the exciting quality that characterised all good Italian tenors. What a pity that di Stefano became flustered at the close of the Flower song, spoiling its most felicitous harmonic touch. Up to that point he had sung it more beautifully than I have heard in years. It was in the last act, however, that he was at his best. His Don Jose was a pitiable, broken victim, only slowly rising to the fury of murderous resentment and despair. Vocally and dramatically this was a notable achievement. Earlier he had seemed stiff and uneasy but he obviously has the makings of a good actor and is already a singer whom the Met should cherish.'[1] Four weeks later on 27th December he 'played the role throughout with an ingenuous, almost boyish grace that made the doomed corporal as attractive and sympathetic as he has appeared in many moons. On the musical side the performance was less unified. There were a number of moments when the surface of a phrase grew choppy with passion which may be alright in Verdi and Puccini but is not the way to sing Bizet; besides the trills were not even attempted in the 'dragon d'Acala' solo. On the credit side, there was many a lovely pianissimo while the Flower Song glowed with passion well spent, plus an awareness of the words that one does not always discern here.'[2] Di Stefano's words were indeed always clear, he used to say that he sees words when others see notes. 'It's no good just singing the music,' he remarked to Patrick O'Connor, when celebrating his 80th birthday, 'you have to sing the words, and sing them from your heart'.

After Don Jose, his Faust was disappointing, reviewed on two occasions in *Musical America* 'seeming out of voice [on 10th December], di Stefano rather walked through his part, attacked many of his notes cautiously and with affected pianissimos; yet, when he made an effort, there was some full-blown, rich singing that suggested how good a Faust he could be.'[3] Four weeks later, on 16th January, he sang 'magnificently at times, less securely in others. He had the volume, the colour and the virtuosity to sing the role excitingly and certain phrases were ravishing but his acting was perfunctory and his French diction outstandingly poor.'[4] In *Tosca* under Mitropoulos' direction *Opera* thought di Stefano 'revealed the warmth and the ringing tones of which he is capable.'[5] *Musical America* agreed: 'He was in exceedingly good voice. But though he made 'E Lucevan' a thrilling experience, the aria became a vocal *tour de force* and made less sense musically.'[6] Best of all, thought *Musical America,* was probably the Duke, 'as congenial a role to him as any, in which he has few peers. His voice is darker than many tenors who tackle the part and it is no less rich and shining. It was functioning flawlessly throughout the performance on 7th January and his phrasing had a true Italianate inflection and bravura if, however it was not as finished and precise as it could have been. He looked and moved well and suggested clearly the carefree lustiness of the dissolute Duke.'[7]

Callas' 'powerful' Norma which opened the 1955/56 Scala season was briefly mentioned in *Opera*. William Weaver in the *Musical Courier* was more forthcoming: 'It had been several years since I heard her in the part, and though she was a stunning Norma in 1950, she has now become a great one. Her interpretation was strikingly dramatic then, but it has deepened and, at certain points, acquired a new lyric tenderness. Callas was always a passionate singer: but now the passion of love in her Norma is equal to the passion for revenge, which formerly made her so terrifyingly effective. On opening night [7th December] she was at the top of her form, so splendid that she brought several gasps of admiration and flurries of unexpected applause [for her recitatives!] from the difficult and often apathetic Milanese audience.' Most memorably was an anguished outburst at that moment in the last scene when Norma unexpectedly chooses to consign herself to the flames. So closely was Maria identified with Norma that many in the audience clearly feared they would lose her also. Nor did the audience always behave during some of Callas' seventeen performances of *Traviata* between 19th January and 6th May according to the *Corriere della Sera*: 'A very exhausted audience, endless applause during the performance and at the end. And may the reader forgive us if we do not take into consideration either the excesses of vociferous idolatry, or those, even more deplorable, of intolerance, noticed especially during and after the first act...'[9] *Opera* again failing to comment on her legendary Violetta, had this to say about her Rosina: 'Excitable, nervous, overpowering, and her familiar unevenness of emission made one regret, rather than forget, the great interpreters of the past.'[10] Peter Hoffer in *Music and Musicians* admitted it was 'far from a conventional conception – Callas played her as a coquette who "knows the ropes" and even flouted tradition to the extent of doing a few steps of dance in which she showed off her ankles. But the voice is in splendid condition and she sings charmingly.'[11]

Meanwhile, di Stefano was returning to Italy where he recorded a wonderful set of fourteen Italian songs in the EMI Milan studios which though issued on LP at the time in Italy never found their way to the UK until their CD release in 1997. Two songs in particular, 'Autunno' by Ernesto de Curtis and 'Passione' by Ernesto Tagliaferri, have a sad beauty, an anguished desperation which bears out the unique essence of di Stefano's singing at its best. Back on stage, first via Rome, he made his debut, opposite Clara Petrella, as Des Grieux in Puccini's version of the opera. According to Cynthia Jolly in *Opera*, the 'fine and unusually good-looking performance made the public nearly delirious. The two singers worked very well together though di Stefano forced a little on a heavy role.'[12] It was certainly more successful than that other debut referred to above – Callas' Rosina in the Scala *Barbiere* taking place on the same night, 16th February. Miss Jolly also thought di Stefano and a new singer, Virginia Zeani, made a 'most good-looking pair in *I Puritani* which followed. But the tenor is oversinging dangerously and though he is always attractive on the stage he does not readily adapt himself to the requirements of a classical role.'[13] Claudio Sartori had similar observations to make on his return to the Scala as Riccardo, opposite Stella, in a Gala *Ballo*: 'Although as usual a sympathetic interpreter, he allowed himself to be carried away by enthusiasm and produced imperfect and less convincing effects.' Within a fortnight, he made his debut as Canio in *Pagliacci* opposite Petrella and under Nino Sanzogno, the 'most agreeable Italian conductor today in the best balanced performance of the season.'[14] With the arrival of *Fedora* with Callas [opposite Corelli] and *Werther* with di Stefano [opposite Petrella], opera-goers were treated to another of those historic periods at La Scala of five operas [*Traviata, Ballo, Pagliacci, Fedora, Werther*] with one or other of their two favourite singers. The prospect of three further EMI recordings to follow would only have added to the excitement. As Peter Hoffer [*Music and Musicians*] wrote: '*Fedora* with Callas in the cast meant full houses and a big success. Once again she proved that even if she is not the greatest singer she certainly is one of the world's greatest actresses. However, the voice seemed to have mellowed, and her upper register has lost some of its strident quality.'[15] Claudio Sartori [*Opera*] agreed: 'Callas and Corelli led the cast, singing and acting with dramatic power, perhaps even overstepping the limits of good style – if indeed good style is desirable in this melodramatic piece'.[16] He also found *Werther* 'a most balanced performance, well conducted by Antonino Votto and with a cast praiseworthy in every respect. Di Stefano made Werther far more of a character than most other singers do.'[17] Before and after La Scala, di Stefano sang Alvaro in *Forza* with Tebaldi, less than happy occasions according to *Opera*: in Palermo he was in 'poor vocal condition and replaced by Giuseppe Vertecchi, for which he sued for breach of contract.'[18] From Florence, James Hinton Jnr reported that the tenor has 'range and delicacy but hardly cuts the figure of seducer, murderer [if only by accident] and soldier of fortune'.[19] Before further performances of Karajan's production of *Lucia* in Vienna, Callas returned after an absence of five years to sing the role at the San Carlo, Naples. Ester Dinacci in *Opera* thought 'her voice, heavily covered in the middle range, was not really suited to Lucia; she becomes too tragic and dramatic a heroine. In the Mad Scene she reached the highest peak in both singing and acting.'[20] The month previously, as we have seen, had also found her wanting, according to the critics of the *Barber* at the Scala. But the broadcast tapes of both performances reveal something much better. As for her EMI recording the following year of the Rossini work, it soon became a classic, showing both her Rosina and Gobbi's Figaro at their most scintillating.

For much of the summer, Callas and di Stefano were together again. Karajan had recently been appointed artistic director of the Staatsoper in addition to his responsibilities in Salzburg and with the Berlin Philharmonic – a huge empire, the wisdom of which was questioned in *Opera*. As Joseph Wechsberg wrote: 'It was perhaps characteristic that Karajan made his triumphal entrance into the Staatsoper conducting an ensemble of Milan's La Scala in three performances of *Lucia*, with Callas and di Stefano. Brilliant, but empty; highly effective but somewhat artificial. I hope it won't be symptomatic for the future of the Vienna Staatsoper.'[21] J.M. McKee, also, in *Opera,* had reservations: 'If this is the finest operatic performance one can see today, it is not altogether satisfactory. Callas on this occasion displayed a shrill and wobbling top register, which detracted from her performance as a whole when one considers the beauty of her glorious singing when she is in the middle of her voice. She played the part with immense grace, and acted movingly, even though one felt that this was only moving acting rather than something the artist was giving from herself. The reason for according Callas such critical attention is that apparently no other artist has ever been paid such a high fee in Vienna before, and so the public has a right to expect the best. Maybe this is the best nowadays! Di Stefano's fine voice sounded well in the new house, though one regrets in his case that some Italian coach has not spent more time over his musical phrasing; one suspects that di Stefano has more intelligence than a number of his tenor colleagues and that further homework would bear fruit.'[22] But Claudia Cassidy of the *Chicago Tribune* was much taken by the occasion: 'There was little of the spontaneous brilliance, the seemingly effortless incandescence, the exquisite shadow play that gave her Chicago Lyric Lucia an indelible radiance in history's hall of song. But there is superb singing of enormous skill over which I later discover to be the kind of sandpaper throat a visitor can acquire in Vienna's sudden, violent and unpredictable squalls of chilly, blowing rain. At one point in the pyrotechnics of the Mad Scene her voice just simply doesn't respond. From our high loge we can see Karajan's instant alertness, the almost pricking ears of the Scala orchestra. But Callas recovers instantly, and the extraordinarily mournful beauty of that voice makes the scene a duet of oboe with the Scala's sensitive flute. You might not have noticed that hazardous moment at all. Just in case you did, a Callas curtain call touches a hand ever so delicately to her throat. The orchestra men are a buzz of amused admiration.'[23]

Six weeks later Karajan was back at the helm for the summer's first EMI recording session to conduct *Il Trovatore*. Thanks to Richard Tucker's post-war disinclination to perform with the maestro, Manrico went to di Stefano who wisely never sang the role on stage. Philip Hope-Wallace takes up this point in *Gramophone* when going through Verdi's requirement for the four greatest singers: 'Di Stefano who sings so well in lyric roles is not the ideal rubusto for Manrico, lacking a stupendous 'Di quella pira' [like del Monaco] or genuine heroism and a bit more finesse [like Bjorling]. But he sings musically, without any faltering or that clumsiness which in actual performance nowadays seems almost inescapable. His 'Mal reggendo' and the whole of the second scene with Azucena are well managed and pleasing. In the opening passages of the prison scene he is perhaps less affecting than Bjorling; his production is rather metallic and the caressing and cajoling tones appropriate to lulling a mother to sleep do not come easily. As to the rest, Signor di Stefano is in his usual form; alert, reasonably tuneful and cutting a strong and on the whole pleasing line. Whether he is your idea of a Manrico must remain a personal choice.' Barbieri and Panerai are marginally preferred to the available competition. Hope-Wallace had quite a few doubts about Karajan's contribution which has subsequently grown steadily in stature. As for the role of Leonora, it was

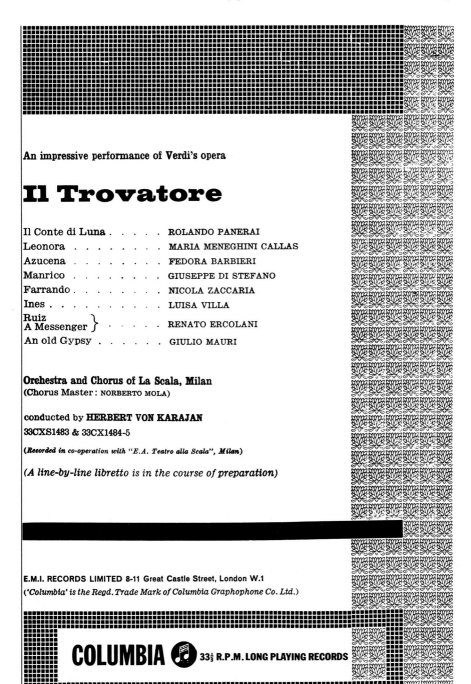

An impressive performance of Verdi's opera

Il Trovatore

Il Conte di Luna . . . . . ROLANDO PANERAI
Leonora . . . . MARIA MENEGHINI CALLAS
Azucena . . . . FEDORA BARBIERI
Manrico . . . . GIUSEPPE DI STEFANO
Farrando . . . . NICOLA ZACCARIA
Ines . . . . LUISA VILLA
Ruiz
A Messenger } . . . . . RENATO ERCOLANI
An old Gypsy . . . . . . GIULIO MAURI

Orchestra and Chorus of La Scala, Milan
(Chorus Master: NORBERTO MOLA)

conducted by **HERBERT VON KARAJAN**
33CXS1483 & 33CX1484-5

(Recorded in co-operation with "E.A. Teatro alla Scala", Milan)

(A line-by-line libretto is in the course of preparation)

E.M.I. RECORDS LIMITED 8-11 Great Castle Street, London W.1
(*'Columbia' is the Regd. Trade Mark of Columbia Graphophone Co. Ltd.*)

COLUMBIA 33⅓ R.P.M. LONG PLAYING RECORDS

one in which he had 'much admired Maria Callas. Her assumption is that of
a great lady, as it should be; and in the two big arias I have heard her phrase the
music like a virtuoso violinist with a mastery which marked her off from the
common sort. Most of that grandeur is evident in this recording. But to enjoy
Mme Callas, you have – if I may commit an Irishism – to like her in the first
place. If you can accept that half closed throat and the occasional, curdling
skirls and the sagging beat on the top notes, all will seem magical. She again
brings to the most hackneyed music a gift of recreating it as if it were being
sung for the first time. She feels the sense of the words [as, for example, neither
Tebaldi nor Milanov seem to sense them at all]. On the other hand, considered
from a purely tonal angle, the purely sensuous side of her singing offers little
here to compare to the ravishing sounds which issue from the Leonoras of
Tebaldi [in 'Tacea la notte'] or Milanov [in the introduction to 'D'amor sull'
ali rosee']. But the actual spanning and placing of the phrases are lovely and in
the rapid and difficult cabaletta to the former aria Mme Callas, who is far
more nippy with her shakes and gruppetti, through sticking to a fairly safe
pace, shows up as a much more practised coloratura singer than either of her
rivals. In the scene with the count which comes after the Miserere, Mme
Callas is altogether astonishing in her realisation of the drama in her dynamic
phrasing, making her rivals sound merely like also-rans in a steeple chase.
Altogether, provided you like Mme Callas' strange vocal production, you are
likely to forget the other two complete Leonoras. Only in one place does she
a little disappoint me; that is her moment of amazement in the Convent
scene, 'E deggio – e posso crederlo?', not nearly as thrilling as expected. But
the working up of the ensemble thereafter is exceptionally clear.'[24] Overall, he
felt that the new Scala set, though not an easy winner over the four-year-old
HMV set, was a decided advance. Desmond Shawe-Taylor did not agree. Harold
Rosenthal in *Opera* did not commit himself but was 'able for the first time to
accept a Karajan operatic recording unreservedly. Maria Callas has always
been an outstanding Leonora, and here her aristocratic performance reaches
truly tragic heights in the last act. Probably for the first time in living memory,
the Leonora remains with Manrico during the singing of 'Di quella pira' and
she sings the few bars between the two verses of that aria. Di Stefano sings the
role of Manrico with his usual competence and musicality. He has not a
natural *tenore rubusto* voice, and the top notes do not ring out with the clarity
of del Monaco, but there is far more variety in his singing.'[25]

Andrew Porter in his *Gramophone* review of their other Verdi recording,
Un ballo in maschera, says he doesn't want to suggest that it is less than a very

THE EMI 'BALLO' September 1956 LA SCALA
Riccardo and Amelia prepare to record with their conductor, Antonino Votto

enjoyable performance and proceeds to make it sound precisely that. For example, he says that Callas 'brings all her dramatic power and imagination to the role of Amelia, but I find her tone monotonous. It is constantly plangent, and rather bitter. The dolent timbre is effective in 'Morro, ma prima in grazia' [though the last note wobbles], but there is no gentle tenderness, no floating beauty of sound, to afford contrast. She is very fine in the *sotto voce* warnings to Riccardo in the last scene.'[26] As one of the few critics who, from the start, understood what Callas was about, his disappointment is strange. Some critics, including J.B.Steane, rate her Amelia as her finest recorded Verdi role. Porter moreover was impressed with di Stefano who 'finds the role of Riccardo very congenial, and though he is sometimes too loud, he is affecting in the big lyrical outbursts, makes a striking effect by observing Verdi's *pp* in the Barcarolle, and sings 'E scherzo od e follia' with airy grace and well-managed laughter in the voice. He shows insensitivity by opening out on the last syllable, the F, of the swaying 'non sai tu che se l'anima mia' in the love duet; neither he nor Callas caresses the phrases of this section, though the climax at 'ebben…si,t'amo' is very exciting.' Harold Rosenthal in *Opera* is fairly enthusiastic about this 'uneven performance, with Callas at her best in the more dramatic portions of the work, especially her scenes with Gobbi. At other moments she sounds tentative and displays a lack of line in the great sweeping curves of Verdi's melodies. Gobbi is an outstanding Renato, and di Stefano finds Riccardo his most congenial role on records to date. We could do with a little more elegance in the Barcarolle and 'E scherzo od e follia' passages, but the tenor is in particularly good voice.'[27] *Musical Times* prefers both Toscanini in *Ballo* and the Decca *Trovatore* to either of the Scala recordings, both of which have since become, fifty years later, top recommendations.

Finally Puccini, Callas and di Stefano in *La bohème*, an opera that the soprano never sang on stage and one which the tenor took to his heart. Both, on this 1956 recording, are wonderful. Philip Hope-Wallace in *Gramophone* loved the 'luminous meaning Callas gives to the words and the variety of tonal nuances she gives to the detail [superior in that to the unchanging beauty of Tebaldi]. No blurting mars this brilliantly realised brilliant Mimi; no conventional vocal pathos at [say] 'sono andati' on the deathbed. The absolute sense of fitness which goes into her contribution to the wonderful pattern which makes up the supper at the café – her tone is like a wonderful oboist, endowed with speech, and at a hundred points of characterisation, this Mimi comes alive and haunts you in a most extraordinary way. As against that if you want a pure swelling up of tone – as distinct from some subtle, artful diminuendo – you won't get it. She is at her squalliest, and Votto at his slowest, in the Mimi-Marcello duet near the start of Act III. The last notes of a marvellously feeling yet unsentimental 'Addio di Mimi' would have given Melba a fit, so wavering are they; and yet I found Callas' Mimi one of the most moving I have ever heard. Di Stefano's Rodolfo may not be mighty stylish at all points, but it sounds handsome, endearing, authentic, and convincing, as if he deeply felt the role. It has ardour, youth and a lovely immediacy which I miss a little in Bjorling.'[28] Harold Rosenthal went even further in *Opera*: 'I find it the most completely satisfying of all the *Bohèmes* to date. Of course one knows that for sheer beauty of voice Tebaldi and de los Angeles are the obvious choice for this music. But Callas *is* Mimi, and her sensitivity and her feeling for words and phrases create for us a fragile moving character. Di Stefano is in splendid voice, and makes a far more ardent poet than his rivals.'[29] *Musical America* agreed: 'Except on his highest and loudest notes, where he is inclined to over-extend himself, di Stefano sets forth his Rodolfo in warm glowing tones and with a combination of power and ease which he projects more successfully in recordings than he does on the stage.'[30]

A THRILLING LA SCALA PERFORMANCE!

LA BOHÈME

PUCCINI

with

MARIA MENEGHINI CALLAS *as Mimi*

GIUSEPPE DI STEFANO *as Rudolph*

ANNA MOFFO *as Musetta*   **ROLANDO PANERAI** *as Marcel*

NICOLA ZACCARIA *as Colline*

and MANUEL SPATAFORA,
CARLO BADIOLI, FRANCO RICCIARDI,
ERALDO CODA, CARLO FORTI

ORCHESTRA AND CHORUS OF LA SCALA, MILAN

(Chorus Master: Norberto Mola)

conducted by **ANTONINO VOTTO**

33CX1464–5

(Recorded in co-operation with " E.A. Teatro alla Scala ", Milan)

COLUMBIA

(Regd. Trade Mark of Columbia Graphophone Co. Ltd.)

33⅓ r.p.m. Long Playing Records

E.M.I. RECORDS LIMITED, 8-11 Great Castle Street, London, W.1

Soprano and tenor then went their separate ways, and this year in reverse –
Maria to the Met for her belated debut, as Norma, and di Stefano to open the
1956 Scala season in a new role, Radames in *Aida* with Stella under Votto.
They would later meet up again at the Scala, but not together on the stage, for
yet another series of performances each to offer the Milanese public.

THE EMI 'BOHÈME' August/September 1956 LA SCALA
Rudolfo: 'E al ritorno?' Mimi: 'Curioso!'

Chapter Thirteen

1957

After a solo RAI Concert broadcast on 27th September, Callas arrived at the Metropolitan Opera to prepare herself for the eagerly awaited first appearances of their New York-born diva, as the local critics were quick to dub her. Her debut took place on 29th October 1956 amid several traumas, political, professional and personal. Her painted portrait appeared on the cover of *Time* magazine when it could easily have been Sir Anthony Eden [British Prime Minister about to invade Egypt], Nikita Krushchev [about to invade Hungary] or Eisenhower [seeking re-election at the White House]. But Callas it was and not altogether for altruistic reasons because the magazine contained a sensationally vicious article featuring family and operatic squabbles designed to rock her debut. It simply added to the general hullabaloo as James Hinton Jnr reported in *Opera*: 'The Metropolitan Opera opened its 1956-57 season with Maria Callas at long last making her New York debut in a revival of *Norma,* an event that before the fact aroused a great deal of excitement, and, after it, extremely mixed reactions that have resulted in some extraordinary [for New York, at any rate] audience behaviour. All autumn the recording-converted Callas acolytes hoarded energies and dollars towards a suitably fervent reception, while admirers of Tebaldi and/or Milanov hoarded theirs towards – whatever. And Miss Callas arrived in great style, under the escort of a new poodle and Signor Meneghini, who stood by while she commented with disdain on the 'boring' lawsuit she faces for alleged breach of a managerial contract signed under counter-alleged duress in the dear, past days of her uncelebrity – a suit that has led to a court order attaching any assets she has or may acquire in New York. It was all very exciting and certainly did no harm at the box-office. The opening *Norma* sold out, at astronomical house benefit prices, with regular subscribers claiming all seats on precedence and leaving the acolytes to scrounge for places in the standing room queue which formed even earlier than usual. Thus the season, and Miss Callas, opened to an audience even more posh than the average for seasonal initiations to the Metropolitan; one said to have been notably quieter and more intent than common, but not one predetermined to build ovations. Nonetheless, at the end there was a demonstration sufficiently long, and almost loud enough, to lead to a break [on whose volition is not quite clear] of the standing Metropolitan rule, in force since partisan troubles in the past few seasons, forbidding solo curtain calls. So far, so good.

The daily press reaction was less than ecstatic. With few exceptions, there were fairly strong critical reservations about the sound of the voice – strong enough in many instances to vitiate the praise offered on other aspects. The occasion was no fiasco, but certainly no triumph comparable to the Callas-can-do-no-wrong carnival set off by her American debut in Chicago two years ago, in the same opera. To some degree, the 'yes–but' response may have been a New York reaction to an overdose of Callas publicity. But if this element entered in, later performances did little to cancel the effect. Although the enthusiasts kept the applause level high, the singing itself confirmed a good many of the other soprano loyalists in their worst expectations, until at one repeat a sniper in the upper reaches of the stage-left side of the house punctuated a curtain call by heaving a small collection of vegetables onto the stage – waiting timidly, however, until Miss Callas was on her way back through the call curtains. No one seems to remember any such incident in earlier history at the Metropolitan, and all sorts of theories have been advanced to explain it. However, vegetables have been bought outside opera houses, and the most reasonable theory is that some zealot of a competitive singer plotted the deed, proving that there are juveniles, however delinquent, capable of going to negative extremes in proving partisan loyalties. Now, perhaps, one will cast a powder puff at Zinka Milanov, and the war will be on. By the fourth *Norma*, Miss Callas had worked considerable improvements on her early form, but what was to be heard came far short of her best, or even average, singing. If voices could be assessed mathematically, I would say that she was a good 25 or 30 per cent below her effectiveness of two seasons past; and although the externals of her acting were familiar their impact attenuated proportionally. She seemed to have reduced her weight still further so that now the impression was of a drawn, nervous woman rather than a svelte, supremely confident one. She began, as she had done before, with a 'Casta diva' that was not in focus, however well phrased by intention, and failed to free up for the cabaletta – usual enough preliminaries to something much finer. Yet there was a difference, and it continued so through the duets with Adalgisa. Apart from its bottled-up moments, the voice lacked body in the middle; and, apart from being familiarly astringent, the top notes were in the main thin and unimpressive. It was as if she were reluctant to put the pressure on except when there was no choice, and then she tended to miss pitches instead of merely shading them, especially at the top. Her compromises were prevailingly vocal rather than musical, and much of the phrasing was as marvellously musical as always in design and shading within a reduced dynamic frame, save for an unfamiliar eagerness to chop off the long notes in a line. But when it was a matter of full-scale attack on difficult *fioriture*, the patent chanciness of the enterprise kept her from sweeping the audience along – except perhaps to help worry about the outcome, which in the Cs after 'Ah! non tremare' was catastrophic. Only in the last act did she do herself anything like justice – 'In mia man' was tremendous, and she sang much better from there on – but the most apposite reaction seemed to be regret that her first impression on New York had to be made under such strain. Musically, and in general artistry, the Callas *Norma* was far superior to those sung recently by Milanov, but still and all not really even good, let alone anything of a order to compel submission.'[1]

Roger Dettmer in *Chicago American* had another view: 'It was a nervous Maria Callas who took to stage – a tremulous sound in the voice reminded one of Butterfly's entrance last November at Chicago. It was an angry Maria Callas, hissed softly but unmistakably at one point during 'Casta diva', who came out for curtain calls to shouts of 'Bravo, del Monaco' and 'Brava, Barbieri'. Then things – magical things, to Chicagoans familiar, but still and incomparably magical – began happening. It was a smouldering Callas in the cave scene who learned that her Roman lover had been dallying in the Druid forests with Adalgisa. Act Three with the duet 'Mira, o Norma' heard the steadiness, intensity and control of Mme Callas' best Chicago appearances take the situation in hand. At this turning point on stage, the audience came over. Act IV with Norma's admission of her own illicit behaviour and that great plea for forgiveness to her father heard a Maria Callas singing whom even Chicago did not hear two years ago. Both her musical and stage performance had the overwhelming power that pulls one to the edge of a seat and leaves one afterwards limp.'[2] Finally, how did *Time* magazine respond? 'Her voice has flaws as the critics eagerly pointed out. Notably, on opening night, the notes became shrill in the upper register but in the low and middle registers she sang with flutelike purity, tender and yet sharply disciplined and in the upper reaches, shrill or not, she flashed a sword-like power that is already legend. In one of the repertory's most strenuous roles, the Callas voice rose from her slender frame with dazzling endurance. No doubt, other great operatic sopranos can coax out of their ample, placid figures tones that aesthetes call more beautiful. But just as the greatest beauties among women do not usually have flawlessly symmetrical features, the greatest voices are not characterised by a flawless marble perfection. Callas' voice and stage presence add up to more than beauty – namely the kind of passionate dedication, the kind of excitement that invariably mark a champ.'[3]

One sentence was all that *Opera* could muster for both *Tosca* and *Lucia*. Once again, let *Time* speak: 'Act II of Tosca was hair-raising. Callas entered Baron Scarpia's den looking like the Queen of the Night in her black velvet and ermine gown and glittering tiara. Her lip curled shrewishly at Scarpia's overtures, but she staggered when she heard her lover's tortured screams. She wound up her big show-stopping aria, 'Vissi d'arte' on her knees just in time to receive the ovation that greeted it. With a start, Callas took the knife from the table, furiously plunged it into Scarpia's chest, then, her head waggling insanely, unable to look directly at the corpse, she placed the candles at his shoulders and made her getaway. When it was over, and everybody else was killed off too, the audience came back to reality and howled like the West Point cheering section while Maria Callas curtsied, hugged herself, and blew kisses through fourteen long curtain calls. Tenor Giuseppe Campora, who had given a vocally beautiful performance, doggedly appeared with her every time, although toward the end he began to look rather tired of keeping up with Callas.'[4] Of *Lucia,* the *Musical Courier* will suffice: 'The 'Regnava nel silenzio' opening air and the following duet with the tenor were delectably and realistically sung; the customarily dull scene with Ashton in Act II held impact and a new appeal. When Callas reached the Mad Scene, one settled back and said, "This is it. This is what we have read about in the stories of divas of the Golden Age. This is at last the true soprano voice as it should be." Dishevelled in appearance [she cares nothing for being constantly a beauty], ravishing in vocal timbre, rivalling the flute in flexible speed, with limpid warmth and cumulative emotional intensity [up until the final note, which went agley], she was superb.'[5]

Callas returned to La Scala for a revival of *La sonnambula* via Covent Garden for two performances of *Norma,* her last with Stignani, and produced from Andrew Porter in *Opera* a warmly appreciative tribute to Callas art. After referring to the personalities and disciplined work habits of previous icons – Lilli Lehmann, Pasta, Malibran – he wrote: 'I venture to suggest that this artist, despite her vocal imperfections, is a creative genius of the first order, whose personal magnetism is such that the critic forgets those vocal imperfections. Because the personality and everything else about the singer is so powerful some of us are enthralled when she is on the stage as with no other operatic artist today, and are convinced that we are in the presence of an artist in the great tradition. I use the word artist advisedly. When all is said and done, opera is more than singing, it is music drama; and Callas' Norma is a dramatic creation of the highest order. Just as I was constantly being told the other week that I should have heard Madame X or Y as Norma, so I am certain that those of us who believe that *this* Norma is just as great in its way will tell our children or grandchildren about it. We will remember the beauty with which she sings the phrase 'E il sacro vischio io mieto' immediately after the words 'Pace v'intimo' just before 'Casta diva'; the soft diminuendo on 'Son io' as she takes the laurel wreath from her brow and makes her confession in the last act; the wealth of meaning she invests in the words 'Oh, rimembranza!' as she lives again through the emotions of being loved by Pollione, while Adalgisa tells her of her illicit love. Then the change from the tender woman to the vindictive wronged mother as she hurls the words 'Tremi tu? e per chi?' at Pollione before the beginning of the magnificent trio; the bitterness with which she begins the scene with Pollione in the last scene, 'In mia man' alfin tu sei', through the heart-broken duet 'Qual cor tradisti', to the final moving plea to Oroveso 'Deh! non volerli vittime'. Callas has, as everyone knows, lost much weight; her voice too has lost some of its body, but instead we have a much more closely-knit instrument, more even in scale than before. There is still the occasionally tendency to a sour note, or to sharp singing, but there is a new-found beauty in the middle voice, and all the old authority and variations of tone and colour. The 'Casta diva' on Saturday was much better sung than at any previous performances in London, but it was the Wednesday performance of this aria that was the best; unfortunately some purists shushed the attempted applause! The duets with Adalgisa were models of their kind, and the give and take between the two women was something to be wondered at.'[6]

By the time Callas arrived back at the Scala for *La sonnambula*, delayed by the soprano's indisposition, di Stefano had appeared in three operas – *Aida*, *Pagliacci* and *Manon Lescaut*. His Radames opposite Stella, which had opened the 1956/57 season, was not a success and was typical of the sort of roles not suited to his voice which, as Claudio Sartori in *Opera* wrote, 'was strained in the characterisation of the role, young and impetuous, but often nearing vulgarity in making too open a sound. The two artists were, however, well controlled in the last act where they sang movingly and with delicacy in their last duet. This made up for all that had gone before.'[7] *Musical America* was supportive: 'Di Stefano has always been a most sympathetic performer and he did well on this important evening, his debut as Radames. His acting and diction were excellent and his last act was most commendable, never forced and with a limpid, lyric quality of voice.'[8] His Des Grieux was, as we would expect, much better although di Stefano was not helped by the conductor, who we read 'frequently allowed his singers that freedom of phrasing which may please the great public, but is lacking in taste and constitutes a fault in style. Di Stefano in particular took advantage of this, being guilty on occasion even of awkward affectation. This was a pity, for we have often had from this tenor exquisite interpretations.'[9] *Musical America* again: 'Di Stefano brought a humanity and pathos to his role and the beauty of his voice in its middle register partly compensated for the rather throaty and forced quality of some of his high notes.'[10] Rather more impressive than either of these Scala appearances had been an ambitious new production in Rome of Mascagni's controversial *Iris* in which Clara Petrella's 'movingly innocent performance was matched by Boris Christoff's sharply-etched Blind Man; di Stefano's lusty singing has become ever-open of late but he was well in character as the handsome Osaka'.[11] Less successful there was his Don Jose opposite Simionato when he 'began without any bloom to his voice but came into his own with the passionate outbursts of Acts III and IV'.[12] Early in March, after much frustrating delay, 'Mme Callas made her triumphant return to La Scala and was greeted with the warmest applause from her public and the circle of admirers which this exceptionally gifted artist draws to the theatre whenever she appears. The revival of *La sonnambula* was particularly well adapted to her personal triumph. This was both on account of the character of Amina, whose portrayal Mme Callas could easily convey without fear of incurring in the middle register a roughness of intonation and ungraciousness of modulation, which she has not yet succeeded in eliminating from her singing, and in which at times she appears rather to indulge with pleasure; and also because of the nature of Visconti's production which succeeded in conjuring up a dreamlike atmosphere surrounding the graceful story, still set in a fourteenth century Arcadian background. Mme Callas created a personality composed of nuances and half-tones, persuasive and of the utmost delicacy.'[13] During the run of six performances EMI recorded the work with the same forces and most of the magic comes through well. The voices are caught exceptionally clearly; the studio cannot match the excitement of the opera house however and Votto certainly doesn't erase memories of Bernstein. But Callas' singing of the two principal arias quite eclipses what she achieved three years before in recital mode.

Four operas now concluded the final two months of the Scala season which was yet again dominated by Callas and di Stefano – she in *Anna Bolena* and *Ifigenia in Tauride*, and he in *Forza* and *Iris* in which *Musical America* noted the tenor 'poured out his beautiful voice almost too generously in the very strenuous part of Osaka.'[14] *Anna Bolena* was the event of the season and was given a 7-page review in *Opera* by Desmond Shawe-Taylor: 'The presence of Maria Callas in the company has lately encouraged a particularly adventurous policy at La Scala, for she is one of the few singers with the voice, technique, style and dramatic power to invest these old tragedies with their proper theatrical force. It was largely [though not wholly] thanks to Mme Callas that Donizetti's *Anna Bolena* was triumphantly revived at La Scala on April 14th after decades of neglect, broken only by one or two provincial productions, notably at Bergamo last year.' Mr Shawe-Taylor, at some length, takes us through the opera's unfamiliar pages from where 'the Queen, advancing herself to the footlights begins to sing a soft cavatina of recollection which suited Madame Callas to perfection and provided her with the first of many triumphs during the evening. We reach the last scene of Act 1 when Anna is discovered in an apparently compromising situation with Percy and Smeaton which was notable for the immense force of outraged dignity which Madame Callas threw into the words of recitative 'Giudici! Ad Anna! Giudici!' It was doubtless in such tremendous moments, of which the score gives no hint, that Pasta too revealed her greatness.' Although he is immensely impressed by Simionato's splendid Giovanna Seymour, especially in the Act 2 scene 1 duet, he has a few quibbles, notably with Rossi-Lemeni's King. 'The final scene in the Tower of London is the greatest thing in the opera and it also showed Madame Callas at the summit of her powers, both as singer and as tragic actress ... she launches into a forceful cabaletta with sequences of rising trills in which she arraigns the guilty couple yet magnanimously pardons them as, with dignity and composure, she leads her companions to the block. Interpreted by such an artist as Maria Callas and directed with perfect taste by Visconti, this was a scene of high tragedy. The whole production,' he concluded, 'showed the Scala at its best. Routine performances there can drop far below the general level, say, of the Metropolitan; but there is perhaps no other house in the world which can rise to a great occasion like this. There was a unity and a grandeur about the long evening which is deeply satisfying. Could *Anna Bolena* enter the international repertory? With Callas, yes; without her, or some comparable soprano of whom as yet there is no sign, no. Many people think it a flaw in these old operas that they depend on the availability of great singers; but what would be the fate of the standard violin and piano concertos if there were scarcely a player who could even get his fingers round the notes, let alone fill them with a lulling charm or a passionate intensity.'[15]

The season ended with *Ifigenia in Tauride,* Callas' final collaboration with Visconti. Lionel Dunlop, a new critic at La Scala, reported in *Opera*: 'With her noble dignity of bearing and authoritative command of the stage, Callas as the humane priestess of the barbaric Scythians, who would see an end to their human sacrifices, was a constant and exciting joy. She is in fine vocal state at present; and, since the *tessitura* of the role lies comfortably within her range, her singing caused none of that momentary discomfort which has sometimes seemed to go with her slimmer figure. Following the opening storm and narration of Ifigenia's dream, she began in tones of the most melting softness, 'O toi, qui prolongeas mes jours', Ifigenia's agonized prayer to Artemis that she would not live to experience the horrors of her dream. Her 'O malheureuse Iphigenie' was another moving experience. Only Callas can invest with so many overtones of meaning a single exclamation as, for example, in Ifigenia's recogition of Orestes, where joy at reunion, sad regret for past separation, horror at his impending sacrifice and an overwhelming love, were all intermingled in the single word "fratello".' [16] After a variety of conductors both in the pit and in the studio, a single RAI concert performance of *Lucia* in Rome brought Serafin back to the studio after two years in the wilderness following the furore over the EMI *Traviata* [though, as already observed, never once on stage].

Following the Scala *Lucia* performances the previous year at the Vienna Staatsoper, di Stefano returned in June 1957 to sing two roles – Don Jose and Puccini's Des Grieux. Joseph Wechsberg reported in *Opera*: 'The hysterical ovations of swooning females after di Stefano's Flower Song reminded one of the early days of Frank Sinatra at New York's Paramount Theatre, where they were less disturbing. Vienna's younger generation is celebrity-crazy and not very discriminating. Di Stefano sang beautifully, giving a fine *bel canto* demonstration, but he is certainly not the greatest singer of the century, as you might have judged by the applause that night. Similar scenes took place during a performance of *Manon Lescaut* performance with di Stefano, Matinis and Berry'. [17] Jean Madeira was the Carmen who once sang small bit parts in some early di Stefano performances at the Met in the 1940's.

Before the Scala Company, including Callas and di Stefano, flew to Edinburgh for the 1957 Festival, it gave performances of *Sonnambula* and *Forza* in Cologne to celebrate the opening of the new opera house. Ralf Steyer was immensely impressed: 'Callas brought conviction even to the unrealities of her role, and beneath the romantic cliches she enabled us to seize and feel the eternal elements of love and passion in all their wonder. Added to this she was in superb voice, and her incomparable artistry conveyed to her audience an atmosphere of quite breathless suspense which was communicated [as she herself admitted] to the singer herself. The final applause was prolonged for nearly an hour. Critics expressed boundless appreciation of her singing and of the musical qualities of the production, while withholding praise for the opera itself and its setting, which met with the harshest disapproval. But the public has a surer instinct, and departed that evening conscious of having enjoyed a rare experience such as the opera fan meets with on only a few occasions in his lifetime.'[18] *Forza* apparently was a twelfth-hour substitute for *Manon Lescaut* under an indisposed Sanzogno which provided nevertheless 'a performance of first-class quality. Leyla Gencer [singing opposite di Stefano for the only time in her career] sang and acted strongly as Leonora. Di Stefano was obliged to force his tone now and then, for the part is over-dramatic for his voice, but he revealed throughout his admirable intellectual and musical mastery, and the limitless *noblesse* of an outstanding artist.'[19] Immediately following this appearance, he recorded *La Gioconda* opposite Milanov at the RCA studios [now part of Polygram]. Milanov, a famous Gioconda at the Met who once boasted that she hadn't any idea what the opera was about, was a trifle too old to do the role complete justice. Philip Hope-Wallace in *Gramophone* thought di Stefano 'much the best of the Enzo Grimaldos and if in the famous tenor baritone duet you think enviously of the combination of power and elegance displayed by singers such as Caruso and Gigli at this moment, you will also have to admit that di Stefano's 'Cielo e mer' alongside the efforts of Messrs. del Monaco and Poggi is a really poetic bit of singing.'[20] Harold Rosenthal in *Opera* absolutely agreed: 'By far the most exciting singing comes from di Stefano, in excellent voice, who makes a rich voiced and pleasant sounding Enzo – surely the best since Gigli.'[21] At precisely this time, Callas was recording *Turandot*, as usual with EMI, which in part might explain the absence of di Stefano who might otherwise have been expected to sing Calaf, a part not yet in his repertoire but which would be within a year, first at Chicago and then to open the 1958-59 Scala season opposite Birgit Nilsson. He had already recorded the two arias successfully except for the climactic top B which only once did he hit 'bang-on', during his second RAI concert on 8th December 1952 alongside Stignani with whom he resurrected the first act duet from *Favorita*. Also with Giordano's two glorious arias, he gave RAI audiences the following year their first taste of his Andrea Chenier, which he debuted in Rome in 1959. In the 1956 concert, he included a rarity – Pietri's 'Io conosco un giardino' from his opera *Maristella* [included in a June '62 recorded recital].

Of Callas' Turandot, Philip Hope-Wallace [*Gramophone*] was cautious: 'To those to whom Mme Callas can do no wrong, the excitement of the set will stand in no need of recommendation from this quarter. Mme Callas has of course her own exciting qualities but lacks steel girder strength and steadiness in the taxing upper ranges of her appalling address before the riddle-posing. The timbre is sometimes hollow and plummy in the easier positions; the emission is wavering and sounds both strained and ill supported in the upper reaches; and her Turandot is here, to my ear, totally unsatisfying – no matter how often elsewhere I may applaud this and that stroke of dramatic truth and imagination. Many people have been looking forward to Mme Callas' Turandot just because something infinitely aristocratic and tragic inherent in the timbre of her voice, at its best, makes one want to hear her interpretation of the ice-bound princess; and to be sure, by the same token all she does is memorable whether for good or ill. I do not necessarily think the role needs ultra heroic treatment in the manner of Eva Turner. I am perfectly prepared to accept a frailer, gentler ice-maid: if only the actual vocal means could seem more *secure*. Of the acting ability – vocally imaginative enunciation of the text – there is never a doubt; the scene between princess and slave where Turandot asks what it is that gives Liù strength is marvellously 'real' and subtle; and in the Alfano pastiche parts which bring this unfinished opera to a conclusion of sorts, Mme Callas brings her own interesting personality sharply to bear, adding stature to the diminishing dramatic interest. But if it's secure and grand singing you want in this role, I have to say that I think you will do better to seek elsewhere.'[22] Harold Rosenthal in *Opera* was much more positive, and rightly so: 'As might have been expected, Turandot is a Callas role *par excellence*. Although there may have been Turandots with larger, more steely and powerful voices than this, I doubt whether any soprano has invested the part with more authority, or just that right mixture of imperiousness and coldness that combine to make the character one of the most difficult to portray in all opera. As is usual with a Callas performance, phrase after phrase takes on a new meaning and the posing of the riddles has a terrifying calculation about it.'[23]

For the other Scala recording that summer – *Manon Lescaut* – there were hitches before and after, but the performance itself brought both Callas and di Stefano together at white heat; act four in particular has seldom if ever received such a blazing account. It was certainly a miracle in execution and also a miracle in delivery because months before the scheduled sessions, EMI had great difficulty in persuading di Stefano to record the work with Callas. They always perform best when at each other's throats. Afterwards, Callas, in increasingly frail voice after the *Turandot* sessions, refused to sanction its release for two and-a-half years. As a top recommendation ever since, she should have

A NEW ROLE — A DAZZLING PERFORMANCE!

PHOTO JEAN-PIERRE LELOIR

with GIUSEPPE DI STEFANO as DES GRIEUX

and Giulio Fioravanti, Franco Calabrese, Dino Formichini, Carlo Forti, Vito Tatone, Fiorenza Cossotto, Giuseppe Morresi

TULLIO SERAFIN conducting the Orchestra and Chorus of La Scala, Milan (RECORDED IN CO-OPERATION WITH 'E. A TEATRO ALLA SCALA', MILAN)

33CX1583-5 33⅓ R P M LONG PLAYING RECORDS AVAILABLE NOVEMBER 6TH (LIBRETTO 6/6)

COLUMBIA

E M I Records Ltd 8 11 Great Castle Street London W1   (Regd. Trade Mark of Columbia Graphophone Co. Ltd.)

had no fears. William Mann reviewed the set for *Gramophone*: 'It is the old story again. Maria Callas' high notes, not so much in the first act as later, are acid in quality and develop what is a beat, if not a wobble. But her singing of Manon's more vivacious passages is beautifully poised and dazzling; she characterises Manon in every mood – the gentle, rather than preoccupied girl, in her first meeting with Des Grieux, the spoilt darling at the beginning of the second act, the woman knowing herself in the wrong but still promising to do better next time though everybody else knows she won't, the kept woman throwing scorn at her protector. And so her performance continues through to, ultimately, the death in the American desert which Puccini had the creative audacity to make an act for two characters alone, a symbol of solitude which makes its point on the gramophone more impressively than any proscenium-bounded stage can ever do. Comparison with Tebaldi is here unkind, because Tebaldi is always herself, warm and opulent and slightly fuller toned. She makes a really lovely noise in all Manon's expansive cantabile music, and that in turn is beyond Callas' reach; but opera is more than vocal euphony, and the much more is where Callas displays herself at every moment of this opera a great artist of the gramophone, an interpreter who removes veils from our eyes and a singing actress who, like all great singers of the century, transforms a gramophone from a wooden box into an experience. Di Stefano does not make a strong impression at his entrance; too close to the mike to give a suggestion of stage effect, he is vocally awkward too, with his shifts of vocal placing in mid-phrase. But he makes a most enjoyable impression in the second and third acts, singing his A minor solo 'Ah, Manon, mi tradisce' with genuine ardour and sustaining with the tension of the third act which explodes in 'Guardate, pazzo son'.[24] Harold Rosenthal for *Opera* also loved the set: 'Serafin gives us a vivid and dramatic reading of the score. The Scala orchestra is in magnificent form and the opening scene captures the atmosphere of the opera straightaway. Callas has never sung Manon on the stage, but unlike many artists who record roles they have never performed in the opera house, she succeeds in creating a vivid personality, a real flesh and blood figure. The differing aspects of Manon's character are admirably realised, and although Callas has not the beautiful, rich creamy tones of Tebaldi, she makes Manon a far more credible character than that singer. Di Stefano is not quite in his best voice; in fact he is disappointing in the first act, but finds almost his best form in the great Act 2 duet. His outburst at the end of act three is very exciting - and made one quickly realise what a long way he had come since his beautifully sung Wilhelm Meister shortly after the war. One regrets the change in a way, for he surely could have been the most beautiful light lyric tenor of our day.'[25] It was their tenth and last complete recording together; indeed, it was Callas' last recording in the mono Scala series; she was to re-record EMI's *Lucia* ['alive as never before'], *Norma* and *Tosca* and Cetra's *La gioconda* and a new recording of *Carmen,* all in stereo. However, the sad fact was that Callas' career at La Scala both on the stage and in the studio was drawing to a close. Complete recordings that she could and should have made for EMI include *Anna Bolena, Il Pirata, Macbeth, Nabucco, La Vestale, I vespri siciliani, Ifigenia* and above all *La traviata.* Instead of which EMI came up with excerpts and issues of live performances, often in poor sound. Di Stefano duly recorded *Forza,* again with Milanov for RCA and re-recorded *Lucia* with Scotto on DG, and *Tosca* with Leontyne Price, under Karajan, for Decca.

Shortly after their *Manon Lescaut,* di Stefano gave a 'beautifully sung' Rodolfo at Verona, 'but his penchant for playing to the gallery completely destroyed the illusion of sincerity'.[26] Three days before, Callas returned to Greece for the first time since she left her homeland at the end of the war to give two recitals at the famous Herodes Atticus Amphitheatre. Both visitor and visited were nervous and edgy after so long and momentous a gap; public misunderstanding over the diva's fee, hot dry weather and a last minute cancellation hardly improved the atmosphere. But on 5th August, Maria finally conquered all. She was then joined by di Stefano for the Scala company's visit to the Edinburgh Festival, she in *Sonnambula,* he in *L'elisir d'amore.* Although they may not have shared the stage together, that did not stop them from sharing the sights of Scotland's capital city. No festival budget, of course, could possibly engage them both in the same opera. Sadly, the writer, at the Festival at the time, failed to get tickets for either. Harold Rosenthal was there: 'It is already past history that the four performances of *Sonnambula* in which Maria Callas sang displayed the prima donna in varying vocal form. Her first night, which opened the festival, did not, according to reliable sources, find her in her best voice, nor was she helped by the lighting plant of the theatre which behaved in a manner more temperamental than any diva. The second performance found her on form and many people will have heard the broadcast [21st August]; her third performance was best forgotten [but surely not on the evidence of the broadcast tapes!]; she herself was unhappy about it and the cold damp Edinburgh weather had evidently afflicted her. The fourth *Sonnambula* [29th August] found Callas at her very best, and she gave a performance that vocally ranked with her last season's Normas in London. Dramatically her interpretation of sweet innocent Amina was a *tour de force,* not least because

EDINBURGH FESTIVAL 1957
Maria and Pippo, in tartan and headgear, sightseeing in the Scottish capital

by very nature Mme Callas is an imperious figure on the stage with a personality
eminently suited for the great tragic and heroic roles in lyric drama. Amina, a
Giselle-like, pathetic figure is miles removed from Norma, Medea, Ifigenia
and the rest; and it says a lot for Callas' genius and personality that she makes
us, by sheer willpower, believe in the person she has created as long as she is
on the stage. But even her greatest admirers, among whom I count myself,

must admit that Amina is not really her role. She is too tall, too elegant and too sophisticated a personality to be ideal for this part. Her singing of 'Come per me sereno' in the first scene was hauntingly beautiful and her 'Ah non credea' in the last, at least on this occasion, a display of *bel canto* singing that was intensely moving. The soprano's natural ability for colouring words and phrases was much in evidence throughout the evening; for example, when the way in which she uttered the words 'L'anello mio–l'anello i me ha tolto' tore at the heart strings. Against all this must be held the not very pleasant quality of some of her top notes and the suspicion that is always present when Callas is a little tired, of a second note lurking not too far away from the one she is singing. But when all is said and done, what a personality, what musicianship, and what intelligence!'[27] Mr Rosenthal's comments on *L'elisir* have already been noted; they were uncannily reproduced in *Musical America*. Scottish newspapers admired di Stefano's 'exemplary character portraiture, excellent singing and spirited acting.'

After a cold and windy Edinburgh, perhaps both singers were pleased to leave for warmer climes. Di Stefano prepared to return to Mexico for the first time since the glory days of 1952. As Otto Mayer-Serra wrote in *Opera:* 'Di Stefano was the big star of the season. He was the only one among the artists who enjoys an immense personal popularity, and has ever since he sang here in 1948 and 1949. He was nervous and strained in his first performance here this season [*La bohème*], due possibly to a completely insufficient Mimi, an inaudible Musetta and a young Italian conductor with whom he disagreed about the tempi. His *L'elisir* was rather over-acted, but he gave a great performance in *Carmen;* his Don Jose was splendid',[28] which he brought from Monterrey. He then returned to Chicago where he sang Enzo opposite Eileen Farrell, and Cavaradossi opposite Steber, which 'showed some effects of vocal indisposition, but was successful in hurling a clarion and thrilling "Vittoria" to the rafters.'[29] He had 'trouble in lightening his voice to match Anna Moffo's Lucia, but he contributed whatever dramatic fire there was to the scene in the Great Hall in Act II after an unbalanced sextet.'[30] Finally, he made his debut as Maurizio in *Adriana Lecouvreur* opposite Tebaldi in which 'he was handsomely garbed but not too vocally secure.'[31]

Callas' departure from Edinbugh was also eventful but much more traumatic; indeed, it had a direct bearing on her break with La Scala itself the following year. Although in his report in *Opera,* Harold Rosenthal had referred to Callas' being released from her engagement on September 3rd, neither he nor anyone else knew that there was in fact no engagement. She had signed for four performances; the Scala and the festival had announced a fifth and hoped Callas would oblige. Tired and exhausted anyway, she absolutely refused. 'Opera star quits Festival' this writer read as he walked along Princes Street. Of course, she did nothing of the kind. But she made two mistakes: first, she agreed to plead ill-health and secondly made straight for Italy where illustrated newspaper reports showed her basking in Venetian sunshine at an Elsa Maxwell party. Ticket holders for September 3rd were not best pleased, and rightly so. The writer met one of them forty years after the event, still fuming. Callas sent her husband to see Ghiringhelli at the Scala to return with an apology; in vain, of course. The crisis simmered on until the curtains rose on the new season on 7th December 1957 with Callas and di Stefano in *Un ballo in maschera*.

Chapter Fourteen

1958

Callas gained some post-Edinburgh comfort from the scheduled recording of *Medea*, even if understandably it is not her most vivid interpretation of the title role. That probably came the following year in Dallas in the wake of her being fired from the Met by its general manager, Rudolf Bing. She had been introduced to the fledgling Texas opera company in 1957 by Nicola Rescigno [who had conducted her in Chicago] for whom she gave a recital, the rehearsal of which survives on disc. Maria had clearly recovered from the traumas of the summer for she is in terrific voice.

The *Opera* Scala critic, Claudio Sartori was back for *Ballo* at the opening of the new season and he made it clear that he did not like what he saw and heard: not the 'usual sumptuous public performance'; not the tradition [tradition?] of 'selecting a Verdi opera'; not the 'gay and festive audience'; above all, not the 'notable group of artists', perhaps the 'finest which the Italian stage today can offer, richly endowed with the rarest gifts, to not one of whom does it occur that for the interpretation of Verdi melodrama, a melo-dramatic nineteenth century style is essential. It would appear,' he added, 'that singers, having discovered the rewards and advantages of recitative and of singing in the style of music drama, now wish to apply what they have absorbed to melodrama.' This was surely a thinly veiled attack on the art of Callas whom he never once mentioned in his review. Di Stefano he did, but only to prove that the production was 'smothered in an atmosphere of irrepressible tedium. 'The limit was reached when di Stefano – in order presumably to display a new and "brilliant" rendering – conceived it necessary to stylise "E scherzo od e follia", that page written and offered to the singer as a supreme proof of his ability to sing and to laugh. Di Stefano neither laughed nor sang; he delivered it smiling graciously, descending at times to a whisper. In spite of that, the audience applauded everything; but the audience, particularly that of the opening night of La Scala, is always a very indulgent one.'[1] Two American critics thought very differently. Ernest de Weerth in *Opera News*: 'As soon as the turbulent Maria Meneghini Callas appeared, extravagantly costumed as ever, we realised that she had set her stamp on Amelia. She was in voice and sang superbly. Callas is never dull. When not held in check she is prone to exaggeration; when guided by an intelligent and trusted *regisseur*, her acting is convincing and exciting. Her personality is without doubt the most imposing

TEATRO ALLA SCALA

ENTE AUTONOMO

STAGIONE LIRICA 1957-58

Repar N 1

N. 1 del Turno B
N. 1 degli abbonati alle 'Prime'

SABATO 7 DICEMBRE 1957 · alle ore 21 precise

SERATA DI GALA PER L'APERTURA DELLA STAGIONE

UN BALLO IN MASCHERA

Melodramma in tre atti

Musica di

GIUSEPPE VERDI

(Proprietà G. Ricordi & C.)

NUOVO ALLESTIMENTO

Personaggi e interpreti

Riccardo, Conte di Warwick, Governatore di Boston	GIUSEPPE DI STEFANO
Renato, creolo, suo segretario e sposo di	ETTORE BASTIANINI
Amelia	MARIA MENEGHINI CALLAS
Ulrica, indovina di razza nera	GIULIETTA SIMIONATO
Oscar, paggio	EUGENIA RATTI
Silvano, marinaio	GIUSEPPE MODESTI
Samuel } nemici del Conte	ANTONIO CASSINELLI
Tom }	MARCO STEFANONI
Un Giudice	ANGELO MERCURIALI
Un servo d'Amelia	ANTONIO RICCI

Deputati · Ufficiali · Marinai · Guardie · Uomini, donne e fanciulli del popolo · Gentiluomini
Aderenti di Samuel e Tom · Servi · Maschere e coppie danzanti

La scena a Boston e nei dintorni · L'azione sulla fine del secolo XVII.

Maestro concertatore e direttore

GIANANDREA GAVAZZENI

Maestro del coro
NORBERTO MOLA

Regia di
MARGHERITA WALLMANN

Direttore dell'allestimento
NICOLA BENOIS

Bozzetti e figurini di
NICOLA BENOIS

Coreografia di
MARGHERITA WALLMANN

Maestro collaboratore
UMBERTO VERGNELLI

Maestro della banda
FRANCO LAZZINI

Maestro suggeritore
VASCO NALDINI

Capo servizio macchinistico
AURELIO CROCE

Attr. scene HANGAR & C. e R. ROUMANI · Calzature PEDRAZZOLI · Parrucche di FELICE SANTORO

Capo servizio elettrico e luci
GIULIO LOPETSI

PREZZI

Platea e palchi esauriti in abbonamento e in prenotazione — Ingresso ai palchi L. 3000

Galleria (ingresso compreso) Poltroncina centrale di I galleria L. 2500

Numerato di I galleria   » 1000   Ingresso L. 350
Numerato di II galleria   » 700   Ingresso » 250

(ai numerati si aggiunge il diritto erariale D - e L in E. F.)

IN PLATEA NON VI SONO POSTI IN PIEDI

È prescritto l'abito da sera per la platea e per i palchi

Il teatro si apre alle ore 20,15 · Le gallerie si aprono alle ore 20.

'UN BALLO IN MASCHERA' 7th December 1957 LA SCALA
Interval reception with President Gronchi [*left*] and conductor, Giandrea Gavazzeni [*right*]

Riccardo: 'Addio, per sempre.'

Congratulations all round from the producer, Margherita Wallmann

The parting of the ways

on the operatic stage today. Others may have more beautiful voices but at the moment there is only one Callas, just as there was only one Mary Garden. Opposite her, di Stefano enthralled his audience vocally and dramatically. His voice when not forced is one of the most lyric and enjoyable of the generation; no tenor in Italy today displays such finesse, few anywhere in such perfect diction. His appearance has youthful charm and elegance, and with maturity he has acquired discrimination. He never overacts. His death scene at the end of the opera was extraordinarily moving.'[2] *Musical America:* 'Di Stefano was a revelation both in his excellent singing and fine appearance. He has improved a great deal vocally since I heard him last season and particularly since he last sang at La Scala. Neither was Callas' long-awaited Amelia a disappointment, for this intelligent artist surmounted the difficulties with superb musicality and artistic phrasing.'[3]

Ballo was their fourth and last collaboration at La Scala; altogether Callas and di Stefano partnered each other in nine operas on stage and ten in the studio. He had one of the most glorious tenor voices of the century; at his best, he was incomparable. Callas was different: even at her worst, she was well nigh incomparable. This disparity, with squabbles in Mexico [*Tosca*], La Scala [*La traviata*], Berlin [*Lucia*], drove them apart and now finally, *Ballo. Un ballo in maschera* is a 'tenor' opera and di Stefano was still playing 'second fiddle' and understandably he had had enough. They never sang together again until the very end of their careers when it was far too late. Even now, as the new year approached, danger signs began to threaten the years of glory, and within a single season. Maria Callas and her husband were probably glad to leave La Scala behind for Christmas and then Rome where she was to open the season with her beloved Norma at a Gala before the President and his wife on 2nd January. As a foretaste of what was to come, she sang the 'Casta diva' on Eurovision, heard by millions of people including the writer who silenced a New Year's Eve party in her honour. Next day, she awoke from the festivities with no voice, and the management with no substitute. 'There is no substitute for La Callas'. Every device was employed to bring back the voice and it obliged in part for the Presidential Gala. Although it lasted the course of 'Casta diva', it could not continue beyond the first interminable interval and was replaced for the next performance by Anita Cerquetti's. Cynthia Jolly saw it all and reported for *Opera:* 'Even the Rome *Messaggero* reporter was not quite sure. Was it 'Via la Callas' [Away with Callas] or 'Viva la Callas' which was being shouted from the gallery among the 'Evviva l'Italias' and 'Viva le cantanti Italiene' which greeted the end of Cerquetti's 'Casta diva' the [second] first night of *Norma*? How did Callas really sing the first act? Over the radio an adequate judgment is difficult. What was clear was that she was singing under effort, specially as the act wore on. She began with an admirably clear-cut recitative taken monumentally slowly, slightly muffed the effect of the 'sacro vischio' but recovered a lovely quality in the opening of 'Casta diva'. The rest – particularly in the *cabaletta* – was a question of covered and hardened tone; nothing that does not happen constantly in performance but which is unacceptable to a perfectionist of Callas' ferocious sensibility. Couple this dissatisfaction with all the other factors [the Corelli-Pirazzini success which ended the act, the over-expectant public, her battle with her own physical state] and the story is told. But as an eminent conductor pointed out, who knows but that with less entreaty and a little more diplomatic firmness she could have been persuaded to go back to reap the inevitable success of the succeeding acts? Feelings were running so high when Cerquetti took over for the second round that she was mistress of all she surveyed, and newspapers next morning were overwhelmingly biased in her favour. Yet in strictest objectivity, it must be said that as a performance it was memorable primarily by virtue of its circumstances. Perhaps the sanest comment on the whole affair comes from a veteran painter who has spent his life in a hotbed of controversy: "Scandals of this sort are necessary. I would almost go so far as to say they need to be encouraged so as to break the monotony of this type of entertainment. Personally I had the time of my life the other evening." Is it a case of 'Via la Callas' or 'Viva la Callas'?' [4]

Callas' scheduled appearances in America provided a very welcome refuge and Ronald Eyer in *Opera* was relieved to report that 'Maria Callas, in *Lucia, Traviata* and *Tosca* has come and gone without a single tantrum or threat of a lawsuit. Her Lucia is one of her best roles, along with Tosca and Norma, but she is somehow not right for Violetta. There is a prevailing demure, sweet quality about this pathetic figure which does not go with the volume and the frequently harsh quality of tone which Callas produces and which stand her in good stead in more starkly dramatic roles. She is a great favourite, however, in whatever she does and always draws a packed house.' [5] But soon she would have to return to Italy where the government had made it clear she was not welcome. Three engagments in the Iberian peninsula – a concert in Madrid and two performances of *Traviata* in Lisbon – helped to put off the evil day. Di Stefano had remained at the Scala since *Ballo* for *Adriana Lecouvreur* and *Madama Butterfly*. And he returned there from a couple of 'reputedly resplendent' [6] performances of *Bohème* at the Teatro dell'Opera, Rome to 'repeat his interpretation of Nemorino, full of wit and wisdom, with an economy of means and exactness of intonation, and, most important of all, with an emotional effect which renders this role one of his finest lyrical achievements. The tumultuous success which he again won should teach him that has no need to force his gifts as a singer to rouse his audience to enthusiasm – which has at times happened to him in other performances at the risk of perfect intonation.'[7]

Meanwhile, as Claudio Sartori observed, 'Maria Meneghini Callas, the famous and much-discussed prima donna had made her reappearance at La Scala in the character of Anne Boleyn. She naturally renewed the triumphant success of her interpretation, particularly in the great scene of the last act, though some justified criticism was not lacking of the eccentricities of style she now systematically adopts, which lead her to exaggerate the dramatic moments and add too great a charm to tender passages.'[8] Perhaps Mr Sartori might have added that on this particular night both of these 'eccentricities' were necessary to overcome the icy hostility of the Milanese audience towards her. However he was completely won over by her final appearances in a new role – Imogene in Bellini's *Il Pirata*, an early work which nevertheless 'contains admirable passages of intimate feeling and moving drama, all expressed with the lyrical emotion of free melody wandering in fresh fields. Maria Callas' interpretation was flawless. Never perhaps has a singer been better adapted by her own means of expression to play the part of Imogene; and never avoided so well those strongly dramatic accents so as to limit herself almost entirely to the meaningful recitatives [which Mme Callas knows how to utter in the only convincing way] and to those lyrical *mezza-voce* sections, meditative and with slackened tempo, which have become a predominating characteristic of her interpretations – though on other occasions such passages have not always justified themselves as necessary and irreplaceable.'[9] Whatever drama there was on stage, however, was nothing to what occurred at the final performance when Callas [who had endured months of mortifying silence from the cold and haughty Ghiringhelli], during the Mad Scene which ends the opera, chose to ignore the 'palco' [scaffold] and curse instead the 'palco' [director's box], at which the sovrintendente brought the safety curtain down between the diva and her clamouring admirers. It was a cruel, savage end to her reign at La Scala, worse even than Rome.

This time she was able to seek refuge in London where she was due to appear in a centenary celebration at the Royal Opera House, Covent Garden and five performances there of *La traviata*. The editor of *Opera* was there: 'The theatre, which always has its own special atmosphere, looked its best. The decorations in the auditorium were far simpler than usual and twice as effective; the audience looked magnificent and was far less stuff-shirted in its behaviour than is generally the case on similiar occasions. All the items were listened to intently, and there was a great deal of genuine enthusiasm which reached its peak in the enormous ovation accorded to Mme Callas after her performance of the Mad Scene from *Puritani*, an example of consummate operatic singing and acting which held the audience spellbound. The Queen of present-day opera was applauded by our own Queen, both of whom were honouring Covent Garden on its hundredth birthday.'[10]

Callas' five wonderful appearances as Violetta opened on 20th June, her first performance since quitting the Scala which, by a most wickedly ironic co-incidence was the very day which marked Renata Tebaldi's prompt return to the Scala company, less than three weeks after Maria left it, to sing *Tosca* opposite di Stefano at the Brussels World Exhibition. Lest this smacks even slightly of treachery on the tenor's part, it must be remembered that this particular performance was in fact di Stefano's thirteenth Cavaradossi opposite Tebaldi and there were eight more to come. Di Stefano's partnership with the Italian diva was indeed considerable, even topping that with Callas: 22 performances at the Scala alone and 30 elsewhere in Rio, Chicago, Philadelphia, Palermo, Florence, Naples and Rome in *Boheme, Onegin, Forza, Adrianna Lecouvreur, Butterfly, Fedora* and *Manon Lescaut*. But of course the recordings have always identified del Monaco with Tebaldi as they have di Stefano with Callas and the Decca artists were soulmates at the can belto school of operatic singing.

During their careers, as of course might be expected, Callas and di Stefano sang opposite a whole host of celebrities. Amongst Callas' 66 tenors, the most important were Mirto Picchi, Mario del Monaco, both stalwart Polliones to her Norma, Franco Corelli, who played a big role in some of Callas' major Scala appearances, Jon Vickers a splendid foil to her Medea, and Valletti an elegant Alfredo. Great tenors like Bjorling [Manrico] and Bergonzi [Edgardo] touched her as she passed by, as did Covent Garden's own James Johnston [Manrico] and Charles Craig [Pollione]. Of the 150 or so ladies who crossed di Stefano's path, there were some stella names. I first heard di Stefano in 1958 opposite Birgit Nilsson in *Tosca* [only their second performance together] and I rather admired his ability to survive that mighty voice. Altogether, he sang 21 performances opposite her in Vienna and La Scala in *Aida, Tosca* and *Turandot*. Other celebrated partners at the Staatsoper were Gré Brouwenstijn [Tosca], Leonie Rysanek [Amelia] and Leontyne Price [Butterfly]. In Mexico 1964, he sang in *Manon* and *Ballo* opposite Montserrat Caballe for the first time. He met the older generation mainly in America – Bido Sayao, Licia Albanese, Eleanor Steber, Erna Berger, Lily Pons and Zinka Milanov. At La Scala, when not singing with Callas, his principal partners were Rosanna Carteri, Clara Petrella and Antonietta Stella. His Covent Garden debut was opposite Régine Crespin in *Tosca* for the first of nine occasions in Europe and South America. But neither Callas nor di Stefano achieved anything greater than they did opposite each other, especially in the recording studios, where between January 1953 and July 1957 they had committed their ten complete operas to disc.

Seven pages in *Opera* allowed Harold Rosenthal to look at the glorious 1958 Covent Garden *Traviata* in detail: 'Whatever one thinks of Maria Callas as an operatic artist there can be no denying that she contributed more to Italian opera in our day than anyone else. Her name is known to the man in the street. In Italy she has been the cause of the revival of long neglected works by Bellini, Donizetti, Cherubini, Spontini and others – and her inter-pretations of the more familiar works in the repertory arouse fierce controversy. She is a sincere and highly intelligent artist; she demands the highest standards from her colleagues and from the opera houses that engage her; she is an untiring worker and seeker after perfection and a highly professional performer. All this has meant that the art of opera, especially Italian opera, benefitted. I am sorry that there have been such divided opinions about her Violetta – but then Callas would not be Callas unless she had this effect on people – and also sorry that some of my colleagues have dwelt at length about the purely vocal side of her first performance, which she herself was the first to admit did not find her in the best of health, while dismissing the interpretation as a whole in a few words. At this time of day we know all about Callas' vocal mechanics, but what we do not all of us seem to realise is that the sum total of her performance of Violetta, no less than any other role, even when she is not singing at her best, represents a great interpretation, conceived as an organic whole, such as only comes our way very, very rarely. The more I read of the criticisms of artists of the last century the more convinced I am that they were not perfect singers. And what of those people who sigh for Melba...or Galli-Curci? Did they ever begin to suggest the tragedy of Violetta as Mme Callas does? Did the round dimpled figure of dal Monte, for example, even touch the fringe of La Dame aux Camelias? Are not some of us forgetting that opera is music-drama and not just *vocalise*? Having been to three of the Callas performances, it was possible to hear that each one was better than its predecessor vocally, and to see how each one differed dramatically. In other

words Callas tries to vary and improve each performance, and although some
of the inflections and nuances remain constant, because the artist has found
the right 'tone' for a certain phrase from the beginning, others assume new
significance as the drama unfolds. As Mme Callas told us in her television
interview with David Webster, she tries to employ a tone for Violetta which
gives the impression of a sick woman who is dying of tuberculosis and I
believe this to be true and not, as some less generous people have suggested,
an excuse she makes because her tone is not a natural Italian one.

In the first act Callas shows us a brittle, highly strung Violetta unable to be
at rest; the charming hostess who talks to as many of her guests as she can,
who does not want to spoil the party when she feels ill, and who can only
joke at first over Alfredo's declaration of love. For this Violetta, love does not
come in the duet but in the middle of the 'Sempre libera' when she hears
Alfredo's 'Amor, amor e palpito'. As Callas uttered the simple word 'Oh!' and
then 'Oh amore!' we knew the truth, just as earlier in the scene when she
looked at herself in the mirror and sighed 'Oh qual pallor' we knew that this
Violetta realised she was a dying woman. And what other Violetta has been
able to use the *coloratura* in 'Un di felice' so naturally to suggest, as Callas does,
the nonchalant carefree life of the courtesan. The second act Violetta had
become softened and was wholly and utterly devoted to her Alfredo. The long
central scene with Germont was outstanding and here Callas was supreme.
From the moment she drew herself proudly to her full height at the words
'Donna son' io, signore, ed in mia casa', through the changing emotions of the
conversation with Germont, to the resigned 'E vero! E vero!', as Germont
pointed out that she would one day grow old and Alfredo would tire of her,
and on to the great moment of renunciation – this was operatic singing and
acting at its greatest. The beginning of 'Dite alla giovine' was a moment of
sheer magic, with the voice curiously suspended in mid-air; and the final
request to Germont to embrace her as a daughter was profoundly moving. In
the writing of the letter and a short scene with Alfredo, Callas achieved a
great intensity. At the first two performances under review the 'Amami Alfredo'
passage was rather subdued; at the final performance, she rode the orchestra,
opened up her voice and achieved the maximum degree of intensity, which
aroused the audience to a spontaneous outburst of applause. In the second
scene of Act 2, Callas successfully depicted the conflicting emotions of Violetta
in the party scene. Again it was the odd word and phrase that assumed a new
significance and at the same time the nervous hands touched her face and
patted her hair. Then in the great ensemble, 'Alfredo, Alfredo di questo core'

was sung as if Violetta's heart was truly breaking'– as indeed was the writer's
from the back of the stalls circle.'Callas' last act was superb. Dramatically one
felt how Violetta suffered, one saw the effort with which the dying woman
dragged herself from bed to dressing table, from dressing table to chair.
'Oh come son mutata' brought a lump to the throat as she eagerly scanned
the tell-tale glass for some glimmer of hope. The reading of the letter was
quiet and intimate, and then came a moving 'Addio del passato'. When Alfredo
was announced, Violetta hurriedly tried to tidy her hair and look her best, and
then came the reunion, with Violetta's hands [and how Callas had made the
most of her beautiful long fingers throughout the evening] clasping at the
longed-for happiness, and hardly believing that Alfredo was a flesh and blood
figure. 'Ah! Gran dio' was sung with terrific intensity – and at the final
performance Callas took the whole phrase in one breath without a break.
The drama moved to its close, and gently Violetta gave Alfredo the locket.
The death scene was almost horrific, the last 'E strano!' was uttered in an
unearthly voice, and as Violetta rose to greet what she thought was a new
life, a glaze came over her eyes, and she literally became a standing corpse.
This was at the first night, but her death scene varied from performance to
performance. If I have spent so much space on this interpretation it is because
I believe that Callas' Violetta deserves to be recorded in such detail; for I am
sure it will go down in operatic history as a very great performance.'[11]

Although it was not recognised at the time, it was also a watershed in the
careers of Callas and di Stefano. Before her fleeting return to La Scala in
December 1960, she gave only a handful of performances: *Medea, Traviata* and
Lucia in Dallas, and *Il pirata* for the New York City Opera, an event which
happily captured her glorious Imogene on tape in the absence of a broadcast
of the ill-fated performances at La Scala. *Opera* reported that 'purely as singing
her performance left a good deal to be desired; her first note might have been
emitted by a Hudson tug-boat. But she improved steadily, so that the final,
inevitable Mad Scene emerged as the kind of performance she alone can give.
Perhaps the most strikingly beautiful piece of singing, though, came with the
quiet duet in which she bids farewell to the husband she has betrayed…
I doubt whether anyone was convinced *Il pirata* deserves more frequent revival,
but to judge by the ovation Mme Callas received afterwards it had given a lot
of harmless, if expensive, pleasure.'[12]

Instead, she embarked on extensive concert tours initiated by her opportunist
husband before he was dispatched in August 1959 after a cruise on Aristotle
Onassis' yacht, *Christina*, which incidentally followed immediately upon the

Greek shipowner's Dorchester Hotel reception after her Covent Garden *Medea*. Harold Rosenthal in *Opera* dealt at some length with the compelling effect of Callas' acting in *Medea* which overcame some very limp conducting and noted for the record that 'her voice was in better shape than last summer [1958], that on the first night she obviously was trying not to make any ugly sounds at all; that her soft singing was often extremely beautiful; that her singing of the Gluck-Mozart like final scene was exciting and electrifying.' [13] And although di Stefano was accorded the singular honour of opening the Scala season in 1958 for the third successive year, as Calaf in *Turandot* opposite Birgit Nilsson, with performances of Rodolfo, and Jenik in *The Bartered Bride* to follow, he, like his famous partner, no longer held sway and found solace in other favourite opera houses – Vienna, Rome, Chicago – with other celebrated sopranos.

Chapter Fifteen

1959–1965

All goods things must, of course, come to an end but neither Callas nor di Stefano could have imagined that their years of glory would have dissolved so quickly. After her sudden dramatic departure in June 1958, Callas made only two further appearances, between 1960 and 1962, at the Scala, in *Poliuto* and *Medea*, a total of ten performances. This compared with 156 she gave there between 1951 and 1958, an average of nearly twenty per year. Her uniquely intense schedules and huge fame had left her exhausted, her voice imperilled, a prey to whatever vicissitudes lay ahead. Di Stefano lingered somewhat longer but having completed a schedule of appearances at the Scala remarkably similar to Callas' – 140 over a similar period with a further forty-six before his last appearance there in *Carmen* in 1972, seven years after Callas' final Tosca at Covent Garden in 1965. Having opened the 1958/59 Scala season with seven performances of *Turandot* and given seven further performances of *Boheme* and *The Bartered Bride*, his appearances were decidedly fitful, a condition imposed by an unfortunate intake of nylon carpeting particles which seriously affected his vocal chords.

Thus they both ceased to be a force at the Scala at much the same time. This is not to suggest that they were inter-dependent because they were not. In fact, their joint appearances had numbered only four at La Scala and a further five elsewhere. Out of Callas' 166 performances and di Stefano's 186 at the Scala, they sang only 18 together. With 29 elsewhere in São Paulo, Mexico City, Italy and Chicago, they numbered a total of 47. Their respective repertoire had little in common, she being the mistress of *bel canto* which he increasingly eschewed. But their domination of the Scala programmes, as we have seen, was very marked and their ten complete recordings blazed a trail world-wide. Chief of Callas' 22 roles sung at La Scala were Violetta [21 performances], Norma [18], Amina [16], Anna Bolena [12], and Medea [10]. Many of her roles, like Alceste, Amelia, Fedora, Ifigenia, Lady Macbeth, Imogene, Giulia, she sang only at the Scala. Of di Stefano's 27 roles there, the most famous were Rodolfo [18 performances], Nemorino [16], Don Jose [16], Riccardo [13]. Alvaro [12], and Cavaradossi [11]. He performed altogether a total of 50 roles; Callas, 41. They made over 500 appearancs in nearly 140 theatres though inevitably only a fraction of these together.

The years between 1958 and 1965 marked a falling-off inevitable at the end of the career of any artist and theirs was all the more pronounced after their prodigious achievements. Alongside her new passionate life with Onassis, Callas sang when she could and not when she had to. Her appearances at Epidauros, La Scala, Covent Garden, the Paris Opéra and the Met were solitary events of great magnitude, shining out amidst a run of concerts which is the lot of the famous. Di Stefano for his part clung to centres where he was loved. As John L. Walsh said of his return to Mexico City in 1965, 'Every artist who has served his public over a considerable period deserves a refuge where he can do no wrong.'[1] And they absolutely deserved no less. Callas, whose high principles had led to trouble with Ghiringhelli at La Scala, Karajan in Vienna, Bing at the Met and others elsewhere, felt differently about Covent Garden which was run by Sir David Webster who was, she said, a gentleman. Her return to the Royal Opera House in 1964 in Zeffirelli's production of *Tosca* was an act of love no less, reflected in Callas' 'warm, feminine heroine, deeply in love with Cavaradossi and ready to sacrifice herself for him,' as Harold Rosenthal wrote in *Opera*: 'She was impulsive and deeply religious: one remembers how she knelt devotedly in prayer; how hardly moving her head she signified her ascent to Scarpia's proposal; how proud she was of her Mario. Yet at the same time she was the girlish and fragile Tosca; and helped by the wonderful second act set, she became a frightened creature, unable to escape from her tormentor, as she beat her clenched fists first on Scarpia, then on the men dragging off Cavaradossi, and finally on the closed door. This same feeling of the trapped creature was again apparent in the last act after the execution, where a huge towering section of the fortress positively dwarfed her, as she looked in vain for a way of escape. There was no way of escape but the battlements. And how in 1964 did she sing? I will be asked. Well, the voice was far better at all the three performances I heard than at any time since the 1958 *Traviatas*. At the performance on 1st February it was at its best, but the voice is so much part of the whole of a Callas performance that one cannot really separate it from the acting. She colours her voice much as a painter does his canvas and if it is still not as large and sumptuous as it once was, it is still an amazing instrument, and its timbre a highly individual.'[2]

The production was taken to Paris and later to the Met with predictable results, reported by Martin Bernheimer in *Opera*: 'As a singularly undistinguished Metropolitan season limped to its merciful end, one event brought momentary life and excitement to the old house on 39th Street: the return of Maria Callas. Predictably, Callas' vintage '65 Tosca divided both press and public, and only her most hysterical devotees pretended that her vocal powers were undiminished. Nevertheless, for two evenings [March 19 and 25], the tattered scenery of the

Met's antique production, the routine of Fausto Cleva's conducting, the absence of a discernible plan of production and the indifferent casting of secondary roles all seemed insignificant. No one in the opulent 'benefit' audience objected that the star was being displayed in unworthy surroundings. The important thing was that she was being displayed at all. The demand for seats was so perplexing that the Met was unable to provide its customary press accommodation. For the first performance, this writer was consigned to an obstructed-view standing location in the Dress Circle. This made conclusive judgment of the performance practically impossible, but it did serve to reinforce certain impressions of Callas' art in its current state. At moments when she was visible as well as audible, which was about 50 per cent of the time, her Tosca was utterly compelling. The voice seemed smaller in size and a bit more limited in colour than when last heard, but, if anything, her capacity for communication through vocal and physical acting had increased. This was a girlish, impetuous Tosca, desperately in love with Cavaradossi and just as desperately frightened by Scarpia. There were no prima-donna mannerisms, no grandiose gestures, and no moments in which the protagonist played to the audience instead of to the other characters. If one was not especially conscious of beautiful singing *per se,* one *was* conscious of a beautiful Tosca. Little else mattered. But whenever Callas moved out of sight, the impression was radically different. Then one suddenly became painfully aware of the vocal limitations: the shortness of breath, the inconsistent focus of tone, the willingness to sacrifice a sustained melodic line for a theatrical half-spoken one, the futile lunges at top notes, and the wobble that crept into the voice whenever she sang loud and/or high notes. Also, one began to notice that the audience was not one hundred per cent sympathetic. With each high-note hurdle, for instance, murmurs of surprise, even derision, greeted the unsuccessful negotiation. The second performance, for which I managed to purchase seats, sustained the previous impression, even though – paradoxically – total vision made it easier to overlook the vocal failures. Whether or not one can overlook them completely, however, depends very much on what one values most in opera. It does seem strange that the bulk of the New York public, which is usually concerned with sound alone, should be so willing to make musical allowances for the sake of the drama. More often it is the other way around. In any case, it now seems unrealistic to suggest that Callas should switch to a lower repertory. After all, the absence of a reliable top does not make a mezzo of a soprano.'[3]

The production then returned to Covent Garden where the great career ended: 'So it has happened at last,' wrote Harold Rosenthal, 'Maria Callas has cancelled a London performance. One really wonders why there has been so much fuss – *most* opera singers cancel performances at some time or other during their careers. What should be remembered is that during the years Callas was at La Scala, she must have sung more than 150 performances without missing one, and there was not a word about that in the press! But Callas has become a legend in her lifetime and I suppose one must expect this kind of publicity. At the Gala on 5 July 1965, Callas sang the first act far more softly than last year, and in the second conserved her meagre vocal resources most cleverly. It was obvious that she was not strong enough vocally or physically to have sung more than the one performance and perhaps it would have been kinder and wiser had she not sung at all on this occasion. I had the feeling that we might well be witnessing her last London stage performance. I hope I am wrong, for she still has the power to illuminate the part she is singing as no other singer can. But how long can she continue with such slender vocal and physical means?'[4] Sadly, we know the answer: she couldn't and didn't.

★   ★   ★

No such abrupt end affected di Stefano's work, which enabled him to achieve a career total of just over a thousand performances. When the Covent Garden curtains fell on the *Tosca* that was in fact to be Callas' final stage performance, he was embarking that night on a run of eight performances of *Carmen* at the Caracalla Baths, Rome. But nevertheless, at almost precisely the same time di Stefano had to severely curtail the number of his performances from the usual fifty or so each year to well below twenty, when he undertook a series of performances of Lehar's *The Land of Smiles*. It was a time of mixed fortunes. He had many friends in Vienna, for example, ever since the visit of the Scala *Lucia* in 1956. Unfortunately, there in September 1958, 'di Stefano's lyric tenor voice [wasn't] right for the metallic demands of Radames; and as Cavaradossi he was again bothered by what was called an indisposition'[5] [though not unduly so to the writer's ears from the standing area at the back of the stalls.] Later in the month, Mitropoulos' *Ballo* was a 'nervous, supercharged job which didn't always help the singers. Di Stefano, opposite a 'glacial' Birgit Nilsson, strained his high notes, but on the whole gave a beautiful, moving performance.'[6] But the following May, 'Stella and di Stefano were disappointing in *Manon Lescaut* and *Ballo*; the tenor had more than a little trouble with his high notes.'[7] There was some consternation in 1960 when he 'broke off after the first act of the second *Ballo* opposite Leonie Rysanek.'[8] But they loved his

Alvaro, with that 'tenorial sweep and mellowness of great beauty. He is one of the very few Italian tenors who give you the illusion of a tenor: most of them shout like pushed up baritones.'[9] At the New Year's *Fledermaus,* he sang 'O sole mio' and 'Dein ist mein ganzes herz' as 'only he can sing it among all the tenors now practising – if he wants to, but he doesn't want to very often,'[10] added *Opera's* Joseph Wechsberg, who had long admired di Stefano. During the summer festival [1961], he gave an 'elegant' Don Jose and as Calaf, with Birgit Nilsson and Leontyne Price, he was 'in good form, hardly straining, singing beautifully, bringing off 'Nessun dorma' with a great sweep and giving a fine portrayal of an elegant prince.' [11] The following year his Cavaradossi with Price and Giuseppe Taddei under Karajan [all later recorded for Decca] had 'moments of greatness. Di Stefano is wonderful; though he does many things wrong according to the book, everything comes out all right. Since we have to have tenors, we should always have di Stefanos who give the complete tenorial illusion.'[12] This did not last with Karajan, though, who turned him down for a Scala *Bohème* in 1963. The following year, as Riccardo, 'in his happy moments, di Stefano is still one of the few real tenors now before the public who tries to give beauty and makes an attempt at *bel canto* but these happy moments do not come very often.'[13] How sad that within a year, Joseph Wechsberg, 'an old di Stefano fan' had 'unhappily to say it was becoming increasingly difficult to have to listen to him.'[14] Time to say 'Goodnight, Vienna'? 1965 was in truth proving a sad year for both singers. Callas' voice by then was silent and in the closing weeks of that year, di Stefano sang four of his great roles – Riccardo, Alvaro, Pinkerton, and Alfredo – for the last time, and three months later his final Cavaradossi.

Time was also running out in America. In October 1958, as Pinkerton, he 'took too long to warm up his voice – and heart.'[15] But his debut as Calaf was a 'foil of vocal splendour and mien.'[15] His four weeks in Chicago [autumn 1959] began badly: 'a raw voiced Don Jose, found in his Canio cupboard'.[16] *Musical America* agreed up to the Flower Song which he 'sang with admirable restraint and artistry. From then on he steadily improved in vocal and dramatic intensity, culminating in the last despairing outburst over the dead body of his beloved Carmen.'[17] Opposite Nilsson in *Turandot,* 'both sang only a measure less than memorably.'[18] And 'not since his Canio of 1958 has di Stefano [as Riccardo] sung so suavely and with so little evidence of strain on top; never before, in Chicago's memory, has he shown such responsible musicianship.'[19] According to *Musical America,* he and Nilsson 'stopped the show with the big duet.'[20] But the following year [1960] he 'disappointed as Cavaradossi except when he was singing softly.'[21] A bad incident spoiled the performance of *Ballo* three years later when di Stefano 'threatened to quit the theatre after catching sight of a picture of Franco Corelli in the programme which pronounced this rival *divo* 'the world's greatest tenor'. Opera at its grandest raged back-stage and it was only after all the programmes had been removed from the auditorium and dumped in di Stefano's dressing-room that the insulted tenor consented to sing. His work proved spotty, with a tendency to tire in sustained passages.'[22] In Dallas they liked the 'practised confidence' of his Pinkerton which 'eased into comfortable voluptuousness only after an unduly long warm-up phase'[23] and his Werther in New Orleans which 'rated admiration for its many artistic nuances but regret that the vocal excesses of the past years have robbed the voice of its former sheen.'[24] The American tour ended unhappily first in Philadelphia where di Stefano 'no longer possesses his former easy lyricism; it is painful to think what this lovely voice was a few years ago. However, he brought an unquestioned authority to his Cavaradossi.'[25] He hit bottom with an unwise return to the Met 'after a long absence in, of all things, *Les Contes d'Hoffmann.* It is doubtful whether di Stefano ever would have been at ease in this very French role, with its high *tessitura* and semi-dramatic declamation. In any case, the di Stefano of today [1965] barely knew the role, and he was not averse from rewriting it when the required notes lay too high for comfort. Furthermore, he seemed uninterested in what was going on round him [with such a supporting cast assembled, one hardly blamed him], and he sounded painfully strained and inaccurate for much of the time. Despite the salvo of applause that greeted his entrance, to which Hoffmann stepped out of character and bowed low, this was a sad come-back for so fine, and so wasted, a talent.'[26] Two visits to Mexico City in 1961 and 1964 brought him some cheer where he 'remained as ever the darling of the public'.[27] After saying he could 'only occasionally share in the frenzy,' John Walsh recorded in *Opera* that he had even read a local review 'admiring di Stefano's manner of attacking tones below pitch and pushing them up to the desired level. An extra *Tosca* and a recital were virtual love-feasts – though I must say that in the recital he sang deliciously.'[28]

It was during this time [18th May 1961] that di Stefano made a 'welcome but much belated Covent Garden debut' as Cavaradossi. Harold Rosenthal was there: 'Di Stefano is above all a highly accomplished professional who clearly enjoys singing. On the first night he was plainly troubled by something, for once or twice in the first act he seemed to lose interest in what he was doing. Then we learned before the last act that he was suffering from bronchitis and had to husband his vocal resources. Nonetheless, he sang his last–act music in a beautiful soft *mezza voce*. His diction is very forward and a joy to listen to, and his large voice, dark in quality, easily fills the house, whether at full volume or at a whisper. One could tell the second performance, when he was clearly far more at ease, that he had thought out the role and was not just walking through it. Indeed, both he and Régine Crespin gave the impression that this Puccini-Sardou drama was a very real thing to them and not, as is so often the case, a boring old job of work to be done for the *n*th time. I would suggest to the tenor, however, that, when he emerges from Scarpia's torture chamber, he should allow his hair to be ruffled, his shirt to be creased and have some bloodstains visible somewhere!'[29] A return was fixed for September 1963 as Calaf and Rodolfo [according to *Opera*], though in the event we got only Rodolfo and only one performance of that because of vocal problems: 'di Stefano is a greatly experienced tenor who some ten years ago was possibly the finest in the world; even when he sang Cavaradossi here two seasons ago, he gave us a great deal of pleasure. On this occasion he was sadly out of voice, and although he tried to enter into the spirit of the evening, he just did not fit in. One still could admire the clear enunciation and the occasional honeyed phrase, but his *mezza voce* singing was inclined to become inaudible and the sheen has all but disappeared from the voice. One hopes this is only a temporary phase, for at 42, he should be at the height of his powers.'[30] Indeed he should, as also Callas, two years younger. But the years of glory had been bought at a heavy price.

On home ground, impressions were mixed. In Rome 1960, his Riccardo was savagely dismissed: 'he made no pretence at acting at all; he walked around the stage like a bored guest at a cocktail party, and he sang always to the audience and never to the other characters. For those who remember the di Stefano of some years ago, it is depressing now to have to listen to the loud and ugly blasting that has replaced the superb *tenore lirico* of the past.'[31] The Rome audience two years later much preferred *Cavalleria rusticana* in an 'old fashioned, blood-and-thunder rendition, with everybody singing at the top of his voice.'[32] But three years after that, di Stefano's once brilliant Des Grieux rather came to grief: 'As usual, di Stefano made little attempt to act; for about half of the opera he was in remarkably good voice, but then signs of wear began to appear, and in the last act he was all at sea.'[33] Other critics were more friendly – Giorgio Gualerzi from Turin: 'di Stefano making a welcome return [in 1961], after an absence of 14 years, as Andrea Chenier, stood out among the singers. But the fascination of his imaginative phrasing and exemplary diction could only partly conceal the tiredness of a voice whose golden quality remains a pleasant memory.'[34] On the evidence of the broadcast tapes, he made a similar impression shortly afterwards in Florence, as he did in Naples as Loris in *Fedora*: 'di Stefano confirmed his extraordinary power to impart elegance, nobility and warmth even into the over-emphasis and rhetoric of this opera.'[35] His performance of the famous 'Amor ti vieta' on the broadcast tapes certainly confirms this – rather better than that recorded in the 1962 recital. He was also the 'excellent'[36] lead there in Pizzetti's new opera which he had premiered at La Scala the previous year. Sadly, he was 'not in good form for his 1962 return to Verona in *Tosca,* the first act almost coming to grief. An apology had to be made on his behalf and he concluded the performance under great difficulties. Later it was announced that he had cancelled, under doctor's orders, all engagements for the ensuing three months.'[37] But this did not prevent him at his next appearance the month after from 'indulging in magnificent open-voiced brinkmanship as Don Johnson in *Fanciulla* at Torre del Lago.'[38] His attempt in Palermo at Rodolfo in Verdi's *Luisa Miller* in the new year, however, was short-lived, as the broadcast tapes suggest.

At the Scala itself, opening the 1958/59 season as Calaf, di Stefano 'sang the more lyrical passages with tonal beauty and emotional sincerity, but in the dramatic moments the warm, velvety sound of his voice did not correspond to the musical requirements of the situation [*Musical America*].'[39] *Opera* more or less agreed: 'di Stefano was more expansive than before but at times relied too much on the generous volume of his voice and was prone to *portamenti*.'[40] Illness postponed his Rodolfo to the third performance when he was 'well rested and in outstanding vocal form which resulted in one of those warm and generous interpretations that only he is able to give, at least as far as the tenors in the Italian field are concerned.'[41] *Musical America* also liked his Jenik: 'an easy triumph'[42] though ironically *Opera* found the tenor 'evidently uneasy'.[43] He made two appearances during the 1959/60 season – in *Tosca* where he 'was allowed by the conductor, Gavazzeni, to woo the gallery with his long-held notes. This may have been legitimate Puccini tenorising but it contrasted violently with Tebaldi's *sognorile* Tosca.'[44] He also presented an 'excellent'[45] Don Jose, again opposite Simionato. On 23rd March 1961, di Stefano 'at last made his reappearance at the Scala after a long absence, giving a good account of the effective but not difficult part of Giuliano'[46] at the premiere of Pizzetti's eagerly-awaited new opera *Il Calzare d'Argento.* The revival of *L'elisir d'amore* in 1964 promised to be 'an interesting one since it marked di Stefano's first performance at La Scala for three years. In the event, the evening did not glitter and an air of anxiety weighed heavily on the house. Di Stefano acquitted himself fairly well, with dignity and skill, but the entire production seemed to be affected by the general uneasiness.'[47] Claudio Sartori was not impressed by a mutilated *Rienzi* where di Stefano 'frequently found the role too strenuous for him.'[48] Saddest of all was the new production of Monteverdi's *L'Incoronazione di Poppea* to celebrate the quartercentenary of the composer's birth when di Stefano was suddenly taken ill and missed the *prima* on 13th January 1967. He sang in two later performances and a few of Nemorino, Rodolfo and Don Jose, but that was all. His last appearance at the Scala, on 21st April 1972, was ten years after Maria's, almost to the day.

★   ★   ★

Callas' return to La Scala was similarly muted. She opened the 1960/61 season in Donizetti's *Poliuto* which, as Harold Rosenthal who was there observed, was 'perhaps a strange choice for Maria Callas to make for her come-back to the scene of her greatest triumphs after an absence of two seasons. Strange, because the role of Paolina is not the title role of the opera; strange, because unlike *Anna Bolena, Il Pirata* or the many other neglected works that Callas has brought back to life, it afforded her few opportunities to re-create musically a great operatic character. She was far from being in good voice at the third performance and although at the fifth the voice was under firmer control, on both occasions her first act was vocally poor. There seemed to be more voice at the singer's disposal than when she was last heard at Covent Garden, but a lot of the time the tone sounded empty and hollow and she seemed to produce more of those strident top notes than usual. Then suddenly would come a few minutes of pure and exquisite singing of phrases so full of significance that little thrills would run down the spine. She was at her very best in the great duet with Severo, the pro-consul and her former lover, and in her appeal to Callistene for clemency at the end of the Act II; and in the glowing intensity of her closing duet with Poliuto there were signs of the Callas we know and admire. Dramatically, too, she produced many of her familiar thrills, yet on both evenings in the first act one had the curious impression that one was witnessing an artificial performance by Callas imitating Callas being Paolina. A strange experience, and one I have never before had at a Callas performance. The audience accorded her an affectionate welcome, and at the second of the two evenings under review, which was her last appearance of the season, she was showered with flowers from the upper gallery.'[49] Her final role was Medea, very properly in that she was its one and only interpreter. But as Claudio Sartori, *Opera's* regular Scala critic, put it: 'Her excursions into fields less suited to her resources have not helped her with it; in particular, they have sapped the vitality of her voice. Anyone who heard the performances of *Medea* some years back and now hears this new production cannot but notice that the youthful impetuosity, the almost savage passion that Callas brought to the character of Medea and to her gestures, words and cries have become somewhat dimmed with the passing of the years. Stylistically, there has perhaps been an improvement: the interpretation is more severe, more homogeneous, the utterance more studied, the characterisation better built up, but all to the detriment of the sincerity and brilliant improvisatory quality that made a miracle of the earlier performances. Formerly one listened only to Callas. Now, thanks to her more modest interpretation, to her new respect for the opera and the character, and her purer singing, there is even time and opportunity to realise that the score of *Medea* is a continuous fabric of gems and a masterpiece. Yet I still believe that when Maria Callas can no longer be Medea, this opera will return to the long oblivion from which it took her to rescue it.'[50] Her fifth and last performance, which marked the end of her career at La Scala was on 3rd June 1962 when di Stefano was completing a run of *Ballo* in Rome. He returned to the Scala to sing a further 15 performances; Maria never did. She had not the vocal strength.

The previous year, however, she gave two performances of the Medea in the ancient Greek theatre of Epidauros in the heart of the Peloponnese mountains. Joan Chisell of the BBC was there: 'To the vast army of tourists who flood the country, Callas is the great international diva, but to the Greeks themselves she is the local girl made good, returning to sing with the opera company in which she started her career among the chorus until spotted by the discerning director Costis Bastias. The result is that tourists and Greeks together, undaunted by the hot and tiring eight-hours journey from Athens and back, flock in their thousands to join in these festival performances under the velvet night sky, sitting on the self-same slopes where pilgrims to the shrine of Aesculapius saw their artistic pleasures in the 4th century B.C. Of Callas, on whom all eyes were turned, it could be said that her performance was a triumph of characterisation in every subtle detail as well as in the great climaxes of heartbroken rage. Some element of vocal steel is inevitable, indeed essential, to realise this virago. But Callas too often allowed the steel to cut too sharply into her tone, notably in the early aria 'Dei tuoi figli la madre' which alone in the opera can win sympathy for Medea as a genuinely distressed, tender-hearted, wronged wife. Her voice warmed as the opera progressed and her last act was a triumphant blend of interpretation and vocal beauty.'[51]

The year before that she had thrilled similar thousands by bringing her incomparable Norma to this ancient site. Jean Demos was bewitched by the splendour and beauty of the occasion and attempted to add to the much that has already been written of the art of Maria Callas: 'To say that it is a highly personal thing and that it depends in large part on extra musical considerations is not to deny that it is art. There are obvious vocal faults: the very wide and slow vibrato on any fortissimo at F or above; the much too audible stroke of the glottis; the exaggerated roll of the 'r'; the uneven scale. But having pointed out these vocal faults one must account for the complete thralldom of a discriminating audience of many thousands. To be sure the vocalism improved as the evening wore on. In the second half the vibrato was less evident because there was less tension and therefore less forcing of the voice. Better *spinto* singing can scarcely be imagined than that of Callas in the great second act duet with Adalgisa. It is easy to say that Callas commands through her dramatic rather than her vocal power but to account for that command is harder. Perhaps the greatest technical factor is the superb timing of bodily movement. In a vast theatre like that of Epidauros, gesture is a close second to the voice as a medium for communicating feelings. Indeed there is no third. But behind the delicate muscular co-ordination which produces the variations in the dynamics and colour of the vocal tone, and behind the compelling gestures, there is in Callas a profound emotional intelligence and a genius for projection. One example among many is the final moment of Act I. Norma concludes a scathing denunciation of Pollione and orders him from her presence with an imperious raising of a right arm which might be hurling Athena's spear. Then the hand crumples, next the forearm, and finally the proud gesture of the goddess becomes a poignant expression of a woman's defeat, broken pride, and anguish. For this moment alone, Callas deserved the laurel wreath and the less comprehensible white doves with which the management saw fit to embellish the long ovation. For the premiere on August 24th [postponed because of rain from August 21st] the great theatre was filled with an audience of more than 12,000 who had travelled the considerable distance from Athens by ship, yacht, car and bus. Almost everyone made this expenditure of time and effort not once but twice since the cloud burst of the twenty-first was not anticipated. In terms of the devotion of an audience as well as the special merits of the presentation, this occasion must be unique in operatic history.'[52]

Soon after Zeffirelli had worked a miracle with the Callas *Tosca* at Covent Garden at the beginning of 1964, he presented her Norma at the Paris Opéra in a spellbinding production of the Bellini masterpiece, in a setting to reflect her supreme greatness in the role. Maybe everyone knew this would not only be the definitive rendering but also the last; and so it was. The editor of *Opera* attended the fifth of eight performances in May and June: 'She had a most sympathetic audience on hand - unlike the preceding Saturday when catcalls and fights developed in the auditorium. Naturally she was uneasy for a good deal of the evening and so were many of her listeners. Indeed I found it difficult to relax during the first act though by the time she reached the Norma-Adalgisa-Pollione trio she had struck form, and as she rounded on Pollione with the words 'Tremi tu? e per chi?', flashing her scornful eyes at him and pointing at him accusingly, the drama flared to life, and we were almost back in 1952. 'Casta diva' had been sung very softly – almost like a lullaby and the *cabaletta* brought a few rasping sounds; the first Norma-Adalgisa duet too was well below her best; then came the trio to which I have referred. As always, the scene with the children was movingly done, but 'Mira, O Norma' especially the *cabaletta* was again not what it used to be. Then in the last scene the miracle happened – in the dramatic recitative before the 'Guerra, guerra' chorus, there was a slight vocal mishap which seem to act as a spur, for from that moment until the end of the evening [some 25 or so minutes] she produced a stream of tone, firmly-based such as I have not heard from her since those first Covent Garden *Normas*. She raged, she pleaded, she was in complete command of the stage, and had an electrifying effect on her companions. The audience went mad, and rightly so, for once again the Callas magic had worked.'[53] The final run of five performances the following year were disgracefully dismissed in Harold Rosenthal's magazine by his *Opera* critic, Stephane Wolff: 'The performances were not good, and there was a great deal of hysterical behaviour from the audience, including a troupe of young girls in white who threw flowers over the orchestra almost every time the diva opened her mouth. Adalgisa was sung by Fiorenza Cossotto and also by Giulietta Simionato – the latter making her Paris debut – with great success.'[54] How the mighty have fallen from when, seven years before, Callas made her Gala debut in this very theatre before the *beau monde*. Claude Rostand wrote in *Musical America*: 'Difficult as it is to believe that Miss Callas made her first appearance in Paris, the announcement of her arrival created a public fever and agitation not caused by any political, sport or atomic event in several years. A month in advance tickets were sold at astronomic prices on the black market. But in justice, it should be added that the proceeds of this gala evening were donated to charitable works of the Legion d'Honneur. The scene of the spectacle was, of course, the stage of the Opéra, but there was just as exciting a spectacle in the auditorium. All Paris, at its most extravagant and elegant, attended – from Brigitte Bardot to the President of the Republic, from the Begum Aga Khan to Charlie Chaplin, from Juliet Greco to Jean Cocteau [He might have added the Duke and Duchess of Windsor, and Aristotle Onassis...]. The evening's programme in itself was nothing but a variety of numbers to give Miss Callas the opportunity to display all the treasures of her virtuosity. It is very regrettable that an artist of her calibre had to make her debut amid so much music-hall atmosphere. It is also regrettable that for such a debut she did not have one of her best nights. The concert opened with the famous 'Casta diva'. A certain unevenness and harshness of her voice did not quite satisfy our expectations, aside from the fact that the voice was not yet warmed up. This was followed by [Leonora's aria from the fourth act of *Trovatore* and] the 'Miserere'. Again her style and phrasing had the utmost in noblesse and grandeur. The first section closed with the great aria from *The Barber of Seville*. From every point of view this was the highlight of the evening. Here she showed herself as the phenomenal, lively, intelligent artist, here she did justice to her reputation. It was pure enchantment, unbelievable virtuosity.'[55] Everett Helm in *Saturday Review* was rather more gracious: 'Let it not be said, near or far, that the spectators did not get their money's worth; it was a very good show indeed. Callas may be difficult, unreasonable, temperamental, impossible, or what you will. But when she is on stage, she is very much *there*. … The ovation she received after the second act of *Tosca* was entirely warranted. 'La Callas' had demonstrated that the prima donna of the 'good old days' is still alive in her person, and *tout Paris* seemed to find delight in this fact and in paying homage to the singer who could elicit such rapture. They hadn't had so much fun since the time of 'La Malibran' … a mere 110 years ago.'[56]

Musical America again, three weeks before, when the concert tour in America was getting into its stride: 'Maria Callas came to San Francisco on Sunday 23rd November 1958, ducked a scheduled press conference that evening, went into seclusion and came out only for her concert in the Civic Auditorium the following Wednesday evening. The large house was not quite sold out. The applause was politely enthusiastic through the programme of operatic arias, and wildly so at the conclusion. One man in the audience jumped on stage and kissed the diva, and this little bit of unscheduled activity was just one of the unusual ingredients in this very peculiar operatic night. The whole performance had a circus touch. After a late start with a perfunctory performance of Verdi's *Forza* Overture by Nicola Rescigno and a skimpy orchestra locally recruited, the lights came up, went down again, and then a spotlight caught hold of a figure wrapped in red satin. It was, of course, Miss Callas and she glided on stage – or slank perhaps – led by the hand of Mr Rescigno. It was only through a distracting veil of arch mannerism that the Callas voice emerged and it did not come through in very good shape. A Beckmesser taking note of all the notes marred by vibrato and/or tremolo and bad intonation would have run out of slates early in the evening.'[57] A recently discovered recording of the succeeding concert in Los Angeles in fact utterly confounds this critic's adverse observations: perhaps he was jaundiced by what he saw rather than by what he heard.

Harold Rosenthal, a year later, took a more serious view: 'At her first London recital at the Royal Festival Hall on 23rd September 1959, the *Don Carlos* item was tentatively begun, and, though her voice is not ideal for this music, she demonstrated, as always, the musical insight and aristocratic phrasing that are the hallmarks of all her performances. The *Pirata* Mad Scene was again a *tour de force*. Another Mad Scene [*Hamlet*] and the Sleep Walking scene from *Macbeth* were both magnificent pieces of singing-acting. In the latter we had a foretaste of what her Lady Macbeth will be like at Covent Garden later in the season. Once again unfortunately she was ill-served by her conductor Nicola Rescigno; and once again one felt that successful as she may be in the concert hall, it is the opera house that is her rightful home.'[58] Sadly, the promised performances of *Macbeth* were just some of the growing number of what might-have-been on the stage, their place too often, too easily and too profitably taken, which Mr Meneghini, unlike Mr Rosenthal, preferred.

Di Stefano, too, was busy. He returned to New York in November 1963 for a concert at Carnegie Hall, 'his first appearance there in many a moon,' *Musical America* reported. 'The tenor presented the sort of aria-canzone programme that makes one cherish Cesare Valletti, though no one in his right mind would expect or even wish di Stefano to attempt the Wolf-Berlioz-Schubert repertory of his colleague Valletti [certainly a wonder among his species]. The audience had gathered to hear a voice, not music, and it was obviously a two way love affair between tenor and flock. They stumped, cheered, whistled and ooed, and he preened, basked in their affection and charmed everyone in sight. He was in excellent voice, though it must be sadly noted that his top above G no longer has the exalted ring and beauty of former Metropolitan days. The high notes, so precious to Italians, came with ease but also with dryness and

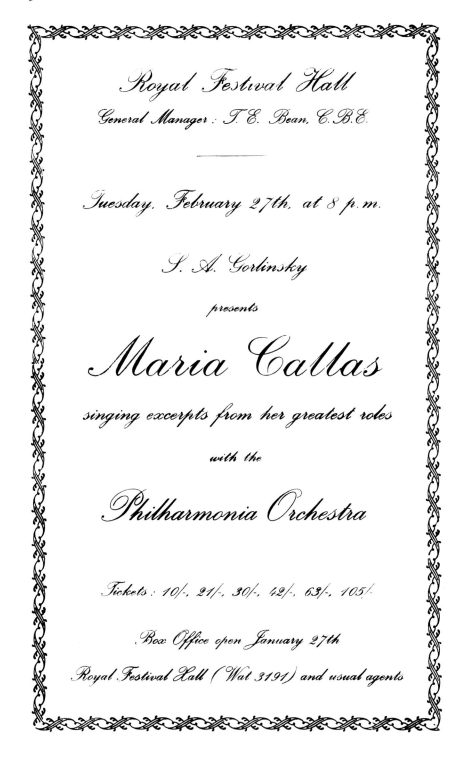

Royal Festival Hall
General Manager : T. E. Bean, C.B.E.

Tuesday, February 27th, at 8 p.m.

S. A. Gorlinsky

presents

Maria Callas

singing excerpts from her greatest roles

with the

Philharmonia Orchestra

Tickets : 10/-, 21/-, 30/-, 42/-, 63/-, 105/-

Box Office open January 27th

Royal Festival Hall (Wat 3191) and usual agents

occasional hollowness. But the middle voice is still one of the most luscious, velvety sounds in opera today, and most of the programme lay in this range. He was heard in arias from *Mignon, Le Roi d'Ys, The Bartered Bride, Eugene Onegin* and *Turandot* and songs by Donizetti, Barrera-Calleja and Friere. Treasurable was di Stefano's singing of the three exquisite Sicilian folk songs. Ivor Newton was the excellent accompanist.'[59]

  Five years later in Vienna, di Stefano's special appeal was articulated in the daily *Kurier* by Karl Lobl: 'Giuseppe di Stefano has always been able to unfold his personality better in the concert hall. What disturbs him – and not only him – about the opera, is being at the mercy of uncomprehending conductors, vain directors, insensitive partners, of being subjected to the arbitrariness of a routine, commercialised business. All this vanishes on the concert stage. There [as on 24th June 1968], di Stefano can be himself: an individualist who sings the soul of the music … With the unmistakable, unique magic of his voice, di Stefano put the spotlight on individuality, charm, musicality and vocal beauty in this concert, all to an equal degree.'[60]

  In addition to the growing emphasis on concerts, was the occasional media event such as 'A Golden Hour from the Royal Opera House' on ITV on 4th November 1962. This did not command much respect from Arthur Jacobs, the assistant editor of *Opera*: 'Earlier in the evening the BBC, in its telerecording of the Royal Variety performance, had given us the curiosity of Eartha Kitt touching [albeit tentatively] a top D flat in a duet from *Rose Marie* with Harry Secombe. It was not, perhaps, more curious than the ATV programme which, despite its title and being compèred by no less a luminary than Sir David Webster, turned out to have slight relationship with Covent Garden's function as we know it. One could imagine the programme originating at some commercial TV tycoon's conference: "Yeah, yeah, we could use the *place* all right, so long as they don't do any opera, of course." So we had [apart from the commercials, including one for electric shavers and one for razor-blades] Jose Greco and his Spanish dance company; Mischa Elman in two violin lollipops; Giuseppe di Stefano and Maria Callas, but not in costume; and [the only point at which the programme touched what Covent Garden's paying customers see] a *pas-de-deux* by Svetlana Beriosova and Donald Macleary of the Royal Ballet. Even the conductor was one who has never performed publicly at the Royal Opera House, Georges Pretre: would Madame Callas have spurned the resident musical staff? Mr di Stefano, apologising for a cold, sang 'Che gelida manina' and two of those appalling Neapolitan ballades; Madame Callas sang 'Tu che le vanita' from *Don Carlos* and [baring her shoulders] the Habanera and Seguidilla from *Carmen*. The latter were charming, with those little freedoms and individual emphases ['il n'a jamais, *jamais* connu de loi'] which are Callas' own. I so much prefer this 'mezzo-soprano' Callas at present that I wished her *Don Carlos* selection had been Eboli's 'O don fatale'; Elisabeth's aria, while delivered with dramatic power, was not without uncomfortable sounds at the top. Georges Pretre put on almost a parody of a

conductor's smiles and come-hither gestures. They were apparently quite wasted on the few players whom the restricted camera-angle permitted us to see; but, oh boy, Liberace had better look out.'[61] Mr Jacobs musical prejudices can probably be ignored. But what we should find of particular interest is that although the records show that the *Cavalleria* duet was recorded, it was not transmitted, thus removing the only evidence to the viewer that either artist was aware of the other. Was time the factor or other, more sensitive, considerations? David Webster benignly spoke of the incomparable Callas; and he spoke of the tenor, di Stefano, as a very rare bird indeed. But never of the two in the same breath which is strange, given their famous partnership.

★ ★ ★

Principally, however, media preoccupation with the couple must reside in the great recorded legacy and many interesting recordings were made during the closing years. One of the first consequences of Callas' break with the Scala in 1958 was the termination of the EMI Scala series which had galvanised the recording world. Whilst it is true that *La gioconda* and the second *Norma* were recorded under the Scala imprimatur, plus a couple of other complete sets, works that in all probability would have been recorded – *Anna Bolena, Il Pirata, La traviata, Macbeth* for example – were offered instead in bleeding chunks. Callas' two recording sessions of Verdi and Mad Scenes [albeit two of her finest recitals] in September at Abbey Road and the Kingsway Hall initiated a stream of recital discs which were warmly embraced by an unknowing public who failed to detect this sinister trend with the release in February 1958 of extracts from *La vestale* and *Medea*. Thereafter came a brilliant recital of French arias in October 1961, side one of which contained mezzo arias, prompting speculation on the future direction of Callas' career. Later releases of more French arias, Mozart/Weber/Beethoven, Verdi [containing some beautifully sung rare music] and Rossini/Donizetti, and another complete *Tosca* put paid to that, although the complete *Carmen* created a distinct hum.

Di Stefano never received similar support from their record company, although ironically his 10 inch LP of eight Neapolitan songs recorded in 1953 was issued six months ahead of Callas' first recital [Puccini arias]. Walter Legge had brought back a tape of five of the songs with him from Italy in June 1953: 'The sooner these are published the better because this artist's brother-in-law has become a director of Decca and Decca are pestering him with offers; so we have to show him all that we can do in selling.'[62] In fact, after this release in 1954, no further attempt to sell a di Stefano recital disc was made until the end of 1959 when a mere 7-inch EP of four Puccini arias was issued. There was never enough material recorded to fill a 12-inch LP [hardly surprising perhaps after the difficulties previously referred to in London in 1947, although five tracks, made in the HMV Milan studios in June 1951, have never seen the light of day] and a face-saving 'Di Stefano at La Scala' LP was issued in May 1962 with 14 tracks culled from the complete recordings. During that time the same company issued six Callas LP recitals, with four more to come in as many years. Only a di Stefano recital in Italian of duets with Rosanna Carteri from *Otello, Iris, Carmen, Pescatori,* and *Faust* was forthcoming, rightly dismissed by *Opera* as an 'unstylish mixed bag'.[63] It was a leftover from the immediate post-war performances of French opera given in Italy, but it is strange that an international record company should have countenanced the practice. Nevertheless, John Steane in *Gramophone* [March'81] admired the tenor's 'sheer stamina'[64] in *Iris* and both he and William Mann praised his Otello which in 1966 di Stefano, like Pavarotti, sang as a live end-of-career indulgence. However the success of the early 10-inch LP lead to further albums of Italian songs which is perhaps where di Stefano's special gifts lay. Thirteen songs previously referred to were recorded in 1956/7 and issued on an LP, but for the Italian market only until they were released on a Testament CD in 1997. A further 25 songs were recorded in 1961 and issued on two LPs for general distribution the following year. W.A. Chislett in *Gramophone* found di Stefano 'in very good form indeed and probably heard to better advantage in songs such as these than in sustained operatic roles.'[65] Especially good is 'Ideale' with its typically soaring rise from F sharp to top A. In 1958 meanwhile, the tenor's new masters, Decca, had recorded 18 songs, many from his native Sicily, including the glorious 'A la barcillunisa' and, for the first time, 'Addio, sogni di gloria', which were released in 1959. They also paid attention to his operatic activities, recording, as well as the complete *Gioconda* and *Forza,* in 1958 an unfinished [owing to illness] *Mefistofele* which didn't come to light until January 1973 when Edward Greenfield was impressed by a 'bonus disc recorded at the very height of di Stefano's career'.[66] A recital of French and Italian arias was also released, but it didn't please *Gramophone's* William Mann who never liked di Stefano. Conversely, Harold Rosenthal in *Opera* said he had not heard di Stefano 'in such good voice for a long time, displaying some of the former beauty of tone and velvety quality of his early 78s which many thought he had lost.'[67] It may well have prompted EMI to issue an LP of love duets with Callas from the complete sets of *Tosca, Cavalleria* and *Boheme.* (33CX1725). For

some reason, Ricordi made a
new recording of *Lucia* with
Scotto in 1959 for DG. Reviewed in *Gramophone* by Philip
Hope-Wallace in September
1961, he thought di Stefano a
'very good choice for the hero,
having heard him do it opposite
Callas in the flesh'.[68] But that
could well have been when it
all began at the Scala in January
1954, before the 'sad vocal
decline'[69] noted by Harold
Rosenthal in *Opera,* with which
the writer has to agree.
DG recorded its own di Stefano
recital in 1962 which, according

33CX1725

to Philip Hope-Wallace contained 'too much undifferentiated all-out singing
to make a really satisfactory effect on the ear'[70] and, sadly, he is right, though
items like the aria from Leoncavallo's *La bohème* are wonderful. When Decca
recorded the Karajan *Tosca,* the result came nearest to rivalling the classic
Callas/di Stefano/Gobbi/de Sabata miracle of 1953. Even Edward Greenfield
later retracted for underestimating the 1962 di Stefano. In 1964, he paid due
attention to the tenor's 'decidedly lusty performance'[71] in an abridged *Manon*
opposite Anna Moffo on RCA. Finally, between 1963 and 1966, a spate of LPs
on Decca and Philips labels of Italian, Neapolitan and Popular Italian songs
was released which found the tenor in variable voice.

    After 1965, the years of glory were but a receding memory, and their
protagonists, Callas and di Stefano, had to live with that. It was far from easy;
after all, both were still only in their forties. They must have wondered what
the future held for two voices ravaged, not by the length of their careers, as
with most singers, but by their intensity and brilliance. She sang from time to
time in the EMI studios in Paris, the results of which trickled through with
other previously discarded material to an ever-hungry public in the Seventies
and beyond. He found a niche in Lehar operetta with *The Land of Smiles,* [and
later *Der Zarewitsch*]. According to Gilles Potvin in *Opera,* the mediocre
production, transferred from Berlin to Expo 67 in Canada, was 'redeemed
only by the singing of di Stefano whose voice has retained much of its former

lustre, apart from a few constricted high notes. Although singing in German, his style has a definite Italian flavour and one can only quibble with his abuse of *mezza-voce*'.[72] When the production settled in the Theater an der Wien, Peter Hutchison's quibble was with the work. 'Lehar can get away splendidly with the unintellectual luxury, the harmless urbanity without responsibility that can make *The Merry Widow* so enjoyable, but this facile and crude gloss on 'the Oriental problem' is the most gruesome thing in musical history after his puerile handling of the responsibilities of monarchy in *Der Zarewitsch*. Any tenor can be sure of cheers for 'Dein ist mein ganzes Herz'. One hopes against hope that this is not the only reason why di Stefano undertook the venture. He openly admits to having little affinity with the German language and it was only with liberal applications of a thick Sicilian accent that he was able to sing it at all.'[73] Andrew Lambert was much more positive when he reviewed the recording of highlights made by Preiser Records in April 1967:'Much has been made of di Stefano's decline from his days as the top Italian tenor, but only in the very occasional slightly strained high note is there anything obviously untoward here. Of course individual listeners may not care for his mannerisms – such as the way syllables are sometimes seemingly forced out one by one – and may find him lacking in subtlety and grace; but I for one thrill to the sheer vocal passion and bravura he brings to this gorgeous music. His German may not be perfect – but then who cared about Tauber's command of the language when singing in English?'[74]

Both singers suffered cruel personal blows to add to the misery of their early withdrawal from the international scene. Maria lost the man she loved to one of the world's adventuresses and di Stefano lost his daughter to the hopeless onslaught of leukaemia. Having gone their separate ways since the 1957 *Ballo*, they met again fifteen years later during Maria's master classes at the Juilliard School in New York. At once the old glory that was theirs came back and they fell in love – which must have recalled many a night on the stage. Their time together began to make more sense of the celebrity they had lost. They co-produced *I vespri siciliani* to open the newly rebuilt Regio, Turin but neither of them knew nearly enough to make a success of it. Singing was their craft and in 1973 that is what they decided to do. "Of course my voice is not what it used to be a few years ago. I know it and so does the public. We are here for exchanging love," said Maria in a radio broadcast the day before their world tour began. Of course, some people misunderstood, expecting the impossible. They don't love Callas and di Stefano; the rest of us do.

WORLD TOUR 1973/74 11th December 1973 CONCERTGEBOUW, AMSTERDAM
There to exchange love

CALLAS & DI STEFANO

[A]   PERFORMANCES AT LA SCALA
Listed chronologically

GDS	15.03.47	[3]	Des Grieux in *Manon* [Massenet] c. Antonio Guarnieri
GDS	02.10.47	[2]	Wilhelm Meister in *Mignon* [Thomas] c. Antonio Guarnieri
MC	07.12.51	[7]	Elena in *I Vespri Siciliani* [Verdi] c. Victor de Sabata
MC	16.01.52	[9]	*Norma* [Bellini] c. Franco Ghione
MC	02.04.52	[4]	Constanza★ in *Il Ratto dal Seraglio* [Mozart] c. Jonel Perlea
MC	07.12.52	[5]	Lady Macbeth★ in *Macbeth* [Verdi] c. de Sabata
GDS	15.12.52	[10]	Rodolfo in *La Boheme* [Puccini] c. de Sabata
MC ⎱	26.12.52	[6]	*La Gioconda* [Ponchielli] c. Antonino Votto
GDS ⎰	26.12.52	[10]	Enzo★ in *La Gioconda* c. Votto
MC	23.02.53	[5]	Leonora in *Il Trovatore* [Verdi] c. Votto
MC	10.12.53	[5]	*Medea* [Cherubini] c. Leonard Bernstein
GDS	16.12.53	[7]	Il Duca in *Rigoletto* [Verdi] c. Nino Sanzogno
MC ⎱	18.01.54	[7]	*Lucia di Lammermoor* [Donizetti] c. Herbert von Karajan
GDS ⎰	18.01.54	[6]	Edgardo in *Lucia di Lammermoor* c. von Karajan
MC	04.04.54	[4]	*Alceste★* [Gluck] c. Carlo Maria Giulini
MC	12.04.54	[5]	Elisabetta di Valois★ in *Don Carlo* [Verdi] c. Votto
GDS	14.04.54	[7]	Cavaradossi in *Tosca* [Puccini] c. Votto
GDS	10.05.54	[4]	Lenski★ in *Eugene Onegin* [Tchaikovsky] c. Artur Rodzinsky
MC	07.12.54	[5]	Giulia★ in *La Vestale* [Spontini] c. Votto
GDS	11.12.54	[6]	Nemorino in *L'Elisir d'Amore* [Donizetti] c. Giulini
MC	08.01.55	[6]	Maddalena★ in *Andrea Chenier* [Giordano] c. Votto
GDS	18.01.55	[6]	Don Jose★ in *Carmen* [Bizet] c. von Karajan
MC	05.03.55	[10]	Amina★ in *La Sonnambula* [Bellini] c. Bernstein
GDS	14.04.55	[3]	Rodolfo in *La Boheme* [Puccini] c. Bernstein
MC	15.04.55	[5]	Fiorilla in *Il Turco in Italia* [Rossini] c. Gianandrea Gavazzeni
GDS	26.04.55	[5]	Alvaro★ in *La Forza del Destino* [Verdi] c. Votto
GDS	10.05.55	[4]	Turiddu in *Cavalleria Rusticana* [Mascagni] c. Votto
MC ⎱	28.05.55	[4]	Violetta in *La Traviata* [Verdi] c. Giulini
GDS ⎰	28.05.55	[1]	Alfredo in *La traviata* c. Guilini
MC	07.12.55	[9]	*Norma* [Bellini] c. Votto
MC	19.01.56	[17]	Violetta in *La Traviata* [Verdi] c. Giulini
MC	16.02.56	[5]	Rosina★ in *Il Barbiere di Siviglia* [Rossini] c. Giulini
GDS	12.04.56	[7]	Riccardo in *Un Ballo in Maschera* [Verdi] c. Gavazzeni
GDS	24.04.56	[6]	Canio★ in *I Pagliacci* [Leoncavallo] c. Sanzogno
MC	21.05.56	[6]	*Fedora★* [Giordano] c. Gavazzeni
GDS	26.05.56	[5]	*Werther* [Massenet] c. Votto
GDS	07.12.56	[7]	Radames★ in *Aida* [Verdi] c. Votto
GDS	22.01.57	[2]	Canio in I Pagliacci [Leoncavallo] c. Sanzogno
GDS	03.02.57	[7]	Des Grieux in *Manon Lescaut* [Puccini] c. Gavazzeni
MC	02.03.57	[6]	Amina in *La Sonnambula* [Bellini] c. Votto
MC	14.04.57	[7]	*Anna Bolena★* [Donizetti] c. Gavazzeni
GDS	23.04.57	[7]	Alvaro in *La Forza del Destino* [Verdi] c. Votto

GDS	23.05.57	[4]	Osaka in Iris [Mascagni] c. Gavazzeni
MC	01.06.57	[4]	*Ifigenia in Tauride★* [Gluck] c. Sanzogno
GDS⟩	07.12.57	[6]	Riccardo in *Un Ballo in Maschera* [Verdi] c. Gavazzeni
MC ⟩	07.12.57	[5]	Amelia★ in *Un Ballo in Maschera* c. Gavazzeni
GDS	04.01.58	[4]	Maurizio in *Adriana Lecouvreur* [Cilea] c. Votto
MC	09.04.58	[5]	*Anna Bolena* [Donizetti] c. Gavazzeni
GDS	14.04.58	[5]	Nemorino in *L'Elisir d'Amore* [Donizetti] c. Sanzogno
GDS	22.04.58	[6]	Pinkerton in *Madama Butterfly* [Puccini] c. Gavazzeni
MC	19.05.58	[5]	Imogene★ in *Il Pirata* [Bellini] c. Votto
GDS	07.12.58	[7]	Calaf in *Turandot* [Puccini] c. Votto
GDS	22.01.59	[4]	Rodolfo in *La Boheme* [Puccini] c. Votto
GDS	02.02.59	[3]	Jenik★ in *The Bartered Bride* [Smetana] c. Lovro von Matacic
GDS	23.07.59	[2]	Don Jose in *Carmen* [Bizet] c. von Matacic
GDS	09.12.59	[4]	Cavaradossi in *Tosca* [Puccini] c. Gavazzeni
GDS	01.02.60	[6]	Don Jose in *Carmen* [Bizet] c. Sanzogno
MC	07.12.60	[5]	Paolina★ in *Poliuto* {Donizetti] c. Votto
GDS	23.03.61	[5]	Giuliano★ in *Il Calzare d'Argento* [Pizzetti] c. Gavazzeni
MC	11.12.61	[5]	*Medea* [Cherubini] c. Schippers
GDS	11.03.64	[4]	Nemorino in *L'Elisir d'Amore* [Donizetti] c. Sanzogno
GDS	04.06.64	[5]	*Rienzi★* [Wagner] c. Hermann Scherchen
GDS	27.01.67	[2]	Nerone★ in *L'Incoronazione di Poppea* [Monteverdi] Bruno Maderna
GDS	22.04.67	[1]	Nemorino in *L'Elisir d'Amore* [Donizetti] c. Antonio Tonini
GDS	02.05 71	[1]	Rodolfo in *La Boheme* [Puccini] c. Nino Verchi
GDS	14.04.72	[2]	Don Jose in *Carmen* [Bizet] c. Georges Pretre

★debut

[B]   OTHER JOINT APPEARANCES
Listed chronologically

MC ⟩	09.09.51	[1]	Violetta in *La Traviata* [Verdi] Theatro Municipal, Sao Paulo
GDS⟩	09.09.51	[1]	Alfredo in *La Traviata* Theatro Municipal, Sao Paulo
MC ⟩	29.05.52	[2]	Elvira in *I Puritani* [Bellini] Palacio de Bellas Artes, Mexico City
GDS⟩	29.05.52	[2]	Arturo★ in *I Puritani* Palacio de Bellas Artes, Mexico City
MC ⟩	03.06.52	[2]	Violetta in *La Traviata* [Verdi] Palacio de Bellas Artes, Mexico City
GDS⟩	03.06.52	[2]	Alfredo in *La Traviata* Palacio de Bellas Artes, Mexico City
MC ⟩	10.06.52	[3]	*Lucia di Lammermoor★* [Donizetti] Palacio de Bellas Artes, Mexico City
GDS⟩	10.06.52	[3]	Edgardo in *Lucia* Palacio de Bellas Artes, Mexico City
MC ⟩	17.06.52	[2]	Gilda★ in *Rigoletto* [Verdi] Palacio de Bellas Artes, Mexico City
GDS⟩	17.06.52	[2]	Il Duca in *Rigoletto* Palacio de Bellas Artes, Mexico City
MC ⟩	28.06.52	[2]	*Tosca* [Puccini] Palacio de Bellas Artes, Mexico City
GDS⟩	28.06.52	[2]	Cavaradossi★ in *Tosca* Palacio de Bellas Artes, Mexico City
MC ⟩	05.02.53	[2]	*Lucia di Lammermoor* [Donizetti] Teatro Communale, Florence
GDS⟩	05.02.53	[2]	Edgardo in *Lucia* Teatro Communale, Florence
MC ⟩	14.03.53	[2]	*Lucia di Lammermoor* [Donizetti] Teatro Carlo Felice, Genoa
GDS⟩	14.03.53	[2]	Edgardo in *Lucia* Teatro Carlo Felice, Genoa

MC	20.07.54	[1]	Margherita★ in *Mefistofele* [Boito] Arena di Verona
GDS	20.07.54	[1]	Faust★ in *Mefistofele* Arena di Verona
MC	15.11.54	[2]	*Lucia di Lammermoor* [Donizetti] Lyric Theater, Chicago
GDS	15.11.54	[2]	Edgardo in *Lucia* Lyric Theater, Chicago
MC	29.09.55	[2]	*Lucia di Lammermoor* [Donizetti] Stadtische Oper, Berlin
GDS	29.09.55	[2]	Edgardo in *Lucia* Stadtische Oper, Berlin
MC	31.10.55	[2]	Elvira in *I Puritani* [Bellini] Lyric Theater, Chicago
GDS	31.10.55	[2]	Arturo in *I Puritani* Lyric Theater, Chicago
MC	11.11.55	[3]	*Madama Butterfly*★ [Puccini] Lyric Theater, Chicago
GDS	11.11.55	[3]	Pinkerton in *Madama Butterfly* Lyric Theater, Chicago
MC	12.06.56	[3]	*Lucia di Lammermoor* [Donizetti] Staatsoper, Vienna
GDS	12.06.56	[3]	Edgardo in *Lucia* Staatsoper, Vienna

★debut

[C]   ROLES AND PERFORMANCES
Listed chronologically

	Debut		**Total**
MC	15.02.41	Beatrice in *Boccaccio* [Suppe] Palas Cinema, Athens	*12*
MC	27.08.42	*Tosca* [Puccini] Summer Theatre, Klafthmonos Square, Athens	*54*
MC	22.04.44	Martha in *Tiefland* [d'Albert] Olympia Theatre. Athens	*11*
MC	06.05 44	Santuzza in *Cavalleria Rusticana* [Mascagni] Olympia Theatre	*2*
MC	05.08.44	Smaragda in *O Protomastoras* [Kalomiras] National Th, Athens	*2*
MC	14.08 44	Leonore in *Fidelio* [Beethoven] Herodes Atticus, Athens	*11*
MC	05.09.45	Laura in *Der Bettelstudent* [Millocker] Summer Theatre, Athens	*7*
GDS	20.04.46	Des Grieux in *Manon* [Massenet] T. Municipal, Reggio Emilia	*70*
GDS	02.05.46	Nadir in *I Pescatori di Perle* [Bizet] La Fenice	*21*
GDS	03.08.46	Il Duca in *Rigoletto* [Verdi] Piazzale del Pavaglione, Lugo	*43*
GDS	04.08.46	Alfredo in *La traviata* [Verdi] Lugo	*35*
GDS	07.09.46	*L'Amico Fritz* [Mascagni] Lugo	*9*
GDS	26.10.46	Elvino in *La Sonnambula* [Bellini] Teatro Communale, Bologna	*14*
GDS	04.05.47	Wilhelm Meister in *Mignon* [Thomas] Teatro dell'Opera, Rome	*21*
MC	02.08.47	*La Gioconda* [Ponchielli] Arena di Verona	*13*
MC	30.12.47	Isolde in *Tristan und Isolde* [Wagner] La Fenice	*12*
MC	29.01.48	*Turandot* [Puccini] La Fenice	*24*
MC	17.04.48	Leonora in *La Forza del Destino* [Verdi] Teatro Rossetti, Trieste	*6*
MC	18.09.48	*Aida* [Verdi] Teatro Lyrico, Turin	*33*
GDS	03.11.48	Rodolfo in *La Boheme* [Puccini] Th. Municipal, Rio de Janiero	*104*
MC	30.11.48	*Norma* [Bellini] Teatro Communale, Florence	*88*
MC	08.01.49	Brunnhilde in *Die Walkure* [Wagner] La Fenice	*6*
MC	19.01.49	Elvira in *I Puritani* [Bellini] La Fenice	*16*
GDS	23.01.49	Nemorino in *L'Elisir d'Amore* [Donizetti] Metropolitan, NY	*48*
GDS	04.02.49	Rinuccio in *Gianni Schicchi* [Puccini] Metropolitan, New York	*7*
MC	26.02.49	Kundry in *Parsifal* [Wagner] Teatro dell'Opera, Rome	*4*
GDS	26.02.49	Fenton in *Falstaff* [Verdi] Metropolitan, New York	*3*
GDS	07.07.49	Almaviva in *Il Barbiere* [Rossini] Palacio de Bellas Artes	*11*
GDS	12.07.49	Fernando in *La Favorita* [Donizetti] Palacio de Bellas Artes,	*2*

GDS	23.07.49	*Werther* [Massenet] Palacio de Bellas Artes, Mexico City	35
GDS	21 11 49	Italian Singer in *Der Rosenkavalier* [Strauss] Metropolitan, NY	3
MC	20.12.49	Abigaille in *Nabucco* [Verdi] San Carlo, Naples	3
GDS	23.12.49	*Faust* [Gounod] Metropolitan, New York	18
MC	20.06.50	Leonora in *Il Trovatore* [Verdi] Palacio de Bellas Artes, Mexico	20
GDS	28.09.50	Edgardo in *Lucia di Lammermoor* {Donizetti} San Francisco	33
MC	19.10.50	Fiorilla in *Il Turco in Italia* [Rossini] Teatro Eliseo, Rome	9
MC	14.01.51	Violetta in *La Traviata* [Verdi] Teatro Communale, Florence	63
MC	26.05.51	Elena in *I Vespri Siciliani* [Verdi] Teatro Communale, Florence	11
MC	09.06.51	Euridice in *Orfeo ed Euridice* [Haydn] Teatro Pergola, Florence	2
GDS	29.09.51	Pinkerton in *Madama Butterfly* Theatro Municipal, Rio de Janiero	28
MC	26.04.52	*Armida* [Rossini] Teatro Communale, Florence	3
GDS	29.05.52	*I Puritani* [see list B above]	9
MC	10.06.52	*Lucia di Lammermoor* [see list B above]	46
MC	17.06.52	*Rigoletto* [see list B above]	2
GDS	28.06.52	*Tosca* [see list B above]	83
MC	07.12.52	*Macbeth* [see list A above]	5
GDS	26.12.52	*La Gioconda* [see list A above]	20
MC	07.05.53	*Medea* [Cherubini] Teatro Communale, Florence	31
MC	04.04.54	*Alceste* [see list A above]	4
MC	12.04.54	*Don Carlo* [see list A above]	5
GDS	10.05.54	*Eugene Onegin* [see list A above]	4
MC	15.07.54	*Mefistofele* [see list B above]	3
GDS	15.07.54	*Mefistofele* [see list B above]	5
GDS	09.10.54	Turiddu in *Cavalleria Rusticana* T. Municipal, Rio de Janeiro	13
MC	07.12.54	*La Vestale* [see list A above]	5
MC	08.01.55	*Andrea Chenier* [see list A above]	6
GDS	18.01.55	*Carmen* [see list A above]	58
GDS	03.03.55	Riccardo in *Un Ballo in Maschera* [Verdi] T. dell 'Opera, Rome	60
MC	05.03.55	*La Sonnambula* [see list A above]	22
GDS	26.04.55	*La Forza del Destino* [see list A above]	27
MC	11.11.55	*Madama Butterfly* [see list B above]	3
MC	16.02.56	*Il Barbiere di Siviglia* [see list A above]	5
GDS	16.02.56	Des Grieux in *Manon Lescaut* [Puccini] Teatro dell'Opera, Rome	31
GDS	24.04.56	*I Pagliacci* [see list A above]	23
MC	21.05.56	*Fedora* [see list A above]	6
GDS	07.12.56	*Aida* [see list A above]	8
GDS	26.12.56	Osaka in *Iris* [Mascagni] Teatro dell'Opera, Rome	8
MC	14.04.57	*Anna Bolena* [see list A above]	12
MC	01.06.57	*Ifigenia in Tauride* [see list A above]	4
GDS	13.11.57	Maurizio in *Adriana Lecouvreur* [Cilea] Lyric Theater, Chicago	8
MC	07.12.57	*Un Ballo in Maschera* [see list A above]	5
MC	19.05.58	*Il Pirata* [see list A above]	7
GDS	18.10.58	Calaf in *Turandot* [Puccini] Lyric Theater, Chicago	16
GDS	02.02.59	*The Bartered Bride* [see list A above]	3
GDS	01.03.59	*Andrea Chenier* [Giordano] Teatro dell'Opera, Rome	20

GDS	23.11.60	Loris in *Fedora* [Giordano] Lyric theatre, Chicago	14
MC	07.12.60	*Poliuto* [see list A above]	5
GDS	23.03.61	*Il Calzare d'Argento* [see list A above]	8
GDS	15.05.62	Dick Johnson in *La Fanciulla del West* [Puccini] Genoa	5
GDS	14.01.63	Rodolfo in *Luisa Miller* [Verdi] Teatro Massimo, Palermo	2
GDS	04.06.64	*Rienzi* [see list A above]	5
GDS	27.01.65	Hoffmann in *The Tales of Hoffmann* [Offenbach] Metropolitan	1
GDS	31.03.66	*Otello* [Verdi] Pasadena	1
GDS	01.09.66	Sou Chong in *Das Land der Lachelus* [Lehar]	63
GDS	27.01.67	*L'Incoronazione di Poppea* [see list A above]	2
GDS	26.07.69	Danilo in *The Merry Widow* [Lehar] San Carlo, Naples	1
GDS	23.02.70	*Der Zarewitsch* [Lehar] Berlin	3
GDS	15.05.72	*Orpheus in the Underworld* [Offenbach] Rome	6
GDS	July '86	The Duke of Urbino in *A Night in Venice* [Strauss] Morbisch	1
GDS	24.07.91	The Narrator in *Le Villi* [Puccini] Siracusa	1
GDS	25.06.92	The Emperor in *Turandot* Caracalla, Rome	1

Maria Callas   41 roles :   590 performances
Giuseppe di Stefano   50 roles : 1015 performances

CONCERTS AND RECITALS
Maria Callas and Giuseppe di Stefano: World Tour 1973 –74

Hamburg [Congress Centrum: 17.10.73]; **Berlin** [Philharmonie: 29.10.73]; **Dusseldorf** [02.11.73]; **Munich** [06.11.73]; **Frankfurt** [Jahrhundert Halle Hochst: 09.11.73]; **Mannheim** [Nationaltheater: 12.11.73]; **Madrid** [Palacio Nacional de Congessos y Exposiciones: 20.11.73]; **London** [26.11.73 & 02.12.73]; **Paris** [07.12.73]; **Amsterdam** [11.12.73]; **Milan** [Instituto Nazionale per lo Studio alla Cure dei Tumori: 20.01.74]; **Stuttgart** [23.01.74]

Philadelphia [02.11.74]; **Toronto** [Massey Hall: 21.02.74]; **Washington** [24.02.74]; **Boston** [Symphony Hall: 27.02.74]; **Chicago** [02.03.74]; **New York** [05.03.74 & 15.04.74]; **Detroit** [Masonic Auditorium: 09.03.74]; **Dallas** [12.03.74]; **Miami Beach** [Auditorium: 21.03.74];**Columbus** [Ohio Theatre: 04.04.74];**Brookville L.I.** [New York, C.W. Post Center Auditorium: 09.04.74]; **Cincinnati** [Music Hall: 18.04.74]; **Seattle** [Opera House: 24.04.74]; **Portland** [Civic Auditorium: 27.04.74]; **Vancouver** [Queen Elizabeth Theatre: 01.05.74]; **Los Angeles** [Shrine Auditorium: 05.05.74]; **San Francisco** [09.05.74]; **Montreal** [Salle Wilfrid Pelletier, Place des Arts: 13.05.74]

Seoul [Auditorium of the University for Women: 05.10.74 & 08.10.74]; **Tokyo** [12.10.74, 19.10.74 & Bunka Kaikan: 27.10.74]; **Fukuoka** [Shimin Kaikan: 24.10.74]; **Osaka** [Festival Hall: 02.11.74]; **Hiroshima** [Yubin Chokin Hall: 07.11.74]; **Sapporo** [Hokkaido Koseinenkin Kaikan: 11.11.74]

CONCERTS AND RECITALS
1942 - 1976
[Listed chronologically]

MC	SALONIKA	Palas Cinema	October '42
MC		White Tower Theatre	August '43
MC	KOSTA MOUSOURI	Summer Theatre	21.07.43
MC	ATHENS	Olympia Theatre	26.09.43; 20.03.45
		Kotopouli-Rex Theatre	12.12.43; 03.08.45
		Herodes Atticus	05.08.57
GDS	CHAUX-DU-FONDS		28.06.46
GDS	TURIN	RAI Auditorium	07.04.47; 21.01.52; 08.12.52; 09.11.53
MC			07.03.49; 13.03.50; 12.03.51; 18.02.52
GDS	MONTREAL★	Forum	05.03.48; 26.11.64
MC			17.10.58
GDS	MIAMI★		21.03.48
GDS	SALT LAKE CITY		06.05.48
GDS	MEXICO CITY	Palacio de Bellas Artes	24.06.49
MC	BUENOS AIRES	Colon	09.07.49
MC	VERONA	Nuovo	31.10.49
GDS	BOSTON★	Statler Hotel	30.11.49
GDS	SAN FRANCISCO	War Memorial Opera House★	01.10.50; 15.10.50; 29.10.50; 22.05.51
MC		Civic Auditorium	26.11.58

Between 5 January and 26 February 1951, **di Stefano** sang concerts in Worcester [Mass.], Des Moines [Iowa], Durham [N. Car.], Greenboro [N. Car.], New Haven [Conn.], Macon [Georgia], and Dallas★.

MC	TRIESTE	Verdi	21.04.51
GDS	FORT WORTH	[Texas]	01.05.51
MC	FLORENCE	Grand Hotel	11.06.51
MC	MEXICO CITY	Radio XEW studios	15.07.51
MC	RIO DE JANEIRO	Municipal	14.09.51

Between 8 October and 1 November 1951, **di Stefano** sang concerts in Spokane [Washington], Boise [Idaho], Portland★ [Oregon], Seattle★, Pasedena [Cal.], St Louis, and Memphis.

MC	MILAN★	Circolo della Stampa	08.02.52
MC		Famiglia Meneghina	10.01.54
MC		RAI studios	27.09.56
GDS			26.11.56; 08.02.60
GDS		Verdi Conservatoire	18.11.84
GDS		[unknown]	21.11.92
MC	LONDON	Italian Embassy	17.11.52
MC		Royal Festival Hall★	23.09.59; 27.02 62; 31.05.63
GDS			11.05.73
MC		St. James' Palace	30.05.61
MC & GDS		Royal Opera House	04.11.62
GDS		Barbican	25.07.88
MC	ROME	Auditorium di Palazzo Pio	16.05.53
GDS		RAI studios	29.11.54;
GDS		[unknown]	19.07.70; 25.05.80; 15.05.81; 23.05.81; 20.11.92
GDS	VIENNA	Staatsoper	1953; 1963; 22.06.68
MC	SAN REMO	Casino	27.12.54
MC	WASHINGTON	Italian Embassy	17.12.56
MC		Constitution Hall★	22.11.58
MC	CHICAGO	Lyric★	15.01.57; 22.01.58
MC	ZURICH	Tonhalle	19.06.57
GDS			22.04.65; 25.04.66
MC	DALLAS	State Fair Music Hall★	21.11.57
MC	MADRID★	Cinema Monumental	24.03.58
		Zarzuela	02.05.58

Between 11 October and 29 November 1958, **Callas** sang concerts in Birmingham [Alabama], Atlanta, Toronto★, Cleveland, Detroit★, Washington★, San Francisco★ and Los Angeles★.

MC	ST. LOUIS	Kiel Auditorium	11.01.59
MC	PHILADELPHIA	Academy of Music★	24.01.59
MC	BARCELONA	Liceo	05.05.59
GDS			05.01.86
GDS	NEW YORK★	Carnegie Hall★	10.05.59; 07.11.63; 11.11.63; 01.09.65; 12.03.72; 13.10.76; 31.10.85
MC		Madison Square Garden	19.05.62
MC	HAMBURG★	Musikhalle	15.05.59; 16.03.62
MC	STUTTGART	Liederhalle★	19.05.59; 23.05.63

MC	MUNICH	Kongress-Saal★	21.05.59; 12.03.62
GDS			07.05.85
MC	WIESBADEN	Kursaal	24.05.59
MC	AMSTERDAM	Concertgebouw★	11.07.59
GDS		Hilversum	23.06.63; 27.01.68
MC	BRUSSELS	de la Monnaie	14.07.59
MC	BILBAO	Coliseo Albia	17.09.59
MC	BERLIN★	Titania Palast	23.10.59
		Deutsche Oper	17.03.63
MC	KANSAS CITY	Midland	28.10.59
GDS	BERGAMO		23.10.61
GDS	PARIS	RTF studios	22.01.62
MC		Th. des Champs-Elysees★	05.06.63
GDS		[unknown]	13.03.87; 16.03.87
MC	ESSEN	Stadtischer Saalbau	19.03.62
MC	BONN	Beethovenhalle	23.03.62
MC	DUSSELDORF	Rheinhalle★	20.05.63
MC	COPENHAGEN	Falkoner Centret	09.06.63
GDS	GHENT		08.03.67; 08.04.76
GDS	HAMILTON		06.05.67
GDS	AUCKLAND		09.05.67; 18.05.67
GDS	WELLINGTON		13.05.67; 20.05.67
GDS	DUNEDIN		16.05.67
GDS	MELBOURNE		26.05.67; 16.11.74; 23 11.74; May '82
GDS	LUCCA		1969

Between 4 & 28 November 1974, **di Stefano** sang concerts in Australia at Perth, Brisbane, Sydney and Adelaide

GDS	TOKYO	NHK Hall★	07.12.75; 18.12.75; 1976

Between 1980 and 1995, **di Stefano** sang in Rome, Palm Springs, Torre del Lago, Naples, Palermo, Modena, Melbourne, Sienna, Verona, Stanford [Conn.], Milan★, Dublin, Munich★, Rucheina, Stockholm, New York★, Barcelona, Busto Arsizio, Paris★, London★, Buxton, Siracusa, Perelada, Santander, Cesena, Mexico, Kremsmunster and fifteen German cities in the 1991 Festival Neapolitan.

★ World Tour venue

THEATRE APPEARANCES
Listed alphabètically

	ADRIA	**Comunale**		
GDS		Pagliacci '70		1
	ATHENS	**Palas Cinema**		
MC		Boccaccio '41		1
		Summer Theatre		
MC		Tosca '42, '43, Der Bettelstudent '45		3
		Olympia Theatre		
MC		Tiefland '44, '45, Cavalleria rusticana '44		3
		Herodes Atticus		
MC		Fidelio '44, O Protomastoras '44		2
	BARCELONA	**Liceu**		
GDS		Manon '46, Sonnambula '46, Rigoletto '46, Ballo '61, Fedora '70		5
	BARI	**Petruzzelli**		
GDS		Manon '53		1
	BENVENUTO			
GDS		Bohème '72		1
	BEOGRAD			
GDS		Carmen '70, Tosca '70		2
	BERGAMO	**Donizetti**		
MC		Traviata '51, Lucia '54,		2
GDS		L'Elisir '53, '61, Bohème '53		3
	BERLIN	**Stadtische Oper**		
MC		Lucia '55★		1
GDS		Lucia '55★		1
		Theater des Westens		
GDS		Tosca '61, Lachens '66, Der Zarewitsch '69, '78		4
	BOLOGNA	**Comunale**		
GDS		Sonnambula '46, Ballo '56, '62, Bohème '62		4
		Duse		
MC		Tosca '50		1
	BRESCIA	**Grand**		
MC		Aida '50		1
	BRUXELLES	**Grand Auditorium**		
GDS		Tosca '58		1
	BUENOS AIRES	Colon		
MC		Turandot '49, Norma '49, Aida '49		3
GDS		Tosca '65		1
	CAGLIARI	**Massimo**		
MC		Traviata '51		1

	CATANIA	**Massimo Bellini**	
MC		Norma '50, '51, Puritani '51, Traviata '52, Lucia '53	5
GDS		Manon '51, L'amico Fritz '52, Manon Lescaut '56	3
	CESENZA	**Comunale**	
GDS		Manon '46, Lucia '69	2
	CHIETI	**Marrucino**	
GDS		L'elisir '74	1
	CHICAGO	**Lyric**	
MC		Norma '54, Traviata '54, Lucia '54★, Puritani '55★, Trovatore '55, Madama Butterfly '55★	6
GDS		Lucia '54★, '57, Tosca '54, '57, '60, Puritani '55★, Bohème '55, Butterfly '55★, '58, Cavalleria '55, Gioconda '57, Adriana Lecouvreur '57, Turandot '58, '59, Pagliacci '58, Carmen '59, '60, Ballo '59, Fedora '60	19
	CINCINNATI	**Zoo Opera Pavilion**	
GDS		Andrea Chenier '59, Manon Lescaut '59	2
	COLOGNE	**Grosses Haus**	
MC		Sonnambula '57	1
GDS		Forza '57	1
	COMO	**Sociale**	
GDS		Manon '48	1
	DALLAS	**State Fair Music Hall**	
MC		Traviata '58, Medea '58, '59, Lucia '59	4
GDS		Butterfly '64	1
	DUBLIN	**Gaiety**	
GDS		Tosca '63	1
	EDINBURGH	**King's**	
MC		Sonnambula '57	1
GDS		L'elisir '57	1
	EPIDAUROS	**Ancient Auditorium**	
MC		Norma '60, Medea '61	2
	ESSEN		
GDS		Lachens '68	1
	FERMO	**Teatrodell'Aquila**	
GDS		Bohème '62, Ballo '62	2
	FLORENCE	**Comunale**	
MC		Norma '48, Traviata '51, Vespri '51, Puritani '52, Armida '52, Lucia '53★, Medea '53	7
GDS		Lucia '53★, Forza '56, Andrea Chenier '62	3
		Pergola	
MC		Orfeo '51	1

	FORLI	Esperia	
GDS		Traviata '46, Bohème '62	2
	FRANKFURT		
GDS		Lachens '79	I
	GENEVA	Grand-Theatre	
GDS		Tosca '63	I
	GENOA	Politeama	
GDS		Rigoletto '46, Werther '63	2
		Grattaciello	
MC		Tristan and Isolde '48	I
		Carlo Felice	
MC		Turandot '48, Lucia '53★, Tosca '54	3
GDS		Lucia '53★, Manon '53, Fanciulla '62	3
		Augustus	
GDS		L'elisir '51	I
	HAMBURG	Staatsoper	
GDS		Tosca '65	I
	HERTFORD	Bushnell Memorial Auditorium	
GDS		Ballo '63, Manon '64	2
	JOHANNESBURG	His Majesty's	
GDS		L'elisir '56	I
	KABENHAVN	Falkoner centret	
GDS		L'elisir '66	I
	LAUSANNE		
GDS		Bohème '62	I
	LISBON	Sao Carlos	
MC		Traviata '58	I
GDS		Bohème '60, Ballo '60	2
	LIVORNO	Teatro la Gran Guardia	
GDS		Bohème '62	I
	LONDON	Royal Opera House, Covent Garden	
MC		Norma '52, '53, '57, Aida '53, Trovatore '53, Traviata '58, Medea '59, Tosca '64, '65	9
GDS		Tosca '61, Bohème '63	2
	LOS ANGELES	Greek	
GDS		Bohème '50, Rigoletto '50, Barbiere '50, Lachens '67	4
	LUCCA	Comunale di Giglio	
GDS		Fedora '69	3
	LUGO	Piazzale del Pavaglione	
GDS		Rigoletto '46, Traviata '46, L'amico Fritz '46	3

MACARATA	**Sferisteria**		
GDS	Carmen '68		1
MANTUA	**Sociale**		
GDS	Andrea Chenier '62		1

MEXICO CITY **Palacio de Bellas Artes**

GDS   Rigoletto '48, Traviata '48, '52★, '61, Manon '48, '52, '57, '64,
Mignon '49, Barbiere '49, Favorita '49, Puritani '52★, Lucia '52★,
Rigoletto '52★, Tosca '52★, '57, '60, '64, Werther '49, '52, '60, '64,
Bohème '49, '52, '57, '60, L'elisir '57, Carmen '57, '61,
Ballo '60, '64, Lucia '60, Cavalleria '61, Andrea Chenier '61,
Butterfly '61   35

MC   Norma '50, Aida '50, '51, Tosca '50, '52★ Trovatore '50,
Traviata '51★, '52 Puritani '52★, Lucia '52★, Rigoletto '52★   11

MILAN   **La Scala**

GDS   Manon '47, Mignon '47, Bohème '52, '55, '59, '71, Gioconda '52★,
Tosca '53, '54, '59, Rigoletto '53, Lucia '54★,
L'elisir '54, '58, '64, '67, Carmen '55, '59, '60, '72, Forza '55, '57,
Cavalleria '55, Traviata '55★, Ballo '56, '57★, Pagliacci '56, '57,
Werther '56, Aida '56, Manon Lescaut '57, Iris '57,
Adriana Lecouvreur '58, Butterfly '58, Turandot '58,
Bartered Bride '59, Calzare '61, Rienzi '64, Poppea '67   39

MC   Aida '50, Vespri '51, Norma '52, '55, Seraglio '52, Macbeth '52,
Gioconda '52, Trovatore '53, Medea '53, '62/3 Lucia '54,
Alceste '54, Don Carlo '54, Vestale '54, Andrea Chenier '55,
Sonnambula '55, '57, Turco '55, Traviata '55, '56, Barbiere '56,
Fedora '56, Anna Bolena '57, '58, Ifigenia '57, Ballo '57,
Pirata '58, Poliuto '60   22

MODENA	**Comunale**		
GDS	Manon '52, Bohème '53		2
MONTE CARLO	**Salle Garnier**		
GDS	Traviata '52		1
MONTERREY	**Florida**		
GDS	Faust '54, Werther '54, Lucia '54, Tosca '54, Carmen '57, '60		6
MONTREAL	**Expo'67**		
GDS	Lachens '67		1
MORBISCH			
GDS	Night in Vienna '88		1
MUNICH	**Nationaltheater**		
GDS	Bohème '70		1

NAPLES   **San Carlo**

GDS   Rigoletto '48, Manon '48, Manon Lescaut '57, Ballo '60,
Fedora '61, Calzare '62, Merry Widow '69,   7

MC   Turandot '49, Nabucco '49, Aida '50, Trovatore '51, Lucia '56 5

		Arena Flegrea	
GDS		Gioconda '53, Tosca '54, '62	3

	NEW ORLEANS Municipal Auditurium		
GDS		Bohème '59, Werther '64	2

	NEW YORK	**Metropolitan**	
GDS		Rigoletto '48, '49, '50, '51, '56, Mignon '48, '49, Traviata '49, '50, '51,L'elisir '49, '50, Gianni Schicchi '49, Falstaff '49, Der Rosenkavalier '49,Faust '49, '51, '55, Bohème '49, '50,'51, Barbiere '50, Manon '51, Butterfly '52, Carmen '55, Tosca '56, Hoffmann '65	27
MC		Norma '56, Tosca '56, '58, '65, Lucia '56, '58, Traviata '58	7
		Carnegie Hall	
MC		Pirata '59	1

	NEWARK		
GDS		Bohème '72	1

	PALERMO	**Massimo**	
MC		Die Walkure '49, Norma '51	2
GDS		Rigoletto '52, Tosca '52, '63, Werther '54, Bohème '55, Manon '55, Cavalleria '56, '63, Forza '56, Luisa Miller '63, Fedora '69	11

	PARIS	**Opera**	
GDS		Faust '54	1
MC		Norma '64, '65, Tosca '65	3

	PARMA	**Regio**	
GDS		Manon '47, Sonnambula '47, L'amico Fritz '47	3
MC		Traviata '51	1

	PASADENA	**Civic Auditorium**	
GDS		Traviata '65, Tosca '66, Otello '66	3

	PERUGIA	**Comunale**	
GDS		Manon '47	1

	PIACENZA	**Municipale**	
GDS		Manon '46	1

	PISA	**Verdi**	
GDS		Pescatori '47, Bohème '53	2
MC		Tosca '50	1

	PHILADELPHIA Academy of Music		
GDS		Tosca '56, '64, Bohème '59, Ballo '63	4
MC		Norma '56	1

	PRAGUE		
GDS		Lachens '68	1

	PURCHASE		
GDS		L'elisir '80	1

RAVENNA **Alighieri**
GDS   Manon '46, Traviata '46, L'amico Fritz '48, Bohème '54   **4**
MC   Forza '54   **I**

REGGIO CALABRIA Cilea
MC   Aida '51   **I**

REGGIO EMILIA Municipal
GDS   Manon '46, L'amico Fritz '46   **2**

RIO DE JANEIRO Municipal
GDS   Rigoletto '48, '51, Traviata '48, Manon '48, '51,
     Bohème '48, '51, '54, Butterfly '51, Tosca '54, Cavalleria '54,   **II**
MC   Norma '51, Tosca '51, Traviata '51   **3**

ROME **Caracalla**
MC   Turandot '48   **I**
GDS   Gioconda '53, Tosca '53, '62, Carmen '65, Turandot
     [Emperor] '92   **5**
     Teatro dell'Opera
GDS   Sonnambula '47, Manon '47, '65, Pescatori '47, Mignon '47,
     Rigoletto '47, '54 Bohème '53, '54, '58, '61, Tosca '54, Lucia '54
     Werther '55, '62, Ballo '55, '59, '60, '62, Manon Lescaut '56,
     '59, '61, Puritani '56, Iris '56, Carmen '57, Pagliacci '58, '72,
     Andrea Chenier '59, Cavalleria '62, Orpheus '71   **30**
MC   Parsifal '49, Tristan and Isolde '50, Norma '50, '53, '58, Aida '50,
     Puritani '52, Traviata '53, Lucia '53, Trovatore '53, Medea '55   **II**
     Eliseo
MC   Turco '50   **I**

ROVIGO **Sociale**
MC   Aida '48   **I**

SALSOMAGGIORE Nuovo
MC   Tosca '50   **I**

SAN FRANCISCO Geary
GDS   Lucia '50, Bohème '50, Lachens '67   **3**

SAN REMO
GDS   Andrea Chenier '62, Lucia '68   **2**

SAO PAULO **Municipal**
GDS   Manon '51, Traviata '51★, Rigoletto '51   **3**
MC   Norma '51, Traviata '51★   **2**

TIMISOARA
GDS   Carmen '71   **I**

TORONTO **O'Keefe Centre**
GDS   Lachens '67   **I**

	TORRE DEL LAGO		
GDS		Fanciulla '62	1
	TRENTON		
GDS		Bohème '72	1
	TREVISO	**Comunale**	
GDS		Andrea Chenier '61	1
	TRIESTE	**Rossetti**	
MC		Forza '48	1
		Verdi	
GDS		Pescatori '47, Manon '50, Bohème '51, Werther '52, Tosca '62, '63	6
MC		Norma '53	1
		Castello di San Giusto	
GDS		Pecheurs '53	1
	TURIN	**Carignano**	
GDS		Mignon '47	1
		Lirico	
MC		Aida '48	1
		Nuovo	
GDS		Andrea Chenier '61, Bohème '63	2
	UDINE	**Puccini**	
MC		Turandot '48	1
	VENICE	**La Fenice**	
GDS		Pescatori '46, Sonnambula '47, Bohème '60	3
MC		Tristan and Isolde '47, Turandot '48, Die Walkure '49, Puritani '49, Norma '50, Traviata '53, Lucia '54, Medea '54	8
	VERONA	**Arena**	
MC		Gioconda '47, '52, Turandot '48, Traviata '52, Aida '53, Trovatore '53, Mefistofele '54★	7
GDS		Pecheurs '50, Bohème '50, '57, Manon '51, Mefistofele '54★, Gioconda '56, Tosca '56, '62	8
	VIAREGGIO	**Politeama**	
GDS		Andrea Chenier '62	1
	VIENNA	**Staatsoper**	
MC		Lucia '56★	1
GDS		Lucia '56★, Manon Lescaut '57, '59, Carmen '57, '58, '59, '60, '61, '65, Tosca '58, '59, '60, '61, '62, '65, Aida '58, Rigoletto '58, Ballo '58, '59, '60, '64, '65, Bohème '60, '61, Traviata '60, '65, Forza '60, '64, '65, Butterfly '60, '64, '65, Fledermaus '60, Turandot '61, '64, Andrea Chenier '65, Pagliacci '65, Cavalleria '65	38
		Volksoper	
GDS		L'elisir '65	1
		Theater der Wien	
GDS		Lachens '67	1

WASHINGTON Constitution Hall
MC   Pirata '59   I

Maria Callas   160 appearances in 49 theatres

Giuseppe di Stefano   353 appearances in 88 theatres

★ Joint appearances

CALLAS & DI STEFANO

DISCOGRAPHY
Listed chronologically

		24.06.46	O, dolce incanto [*Manon*-Massenet]	
			All piano accompanied	
	GDS		**The Young di Stefano**	*Testament SBT 1096*
		1944/45	Se vuoi goder la vita [Bixio]★	
		1944/45	Mamma [Bixio]★	
		1944/45	Una furtive lagrima [*L'elisir*-Donizetti]★	
		09.04.46	Vola, Vola, Vola [Bixio]	
		09.04.46	Canto, ma sotto voce [Bixio]	
		25.06.46	Ed anche Beppe amo [*L'amico Fritz*-Mascagni]★	
12		25.06.46	O, dolce incanto [*Manon*-Massenet]★	
17, 93		30.11.47	E la solita storia [*L'arlesiana*-Cilea]	
17		30.11.47	Ah! Non credevi tu! [*Mignon*-Thomas]	
17		04.12.47	Addio, Mignon, fa' core [*Mignon*-Thomas]	
17		04.12 47	A la Barcillunisa [arr. Favara]	
17		04.12.47	Cantu a timuni [arr. Favara]	
17		06.12.47	E lucevan le stelle [*Tosca*-Puccini]	
17		11.12.47	Io son Solo!...Ah! dispar [*Manon*-Massenet]	
33		12.12.50	Abballati [arr. Favara]	
33		12.12.50	Mutteti di lu Paliu [arr, Favara]	
		20.06.55	Una parola sola!...Or son sei mesi [*La Fanciulla del West*-Puccini]	
		22.06.55	Ce'ella mi creda libero [*La Fanciulla del West*-Puccini]	
92		22.06.55	La vito e inferno...Oh tu che in seno [*La forza del destino*-Verdi]	
92		22.06.55	Avete torto!...Firenze e come un albero [*Gianni Schicchi*-Puccini]	
		22.06.55	Non piangere, Liu [*Turandot*-Puccini]	
118		32.06.55	Nessun dorma! [*Turandot*-Puccini]	
100		04.04.56	Passione [Tagliaferri]	
			★piano accompanied	
12	**GDS**	03.09.44	**L'ELISIR D'AMORE [Donizetti]** c. Ackermann	
				Bongiovanni GB1141-2
	GDS	1944	Vieni sul mar [Maatner]	*LR CD 1010*
12	**GDS**	18.02.45	**IL TABARRO [Puccini]** c. Ackermann	*VA 1226*
	GDS	04.09.46	Maria Cristina [Bixio]	*Bongiovanni GB1154.2*
		04.09.46	Il valzer del quarto di Luna [Bixio]	
	GDS	04.09.46	Cherie [Tieri]	*G.O.P.810 CD2*
		04.09.46	Voglio sognar [Tieri]	
	GDS		**Unreleased Jewels**	*Preiser 93426*
		28.06.45	Se vuoi goder la vita [Bixio]	
		28.06.45	O sole mio [di Capua]	
		05.07.45	Visione veneziana [Brogi]★	
		28.06.46	Serenata del burattino [Mignone]★	
		28.06.46	La leggenda del pastore [Bianca]★	
		28.06.46	Mamma [Bixio]★	
		28.06.46	Dicitencello vuie [Falvo]★	
		28.06.46	Musica proibita [Gastaldon]★	
			★piano accompanied	

| 13 | **GDS** | 13.09.46 | **PAGANINI [abridged-Lehar]]** c.Victor Desorzens |
| | | | *Preiser 93426* |

| 15 | **GDS** | 15.03.47 | **MANON [Massenet]**live hghts Scala with Favero |
| | | | *Myto 1 MCD 905.26* |

	GDS		**Opera Arias** *EMI CDM 763105.2*
17		09.12.47	De' miei bollenti spiriti [*Traviata*-Verdi]
156		Jun '57	Non hai comresso [*Pescatori*-Bizet[with Carteri
			+ 16 tracks from EMI recordings

| 20 | **GDS** | 22.06.48 | **RIGOLETTO [Verdi]** live Mexico City with O'Connor |
| | | | c. Cellini   *GAO 128/9* |

| 20 | **GDS** | 01.07.48 | **LA TRAVIATA [Verdi]** live excs Mexico City with |
| | | | O'Connor   *Fono 1002* |

| 20 | **GDS** | 06.07.48 | **MANON [Massenet]** live Mexico City with Gonzales |
| | | | c.Cellini   *G.O.P. 813 CD 2* |

| 22 | **GDS** | 01.01.49 | **LA TRAVIATA [Verdi]** live Met with Steber, Merrill |
| | | | *Naxos 8110115-16* |

| 23 | **GDS** | 26.02.49 | **FALSTAFF [Verdi]** live Met with Warren c. Reiner |
| | | | *Arlecchino ARLA85-A86* |

| 23 | **GDS** | 12.03.49 | **GIANNI SCHICCHI [Puccini]** c. Giuseppe Antonicelli |
| | | | *G.O.P.830 CD2* |

| 24 | **MC** | 20.05.49 | **TURANDOT [Puccini]** live excs Buenos Aires c. Serafin |
| | | | *Archipel ARPCD 0005* |

| 24 | **MC** | 17.06.49 | **NORMA [Bellini]** live excs Buenos Aires with Barbieri |
| | | | c.Serafin   *Divina DVN-12* |

	GDS		**The Glory of Italy** live *Cantabile BIM-704-2 [2 CDs]*
24		25.06.49	*Mexico Radio*
			Santa Lucia [Cottrau]
			Ay, ay, ay [Perez-Freire]
			Core 'ngrato [Cardillo]
			Mamma mia, che vo sape [Nutile]
			Estrellita [Ponce]
			Tu, ca' nun chiagne! [de Curtis]
		29.11.54	*RAI Rome*
			Fra poco [*Lucia*-Donizetti]
			Firenze e come [*Gianni Schicchi*-Puccini]
			Non piangere Liu [*Turandot*-Puccini]
			+ 29 tracks from RAI recitals, San Francisco, Mexico City
			and La Scala

| 24 | **GDS** | 28.06.49 | **MIGNON [Thomas]** live Mexico with Simionato |
| | | | c. Picco   *Gebbhardt JGCD 0005* |

| 24 | **GDS** | 07.07.49 | **IL BARBIERE DI SIVIGLIA [Rossini]** live excs |
| | | | Mexico, c. Cellini   *GOP 817CD2* |

24	**GDS**	12.07.49	**LA FAVORITA [Donizetti]** with Simionato c. Cellini

                                                        SRO 812-2

24 GDS 23.07.49 WERTHER [Massenet] live Mexico City with
Simionato c. Cellini   *G.O.P.817 CD2*

MC   **Callas Edition Vol.1**   *CED 100341 [3CDs]*

08–10.11.49 *Cetra records*
Liebestod [*Tristan and Isolde*-Wagner]
Casta diva Ah! bello [*Norma*-Bellini]
26   Mad Scene [*I Puritani*-Bellini]

12.03.51 *RAI Turin*
Variations on Deh torna [Proch]
Io son Titania [*Mignon*-Thomas]
Ecco l'orrido campo…[*Ballo*-Verdi]

50   18.02.52 *RAI Rome*
Vieni t'affretta [*Macbeth*-Verdi]
Mad scene [*Lucia*-Donizetti]
Anch'io dischiuso [*Nabucco*-Verdi]
Dov'e l'indiana bruna [*Lakme*-Delibes]

40   27.12.54 *RAI San Remo*
Tutte le torture [*Il seraglio*-Mozart]
Ombra leggiera [*Dinorah* –Meyerbeer]
Depuis le jour [*Louise*-Charpentier]
D'amore al dolce impero [*Armida*-Rossini]

27.12.56 *RAI Milan*
Tu che invoco [*La vestale*-Spontini]
Bel raggio [*Semiramide*-Rossini]
Mad scene [*Hamlet*-Thomas]
Vieni al tempio [*I puritani*-Bellini]

122   05.08.57 *Athens Concert*
Oh sventura Ifigenia [*Ifigenia in Tauride*-Gluck]
D'amor sull'ali rosee [*Il trovatore*-Verdi]
Pace, pace mio dio [*Forza*-Verdi]
Liebestod [*Tristan*-Wagner]
Regnava nel silenzio [*Lucia*-Donizetti]
Mad scene [*Hamlet*-Thomas]

26 GDS 03.12.49 DER ROSENKAVALIER [Strauss] with Steber,
Stevens, c. Reiner   *LYS 425-7*

27 MC 20.12.49 NABUCCO [Verdi[live Naples with Bechi c. Gui
Archipel ARPCD 0001-2

26 GDS 31.12.49 FAUST [Gounod] with Kirsten, Tajo, Warren c. Pelletier
Arkadia MP 478.2

30 MC 23.05.50 NORMA [Bellini] live Mexico City with Simionato
Golden Melodram GM 2.0015

| 30 | MC | 30.05.50 | **AIDA [Verdi]** live Mexico City with Simionato, Baum |
| | | | *Golden Melodram GM.20015* |

| 30 | MC | 30.05.50 | **AIDA [Verdi]** live excs Mexico City |
| | | | *Archipel ARPCD 0005* |

| 31 | MC | 08.06.50 | **TOSCA [Verdi]** live Mexico City with Filippchi, Weede |
| | | | c. Mugnai   *GM 2.0015* |

| 31 | MC | 20.06.50 | **IL TROVATORE [Verdi]** live Mexico with Simionato, |
| | | | Baum, Warren,   *GM 2.0015* |

| 31 | MC | 27.07.50 | **IL TROVATORE [Verdi]** live excs Mexico c. Picco |
| | | | *Archipel ARPCD0010* |

	GDS		**San Francisco recitals** live *Myto 1 MCD 924.67*
		01.10.50	Salut! Demeure [*Faust*-Gounod]
32		01.10.50	M'appari [*Martha*-Flotow]
		01.10.50	Che gelida manina…[*Bohème* Puccini] with Sayao
32		15.10.50	O Souverain [*Le Cid*-Massenet]
		15.10.50	Parmi veder [*Rigoletto*-Verdi]
		15.10.50	Love duet [*Madama Butterfly*-Puccini] with Tebaldi
		29.10.50	Cielo e mar [*Gioconda*-Ponchielli]
		29.10.50	E lucevan le stelle [*Tosca*-Puccini]
		29.10.50	Love duet [*Lucia*-Donizetti] with L. Pons

| 32 | MC | 02.10.50 | **AIDA [Verdi]** live excs Rome with Stignani, Picchi |
| | | | c. Bellezza   *Melodram 26109* |

	GDS	12.12.50	A la Vallelunghisa [arr. Favara] *LR CD 1010*
		12.12.50	A la Barcillunisa [arr. Favara]
		12.12.50	Cantu a Timuni [arr. Favara]

| 21 | MC | 20/21 Nov '50 | **PARSIFAL [Wagner]** with Baldelli, Christoff, cond Gui |
| | | | *Virtuoso 2699232* |

| 50 | MC | 27.01.51 | **IL TROVATORE [Verdi]** live Naples with Lauri-Volpi |
| | | | *Melodram CDM 26001* |

| 33 | GDS | 27.01.51 | **REQUIEM [Verdi]** live Carnegie Hall c. Toscanini |
| | | | *RCA GD 60299* |

| 33 | GDS | 17.03.51 | **LA BOHÈME [Puccini]** live Metropolitan c. Antonicelli |
| | | | *CDM 270108* |

| 34 | GDS | 23.03.51 | Dunque e proprio finita? [*La Bohème* –Puccini] |
| | | | RCA Victor c. Cellini   *MET 224* |

| 32 | MC | 30.05.51 | **I VESPRI SICILIANI [Verdi]** live Florence with Christoff. |
| | | | *Archipel ARPCD 0016-3* |

| 35 | MC | 03.07.51 | **AIDA [Verdi]** live Mexico City with del Monaco. |
| | | | *Archipel ARPCD 0020-2* |

| 35 | MC | 17.07.51 | **LA TRAVIATA [Verdi]** live Mexico with Valletti, Taddei |
| | | | *Archipel ARPCD 018* |

35	MC	24.09.51	TOSCA [Puccini] live hghts Rio with Poggi, Silveri, c.Votto
			ArchipelARPCD 0026

	MC	07.12.51	I VESPRI SICILIANI [Verdi] live Scala c. de Sabata *n/a*

38	GDS	15.12.51	MANON [Massenet] live Met with Albanese c. Cleva
			GDS 2 CD 1010

	GDS		**Historical recordings**	*Gala GL 303*
38		15.03.52	Che gelida manina [*Bohème*-Puccini]	
114		07.12.56	Celeste Aida [*Aida*-Verdi]	
145		07.12.58	Non piangere Liu [*Turandot*-Puccini]	
		10.10.61	Una furtiva lagrima [*L'elisir*-Donizetti]	
			+ 12 tracks live	

40	MC	26.04.52	ARMIDA [Rossini] live Florence c. Serafin
			SakkarisSR.DIVA 1105/6

42	MC+GDS	29.05.52	I PURITANI [Bellini] live Mexico City c. Picco
			ARPCD 0047.2

44	MC+GDS	03.06.52	LA TRAVIATA [Verdi] live Mexico City c. Mugnai
			ARPCD 0048.2

42	MC+GDS	10.06.52	LUCIA DI LAMMERMOOR [Donizetti] live Mexico
			Myto2MCD 913.40

44	MC+GDS	17.06.52	RIGOLETTO [Verdi] live Mexico City c.Mugna
			ARPCD 0061.2

44	MC+GDS	01.07.52	TOSCA [Puccini] live Mexico City with Campolonghi
			ARPCD 0049.2

49	MC	Sept '52	LA GIOCONDA [Ponchielli] with Barbieri, Poggi.
			Hommage 001837 HOM

53-4	MC	18.11.52	NORMA [Bellini] live Covent Garden with Stignani c. Gui
			Sakkaris PR.SR.277/8

46	MC	07.12.52	MACBETH [Verdi] live La Scala with Masherini c. de Sabata
			EMI CMS 566447.2

	GDS		**RAI recitals**	*GDS 1205*
118		08.12.52	Nessun dorma [*Turandot*-Puccini]	
		08.12.52	Ah, mio bene [*La favorita*-Donizetti] with Stignani	
		09.11 53	Apei le tua finestra [*Iris*-Mascagni]	
118		09.11.53	Come un bel di di maggio [*Andrea Chenier*-Giordano]	
		09.11.53	O tu che in seno agl angeli [*Forza*-Verdi]	
		09.11.53	Vieni fra queste braccia [Puritani-*Bellini*] with Carosio	
		26.11.56	Ma se m'e forza perderti [*Ballo*-Verdi]	
118		06.11.56	Un di all'azzuro spazio [*Andrea Chenier*-Giordano]	
118		26.11.56	Io conosco un giardino [*Maristella*-Pietri]	
		26.11.56	Nessun dorma [*Turandot*-Puccini]	

	MC		**The EMI Rarities**	*EMI CMS 566468*
		27.01.53	Non mi dir [*Don Giovanni*-Mozart]	
		Sept '58	Sleepwalking scene [*Macbeth*-Verdi]	
		Jul '60	Bel raggio [*Semiramide*-Rossini]	
		Jul '60	Arrigo ah, parli a un core [*Vespri*-Verdi]	
		Nov '61	Com'e bello [*Lucrezia Borgia*-Donizetti]	
		Nov '61	Selva opaca [*Guglielmo Tell*-Rossini]	
		Nov '61	Bel raggio [*Semiramide*-Rossini]	
		Nov '61	Sorgete[*Il pirata*-Bellini]	
		Apr '62	O don fatale [*Don Carlo*-Verdi]	
		Apr '62	Naqui all'affanno [*La cenerentola*-Rossini]	
		Apr '62	Ocean! Thou mighty monster [*Oberon*-Weber]	
		Jun '64	Pur ti riveggio [*Aida*-Verdi]	
		Jan '65	Te, vergin santa [*I Lombardi*-Verdi]	
		Jan '65	D'amor sull'ali rosee [*Trovatore*-Verdi]	
		Feb '69	Arrigo! Ah, parli a un core [*Vespri*-Verdi]	
		Feb '69	Liberamente or piangi [*Attila*-Verdi]	
		Feb '69	Te, vergin santa [*I Lombardi*-Verdi]	

62-4	MC+GDS	Feb/Mar '53	**LUCIA DI LAMMERMOOR [Donizetti]** c. Serafin	
				EMI CMS 566441.2]

50	**MC**	23.02.53	**IL TROVATORE [Verdi]** live Scala with Stignani, c.Votto	
				Myto 2MCD 902.13

50-2	**MC+GDS**	Mar '53	**I PURITANI [Bellini]** with Panerai c. Serafin	
65-8				*EMI CDS 556275.2*
			Highlights	*EMI CDM 566665.2*

55	**GDS**		**Neapolitan Songs**	*Testament SBT 1097*
		Apr '53	Tu, ca nun chiagne [de Curtis]	
		Apr '53	Core 'ngrato [Cardillo]	
		Apr '53	Dicitencello vuje [Flavo]	
		Apr '53	Marechiare [Tosti]	
		Apr '53	Torna a Surriento [de Curtis]	
		Jun '53	'O sole mio [di Capua]	
		Jun '53	Santa Lucia luntana [Mario]	
		Jun '53	I' te vurria vasa [di Capua]	
100		Apr '56	Silenzio cantatore [Lama]	
		Apr '56	Chiove [Nardella]	
		Apr '56	'O paese d''o sole [D'Annibale]	
		Apr '56	Maria, mari' [di Capua]	
		Apr '56	'Na sera 'e maggio [Cioff]	
		Apr '56	Santa Lucia	
		Apr '56	Senza nisciuno [de Curtis]	
		May '56	Fenesta che lucive [Bellini]	
		May '56	Piscatore 'e pusilecco [Tagliaferri]	
		Nov '56	Voce 'e notte [de Curtis]	
		Nov '56	O Maranariello [Gambardella]	

100		May '57	Autunno [de Curtis]
		May '57	'E pallume [Persico]

52	**MC**	07.05.53	**MEDEA [Cherubini]** live Florence c. Gui

Golden Melodram GM 2.0037

54	**MC**	10.06.53	**AIDA [Verdi]** live Covent Garden c. Barbirolli

Golden Melodram GM 2.0035

56-7	**MC+GDS** Aug '53	**CAVALLERIA RUSTICANA [Mascagni]** c. Serafin

EMI CDS 556287.2

57-9	**MC+GDS** Aug '53	**TOSCA [Puccini]** with Gobbi c. de Sabata

EMI CMS 567756.2

61	**MC**	Sept '53	**LA TRAVIATA [Verdi]** with F. Albanese, Savarese c. Santini

Warner Fonit Cetra

60	**MC**	19.11.53	**NORMA [Bellini]** live Trieste with Nicolai, Corelli, Christoff c. Votto

Divina DVN3

5	**MC**	10.12.53	**MEDEA [Cherubini]** live La Scala with Penno c. Bernstein

Fonit Cetra 101

5-10	**MC+GDS** 18.01.54	**LUCIA DI LAMMERMOOR [Donizetti]** live La Scala c. Karajan

SRO 831/2

69	**MC**	04.04.54	**ALCESTE [Gluck]** live La Scala c. Giulini

Golden Melodram GM 2.0019

71	**MC**	Apr/May '54	**NORMA [Bellini]** with Stignani, Filippeschi c. Serafin

EMI CDS 556271

70	**GDS**	03.06.54	La Strada del Cuore [Nino Gatti]	*G.O.P.810 CD2*

71-5	**MC+GDS** Jun '54	**I PAGLIACCI [Leoncavallo]** with Gobbi, Panerai c. Serafin

EMI CDS556287.2

60	**GDS**	Jun '54	**REQUIEM [Verdi]** with Schwarzkopf, Siepi c. de Sabata

EMI CHS 565506

76-7	**GDS**	Aug '54	**MADAMA BUTTERFLY [Puccini]** with de los Angeles, Gobbi

Testament SBT 2168

76	**MC**	Aug '54	**LA FORZA DEL DESTINO [Verdi]** with Tucker c. Serafin

EMI CDS 556323.2

76	**MC**	Sept '54	**IL TURCO IN ITALIA [Rossini]** with Rossi-Lemeni

EMI CDS 556313.2

78	**MC**	Sept '54	**Puccini arias**	*EMI CDM 566463.2*

In quelle trine morbide [*Manon Lescaut*]
Solo, perduta, abbandonata [*Manon Lescaut*]
Signore ascolta [*Turandot*]
Tu che di gel cinta [*Turandot*]
In questa reggia [*Turandot*]
O mio babbini caro [*Gianni Schicchi*]

Si, chiamano Mimi [*La bohème*]
Donde lieta usci [*La bohème*]
Un bel di [*Madama Butterfly*]
Tu, tu, piccolo Iddio! [*Madama Butterfly*]
Senza mamma [*Suor Angelica*]

78	**MC**	Sept '54	**Lyric and coloratura arias**	*EMI CDM 566458.2*

Io sono l'umile ancella [*Adriana Lecouvreur*-Cilea]
Povero fiori [*Adriana Lecouvreur*-Cilea]
78   Ebben? Ne andro lontano [*La Wally*-Catalani]
La mamma morta [*Andrea Chenier*-Giordano]
L'altra notte [*Mefistofele*-Boito]
Una poco voce fa [*Il Barbiere di Siviglia*-Rossini]
Aria delle campanelle [*Lakme*-Delibes]
Ombra leggera [*Dinorah*-Meyerbeer]
Bolero [*I Vespri Siciliani*-Verdi]

	GDS	21.09.54	**TOSCA [Puccini]** live Rio de Janiero with Tebaldi, Taddei c. Fabritiis	*ROM101*
118	**GDS**	29.11.54	**RAI Rome**	*Fonit Cetra CDC 8*

Firenze e come un albergo [*Gianni Schicchi*- Puccini]
In un coupe? [*Bohème*-Puccini] with Taddei
Non piangere Liu [*Turandot*-Puccini]
Tutta su me ti posa…Fra le tue braccia [*Manon Lescaut*
  Puccini] with Tebaldi

81	**MC**	07.12.54	**LA VESTALE [Spontini]** live La Scala with Corelli c. Votto	*Sakkaris PR.SR.281/2*
82	**MC**	08.01.55	**ANDREA CHENIER [Giordano]** live Scala, del Monaco	*GM 2.0006*
82	**GDS**	18.01.55	**CARMEN [Bizet]** live hghts La Scala with Simionato c. Karajan	*CDKAR221.3*
82	**MC**	05.03.55	**LA SONNAMBULA [Bellini]** live La Scala, c. Bernstein	*Myto 2 MCD 890.06*
83	**GDS**	26.04.55	**LA FORZA DEL DESTINO [Verdi]** live La Scala with Tebaldi	*GDS 3CD 103*
83	**GDS**	10.05.55	**CAVALLERIA RUSTICANA [Mascagni]** live Scala with Simionato	*1MCD 981.180*
155	**MC**	Jun '55	**Callas at La Scala**	*EMI CDM 566457.2*

Dei tuoi figli [*Medea*-Cherubini]
Tu che invoco [*La vestale*-Spontini]
O Nume tutelar [*La vestale*-Spontini]
Caro oggetto [*La vestale*-Spontini]
115   Come per me sereno [*La sonnambula*-Bellini]
Ah! non credea mirati…Ah! non giunge [*La sonnambula*-Bellini]

| 85 | MC+GDS | 28.05.55 | **LA TRAVIATA [Verdi]** live Scala c. Giulini |
| | | | *EMI CMS566450.2* |

| 85 | MC | 29.06.55 | **NORMA [Bellini]** live RAI Rome with Stignani, del Monaco |
| | | | *Hommage 7001830* |

| 85 | MC | Aug '55 | **MADAMA BUTTERFLY [Puccini]** with Gedda c. Karajan |
| | | | *EMI CDS 556298.2* |

85	MC	Aug '55	**AIDA [Verdi]** with Barbieri, Tucker, Gobbi c. Serafin
			MI CDS 556316.2
			Highlights *EMI CDM 566668.2*

88-91	MC+GDS	Sept '55	**RIGOLETTO [Verdi]** with Gobbi c. Serafin
			EMI CDS 556327.2
			Highlights *EMI CDM 566667.2*

| 92 | GDS | Sept '55 | **LA TRAVIATA [Verdi]** with Stella, Gobbi c. Serafin |
| | | | *Testament SBT 2211* |

| 92 | GDS | Sept '55 | **L'ELISIR D'AMORE [Donizetti]** c. Molinari-Pradelli |
| | | | *Decca 443542.2* |

| 93-4 | MC+GDS | 29.09.55 | **LUCIA DI LAMMERMOOR [Donizetti]** live Berlin |
| | | | c. Karajan   *EMI CMS 566441.2* |

| 99 | MC | 07.12.55 | **NORMA [Bellini]** live La Scala with Simionato, del Monaco |
| | | | *Gala GL 100.511* |

| 99 | MC | 19.01.56 | **LA TRAVIATA [Verdi[** live La Scala with Raimondi c. Giulini |
| | | | *Myto 2MCD890.03* |

| 99 | MC | 16.02.56 | **IL BARBIERE DI SIVIGLIA [Rossini]** live Scala with |
| | | | Gobbi.   *DIVA 1103/4* |

| 101 | MC | 22.03.56 | **LUCIA DI LAMMERMOOR [Donizetti]** live Naples |
| | | | c. Molinari-Pradelli   *2MCD903 19* |

| 100 | GDS | 24.04.56 | **I PAGLIACCI [Leoncavallo]** live La Scala c. Sanzogno |
| | | | *IMCD 012.244* |

| 101 | GDS | 08.06.56 | **LA FORZA DEL DESTINO [Verdi]** live Florence |
| | | | with Tebaldi   *Mel. 37010* |

| | GDS | 1956 | Santo natal! notte d'opal [Gruber]   *LR CD 1010* |
| | | | Tu scendi dalle stelle [de Liguori] |

102	MC+GDS	Aug '56	**IL TROVATORE [Verdi]** with Barbieri, Panerai c. Karajan
			EMI CDS 556333.2
			Highlights *EMI CDM 566669.2*

107	MC+GDS	Aug/Sept '56	**LA BOHÈME [Puccini]** Moffo, Panerai c. Votto
			EMI CDS 556295.2
			Highlights *EMI CDM 566670.2*

| 104 | MC+GDS | Sept '56 | **UN BALLO IN MASCHERA [Verdi]** w. Gobbi c. Serafin |
| | | | *EMI CDS 556322.2* |

| 114 | GDS | 07.12.56 | **AIDA [Verdi]** live La Scala with Stella, Simionato c.Votto *Legato LCD 204-2* |

| 113 | MC | 08.12.56 | **LUCIA DI LAMMERMOOR [Donizetti]** live Met c.Cleva *Melodram 26034* |

| 115 | GDS | 26.12.56 | **IRIS [Mascagni]** live Rome with Petrella, Christoff, c. Gavazzeni   *051-043* |

| 101 | MC | Feb '57 | **IL BARBIERE DI SIVIGLIA [Rossini]** with Gobbi c. Galliera   *EMI CDS 556310.2* Highlights   *EMI CDM 566671.2* |

| 115 | MC | Mar '57 | **LA SONNAMBULA [Bellini]** with Monti, Zaccaria c.Votto   *EMI CDS 556278.2* |

| | GDS | 09.03.57 | **MANON LESCAUT [Puccini]** live Naples with Petrella c.Bellezza   *GDS 21050* |

| 116 | MC | 17.04.57 | **ANNA BOLENA [Donizetti]** with Simionato,c. Gavazzeni *EMI CMS 566471.2* |

| 117 | MC | 01.06.57 | **IFIGENIA IN TAURIDE [Gluck]** live La Scala c. Sanzogno *Divina DVN-11* |

| 156 | GDS | 05.06.57 | Oh,come al tuo sottile corpo [*Iris*-Mascagni] with Carteri *MET 224* |

| 101 | MC | 26.06.57 | **LUCIA DI LAMMERMOOR [Donizetti]** live Naples Fernandi   *PR.SR 271/2* |

| 117 | MC | 04.07.57 | **LA SONNAMBULA [Bellini]** live Cologne c.Votto *SakkarisPR.SR.279/280* |

| 118 | GDS | 05.07.57 | **LA FORZA DEL DESTINO [Verdi]** live Cologne, with Gencer.   *LS 4035137* |

| 119 | MC | Jul '57 | **TURANDOT [Puccini]** with Schwarzkopf, Fernandi c. Serafin   *EMI CDS 556307.2* |

| 118 | GDS | Jul '57 | **LA GIOCONDA [Ponchielli]** with Milanov, Warren c.Previtali   *Decca 444 598.2* |

| 119 | MC+GDS | Jul '57 | **MANON LESCAUT [Puccini]** with Fioravanti c. Serafin *EMI CDS 556301.2* |

| 122 | MC | 21.08.57 | **LA SONNAMBULA [Bellini]** live Edinburgh c.Votto *Divina DVN-9* |

| 122 | MC | 26.08.57 | **LA SONNAMBULA [Bellini]** live Edinburgh c.Votto *Divina DVN-6* |

| 126 | MC | Sept '57 | **MEDEA [Cherubini]** with Scotto, Picchi c. Serafin *EMI CMS 566435* |

| | MC | | **Callas Edition Vol 2**   *CED 100342 [3 CDs]* |
| 126 | | 20.11.57 | *Dallas rehearsal* |

Tutte le torture [*Seraglio*-Mozart]
Mad scene [*Puritani*-Bellini]
Vieni t'affretta! [*Macbeth*-Verdi]
Ah! fors'e lui...Sempre libera [*Traviata*-Verdi]
Mad Scene [*Anna Bolena*-Donizetti]

| 150 | | 19.12.58 | *Paris Gala* |

Casta diva...[*Norma*-Bellini]
D'amor sull'ai rosee...-[*Trovatore*-Verdi]
Una voce poco fa [*Barbiere* Rossini]
Act II [*Tosca*-Puccini]

15.05.59   *Hamburg Concert*
Tu che invoco [*Vestale*-Spontini]
Vieni t'affretta [*Macbeth*-Verdi]
Una voce poco fa [*Barbiere*-Rossini]
Tu che la vanita [*Don Carlo*-Verdi]
Mad scene [*Pirata*-Bellini]

| 126 | **MC+GDS** | 07.12.57 | **UN BALLO IN MASCHERA [Verdi]** live Scala |
| | | | c. Gavazzeni   *PR.SR.273/4* |

	MC		**Callas Edition Vol 3** *CED 100343 [3 CDs]*
130		31.12.57	Casta diva [*Norma*-Bellini] RAI TV Rome
130		02.01.58	**NORMA [Bellini –Act I]** live Rome c. Santini
		19.05.59	*Stuttgart*

Tu che invoco [*Vestale*-Spontini]
Vieni t'affretta [*Macbeth*-Verdi]
Una voce poco fa [*Barbiere*-Rossini]
Tu che la vanita [*Don Carlo-Verdi*]
Mad scene [*Pirata*-Bellini]

23.09.59   *London*

| 151 | | | Una macchia e qui tuttora [*Macbeth*-Verdi] |

Mad Scene [[*Hamlet*-Thomas]

| 131 | **MC** | 27.03.58 | **LA TRAVIATA [Verdi]** live Lisbon with Kraus, c. Ghione |
| | | | *EMI CDS 556330.2* |

| 156 | **GDS** | Jun '58 | **MEFISTOFELE [Boito]** with Tebaldi, Siepi c. Serafin |
| | | | *Decca 458.242.2* |

| 133 | **GDS** | 20.06.58 | **TOSCA [Puccini]** live Scala Brussels with Tebaldi c. Gavazzeni |
| | | | LCD 209 |

| 134-6 | **MC** | 20.06.58 | **LA TRAVIATA [Verdi]** live Covent Garden with Valletti |
| | | | *Sakkaris PR.SR.259/6* |

| 156 | **GDS** | | **Torna a Surriento**   *Decca 455 482.2* |
| | | Jul '58 | CD2 |

Parlami d'amore Mariu [Bixio]
Munasterio 'e Santa-Chiara [Barberis]
Firenze sogna [Cesarini]
Canta pe'me [de Curtis]
Che t'aggia di! [Nardella]

			Come e bello [Simi]	
			'A canzone 'e Napule [de Curtis]	
			Sicilia bedda [Vancheri]	
			Ti voglio tanto bene [de Curtis]	
			Fili d'oro [Buongiovanni]	
			Chitarra romana [di Lazzaro]	
156			Addio, sogni di gloria [Rivi]	
			A la barcillunisa [trad. arr. Favara]	
			Nota di li lavannari [trad. arr. Favara]	
			A la vallelunghisa [trad. arr. Favara]	
			Muttetti di lu paliu [trad. arr. Favara]	
			Chiovu "abballati" [trad. arr. Favara]	
			Cantu a timuni [trad.arr. Favara]	
			Aug/Sept '64 CD1	
			Torna a Surriento [de Curtis]	
			Tu ca' nun chigne [de Curtis]	
			Sona chitarra [de Curtis]	
			Lacreme napulitane [Buongiovanni]	
			Napule canta [Tagliaferri]	
			'O surdato 'nnammurato [Califano]	
			Catari, catari [Cardillo]	
			Pusilleco [Tagliaferri]	
			Era di maggio matenata [Costa]	
			Scetate [Costa]	
			Addio mia bella Napoli [Valente]	

| 76 | **GDS** | Aug '58 | **LA FORZA DEL DESTINO [Verdi]** with Milanov | |
| | | | c.Previtali | *Decca 443 678.2* |

156	**GDS**	Sept/Nov '58	**Grandi voci**	*Decca 440.403.2*
			Un di, all'azzurro spazio [*Andrea Chenier*-Giordano]	
			Come un bel di di maggio [*Andrea Chenier*-Giordano]	
			Recondita armonia [*Tosca*-Puccini]	
			E lucevan le stelle [*Tosca*]	
			Non piangere Liu [*Turandot*-Puccini]	
			Nessun dorma [*Turandot*]	
			Pourquoi me reveiller [*Werther*-Massenet]	
			En fermant les yeux [*Manon*-Massenet]	
			La fleur que tu m'avais jetee [*Carmen*-Bizet]	
			Salut! Demeure [*Faust*-Gounod]	
			De mon amie [*Pecheurs*-Bizet]	
			+ 5 tracks [Decca]	

155	**MC**	Sept '58	**Verdi I**	*EMI CDM 566462.2*
			Vieni t'affretta [*Macbeth*]	
			La luce langue [*Macbeth*]	
			Sleepwalking scene [*Macbeth*]	
			Ernani, Ernani involami [*Ernani*]	
			Anch'io dischiuso [*Nabucco*]	
			Tu che la vanita [*Don Carlo*]	

155	MC	Sept '58	**Mad Scenes**	*EMI CDM 566459*

Anna Bolena [Donizetti]
Hamlet [Thonas]
Il pirata [Bellini]

126	MC	06.11.58	**MEDEA [Cherubini]** live Dallas with Vickers.

Gala GL 100.521

151	MC	29.11.58	**Los Angeles Concert** live c. Rescigno	*VAI audio VAIA 1182*

Tu che invoco [*Vestale*-Spontini]
Vieni, t'affretta [*Macbeth*-Verdi]
Una voce poco fa [*Barbiere*-Rossini]
L'altra notte [*Mefistofele*-Boito]
Quando m'en vo' [*Bohème*-Puccini]
Mad Scene [*Hamlet*-Thomas]

145	GDS	07.12.58	**TURANDOT [Puccini]** live La Scala with Nilsson c. Votto

OPD 1256

136	MC	27.01.59	**IL PIRATA [Bellini]** live Carnegie Hall c. Rescigno

Sakkaris PR.SR.283/4

122	MC	Mar '59	**LUCIA DI LAMMERMOOR [Donizetti]** with Tagliavini

EMI CDS 556284.2
Highlights   *EMI CDM 566664.2*

137	MC	30.06.59	**MEDEA [Cherubini]** live Covent Garden with Carlyle, Vickers.

PS.SR.267/8

	MC		**Callas Edition Vol 4**	*CED 100344 [3 CDs]*

		11.07 59	*Amsterdam concert*

Tu che invoco [*La vestale*-Spontini]
Ernani, Ernani, involami [*Ernani*-Verdi]
Tu che la vanita [*Don Carlo*-Verdi]
Mad scene [*Pirata*-Bellini]

03.10.59   *Wood Green Theatre, London*
Si. Mi chiamano Mimi [*Bohème*-Puccini]
L'altra notte [*Mefistofele*-Boito]

30.05.61   *St James Palace, London*
Pleurez, mes yeux [*Le Cid*-Massenet]
Tu che la vanita [*Don Carlo*-Verdi]
L'altro notte [*Mefistofele*-Boito]

152   27.02.62   *Royal Festival Hall*
Ocean! Thou mighty monster [*Oberon*-Weber]
Pleurez, mes yeux [*Le Cid*-Massenet]
Nacqui all'affanno [*La cenerentola*-Rossini]
La luce langue [*Macbeth*-Verdi]
Mad scene [*Anna Bolena*-Donizetti]

153		04.11.62	*Royal Opera House, Covent Garden* Tu che la vanita [*Don Carlo*-Verdi] Habanera [*Carmen*-Bizet] Seguedille [*Carmen*]
49	MC	Sept '59	**LA GIOCONDA [Ponchielli]** with Ferraro, Cappucilli c. Votto *EMI CDS 556291.2*
157	GDS	Sept '59	**LUCIA DI LAMMERMOOR [Donizetti]** with Scotto c. Sanzogno *LS 34713*
	GDS	12.11.59	**LA BOHEME [Puccini]** live New Orleans with Albanese *VAI 1188-2*
145	GDS	09.12.59	**TOSCA [Puccini]** live Scala with Tebaldi *OPD 1162*
	GDS	02.08.60	**UN BALLO IN MASCHERA [Verdi]** live Mexico City *GDS CD 21039*
71	MC	Sept '60	**NORMA [Bellini]** with Ludwig, Corelli c. Serafin *EMI CMS 566428.2* Highlights *EMI CDM 566662.2*
142	GDS	23.09.60	**LA FORZA DEL DESTINO [Verdi]** live Vienna c. Mitropoulos *2MCD 002.228*
146	MC	07.12.60	**POLIUTO [Donizetti]** live La Scala with Corelli c. Votto *EMI CMS 565448.2*
142	GDS	31.12.60	**DIE FLEDERMAUS [Strauss]** live c. Karajan *RCA 74321 61949.2*
155	MC	Mar/Apr '61	**Callas à Paris I** *EMI CDM 566466.2* J'ai perdu mon Eurydice [*Orfeo*-Gluck[Divinites du Styx [*Alceste*-Gluck] Habanera [*Carmen* Bizet] Seguidilla [*Carmen*] Printemps qui commence [*Samsom et Dalila*-Saint-Saens] Amour! Veins aider ma faiblesse [*Samson et Dalila*] Mon coeur s'ouvre a ta voix [*Samson et Dalila*] Ah! je veux vivre [*Romeo et Juliette*] Je suis Titania [*Mignon*-Thomas] Pleurez, mes yeux [*Le Cid*-Massenet] Depuis le jour [*Louise*-Charpentier]
	GDS	Apr/Jul '61	**Neapolitan & other songs** *Testament SBT 1098* Lolita [Peccia]
156			Ideale [Tosti] L'Ultima canzone [Tosti] Aprile [Tosti] Luna d'estate [Tosti] La serenata [Tosti] Matinata {Leoncavallo] Non t'amo piu [Tosti]

Malia [Tosti]
Chanson de l'adieu [Tosti]
'A Vucchella [Tosti]
Musica proibita [Gastaldon]
Funicula, funiculi [Denza]
Luna nova [Costa]
Mamma mia, che vo' sape [Nutile]
Torna [Valente]
Carmela [de Curtis]
Guapparia [Falva]
Mandulinata a Napule [Tagliaferri]
L' m'arricordo 'e napule [Joe]
Pecche? [Pennino]
Anema 'e core [d'Esposito]
Me so' 'mbriacato 'e sole [d'Esposito]
Vurria [Rendine]

142	GDS	22.06.61	**TURANDOT [Puccini]** live Vienna with Nilsson, L. Price
			Myto 2MCD 014.250
	GDS	02.10.61	Recondita armonia; E lucevan [*Tosca*-Puccini]live Berlin
			c. de Fabritiis *GDS CD101*
	GDS	10.10.61	**L'ELISIR D'AMORE [Donizetti]** live Bergamo c. Gavazzeni
			OS 4712
147	MC	14.12.61	**MEDEA [Cherubini]** live La Scala with Vickers,
			c. Schippers *Ombra*
145	GDS	14.12.61	**FEDORA [Giordano]** live Naples with Tebaldi c. Basile
			Arkadia HP 608.2
144	GDS	04.01.62	**ANDREA CHENIER [Giordano]** live hghts Florence
			with Fineschi *HP 608.2*
	MC		**Callas Edition Vol 5** *CED 100345 [3 CDs]*
		16.03.62	*Hamburg*
			Pleurez mes yeux [*Le Cid* Massenet]
			Habanera [*Carmen*-Bizet]
			Segueille [*Carmen*]
			Ernani! Ernani, involami [*Ernani*-Verdi]
			Nacqui all'affanno [*La cenerentola*-Rossini]
			O don fatale [*Don Carlo*-Verdi]
		19.05.62	*Madison Square Garden*
			Habanera [*Carmen*-Bizet]
			Segueille [*Carmen*]
		17.05.63	*Berlin*
			Bel raggio [*Semiramide*-Rossini]
			Anch'io dschiuso [*Nabucco*-Verdi]
			Quando m'en vo [*Bohème*-Puccini]
			Tu? tu? Piccolo iddio! [*Madama Butterfly*-Puccini]

		23.05.63	*Stuttgart*
			Bel raggio [*Semiramide*-Rossini]
			Casta Diva [*Norma*-Bellini]
			Anch'io dischiuso [*Nabucco*-Verdi]
			Quando m'en vo [*Bohème*-Puccini]
			Tu? tu? Piccolo iddio! [*Madama Butterfly*-Puccini]
		31.05.63	*Royal Festival Hall, London*
			Bel raggio [*Semiramide*-Rossini]

		09.06.63	*Copenhagen*
			Casta diva [*Norma*-Bellini]
			Anch'io dischiuso [*Nabucco*-Verdi]
			Quando m'en vo [*Bohème*-Puccini]
			Tu? tu? Piccolo iddio! [*Madama Butterfly*-Puccini]

		05.06.63	*Paris*
			Bel raggio [*Semiramide*-Rossini]
			Nacqui all'affanno [*La cenerentola*-Rossini]
			Adieu, notre petite table [*Manon*-Massenet]
			Werther! Ces letters [*Werther*-Massenet]
			Anch'io dischiuso [*Nabucco*-Verdi]
			Quando m'en vo [*Bohème*-Puccini]
			Tu? tu? Piccolo iddio! [*Madama Butterfly*-Puccini]
			O mio babbino caro [*Gianni Schicchi*-Puccini]

		18.05.65	*RFT Studios, Paris*
			Adieu, notre petite table [*Manon*-Massenet]
			Ah! non credea mirati [*Sonnambula*-Bellini]
			O mio babbino caro [*Gianni Schicchi*-Puccini]

	GDS	Jun '62	**The Singers** *Decca 467 908.2*
			Celeste Aida [*Aida*-Verdi]
			Quando le sere placido [*Luisa Miller*-Verdi]
156			Dio! Mi potevi scagliar [*Otello*-Verdi]
			Niun mi tema [*Otello*]
			Giunto sul passo estremo [*Mefistofele*-Boito]
			O paradiso! [*L'Africana*-Meyerbeer]
			Cielo e mar! [*Gioconda*-Ponchielli]
			Or son sei mesi [*Fanciulla*-Puccini]
			La dolissima effigie [*Adriana Lecouvreur*-Cilea]
157			Testa adorata [*La bohème*-Leoncavallo]
			Amor te vieta [*Fedora*-Giordano]
			Io conosco un giardino [*Maristella*-Pietri]
			Davvero, quanto grande e la miseria [*Il calzare d'argento*-Pizzetti]

157	**GDS**	Sept '62	**TOSCA [Puccini]** with L.Price, Taddei c. Karajan
			Decca 452.620.2
			Highlights *452 728.2*

| 145 | **GDS** | 14.01.63 | **LUISA MILLER [Verdi]** live Palermo with Stella c. Sanzogno |
| | | | *GDS 21033* |

155	MC	May '63	**Callas à Paris II**	*EMI CDM 566457.2*

O malheureuse Iphigenie [*Iphigenie en Tauride*-Gluck]
D'amour l'ardente flame [*La Damnation de Faust*-Berlioz]
Comme autrefois [*Pecheurs*-Bizet]
Adieu, notre petite table[*Manon*-massenet]
Je marche sur tous les chemins [*Manon*]
Werther! Qui m'aurait dit…[*Werther*-Massenet]
Ballade of the King of Tule and the Jewel Song [*Faust*-Gounod]

	GDS	Aug '63	**MANON [Massenet]** with Moffo c. Leibwitz	
157			Ah fuyez	*MET 224*
157			Ah1 des Grieux! O Manon!..Nous reparlerons du passé	
				MET 227

157	**GDS**	Sept '63	**Italian songs**	*Ricordi SVCD 18*

Mille cherubini in coro [Schubert]
Mamma [Bixio]
Rondine al nido [de Crescenzo]
Serenata [Drigo]
Non ti scordar di me [de Curtis]
Se vuoi goder la vita [Bixio]
La canzone dell'amore [Bixio]
Malinconia d'amore [d'Anzi]
'E rrose e tu [Rendine]
Incantesimo [Olivieri]
Tristezze [Chopin]
Tu no mi lascerai [d'Anzi]

155	MC Dec'63/Jan '64	**Mozart, Beethoven, Weber**	*EMI CDM 566465.2*

Ah! perfido, Op. 65 [Beethoven]
Ocean! Thou mighty monster [*Oberon*-Weber]
Porgi amor [*Le nozze di Figaro*-Mozart]
Or sai chi l'onore [*Don Giovanni*-Mozart]
Non mi dir [*Don Giovanni*]
Mi tradi [*Don Giovanni*]

155	MC Dec'63/Feb '64	**Verdi II**	*EMI CDM 566461.2*

Willow Song and Ave Maria [*Otello*]
Salvami, salvami tu gran Dio! [*Aroldo*]
O cielo! Dove son io? [*Aroldo*]
Non pianger, mia compagna [*Don Carlo*]
O don fatale [*Don Carlo*]

155	MC Dec'63/Apr '64	**Rossini & Donizetti arias**	*EMI CDM 566464.1*

Non piu mesta [*La cenerentola*-Rossini]
Selva opaca [*Guglielmo Tell*-Rossini]
Bel raggio [*Semiramide*-Rossini]
Convien partir [*La figlia del reggimento*-Donizetti]
Com'e bello [*Lucrezia Borgia*-Donizetti]
Prendi, prendi per me [*L'elisir d'amore*-Donizetti]

139	**MC**	21.01.64	**TOSCA [Puccini]** live Cioni, Gobbi, c. Cillario
			Sakkaris PR.SR. 265/6

	MC		**Verdi III**	*EMI CDM 566462.2*
		Apr '64	Liberamente or piangi [*Attila*]	
		Apr '64	Ecco l'orrido campo…[*Ballo*]	
		Apr '64	Morro, ma prima in grazia [*Ballo*]	
		Apr '64	Ritorna vincitor! [*Aida*]	
		Jan '65	O madre, dal cielo soccorri [*I Lombardi*]	
		Jan '65	Tacea la notte [*Trovatore*]	
		Mar '69	Non so le tetre [*Il corsaro*]	
		Mar '69	Vola talor dal carcere [*Il corsaro*]	

146	**GDS**	04.06.64	**RIENZI [Wagner]** live La Scala, c. Scherchen *GDS 21038*

122	**MC**	Jul '64	**CARMEN [Bizet[** with Gedda, Guiot, Massard c. Pretre
			EMI CDS 552681.2
			Highlights *EMI CDM 5666653.2*

122	**MC**	Dec '64	**TOSCA [Puccini]** with Bergonzi, Gobbi c. Pretre
			EMI CMS 566444.2
			Highlights *EMI CDM 566666.2*

139	**MC**	19.03.65	**TOSCA [Puccini]** live Met with Corelli c. Cleva
			Melodram 26030

139	**MC**	25.03.65	**TOSCA [Puccini]** live Met with Tucker c. Cleva
			Melodram 26035

149	**MC**	14.05.65	**NORMA [Bellini]** live excs Paris with Simionato c. Pretre
			Divina DVN-10

149	**MC**	17.05.65	**NORMA [Bellini]** live excs Paris with Simionato c. Pretre
			Divina DVN-10

149	**MC**	21.05.65	**NORMA [Bellini]** live highlights Paris with Cossotto c. Pretre
			Divina DVN-10

149	**MC**	29.05.65	**NORMA [Bellini]** live Paris with Cossotto c. Pretre *Gala*
			Divina DVN-15

141	**MC**	05.07.65	**TOSCA [Puccini]** live Covent Garden with Cioni,
			Gobbi c. Pretre *Divina DVN-2*

157	**GDS**	Feb '66	**Le piu belle canzoni** *DV More Record CD DV 5816*
			Addio, mio balla Napoli [Valente]
			Canzone appassiunate [Mario]
			Comme facette mammeta [Gambardello]
			Dicitencello vuie [Falvo]
			'E rrose e tu [Rendine]
			I'te vurria vasa [de Capua]
			Napule ca se ne va [Tagliaferri]
			Nuttata 'e sentimento [Capolongo]
			O mese d''e rrose [Bonavolonta]

'O sole mio [di Capua]
Tutta pe' mme! [Lama]
Vierno [Acampora]

157   **GDS**   Dec '66   **Il nostro concerto**   *Replay Music RMCD 8007*
Amore, scusami [Pallavicini]
Arrivederci [Calabrese]
Il cielo in una stanza [Toang]
Come sinfonia [Donaggio]
Concerto d'autunno [Danpa]
E se domain [Calabrese]
Io che amo solo te [Endrigo]
Il mondo [Meccia]
Noi [Malgoni]
T'ho voluto bene [Redi]
Il nostro concerto [Calabrese]
Sedici anni [Zanfagna]

146   **GDS**   27.01.67   **L'INCORONAZIONE DI POPPEA [Monteverdi]**live
Scala   *IMCD 905.31*

158   **GDS**   Apr '67   **DAS LAND DES LACHELNS [Lehar]** Highlights,
c. Lambrecht   *Preiser 93144*

    GDS   Apr '67   **DER ZAREWITSCH [Lehar]** Highlights, c. Scherzer
Koch 3-1273.2

153   **GDS**   Jun '68   **Liederabend, Vienna**   *Koch 3-1833.2*
Vaga Luna che inargente [Bellini]
Dolente imagine di fille mia [Bellini]
Il poveretto [Verdi]
Stornello [Verdi]
Ici bas [Faure]
Chanson d'Avril [Bizet]
Absence [Berlioz]
Three Sicilian folksongs [arr. Favara]
Non t'amo piu [Tosti]
Chanson d'adieu [Tosti]
Luna d'estate [Tosti]
Carmela [de Curtis]
Core'ngrato [Cardillo]
Piano accompanied by Rudolf Bibl

    GDS   16.09.69   **FEDORA [Giordano]** live Lucca with Olivero   *OPD 1260*

158   **MC** Oct '71 to Mar '72 **Julliard Master Classes**   *CMS 565802.2*

    MC+GDS 2-7.05.73   Ah! per sempre [*Forza*-Verdi]   *House of Opera CD373S*
Quale o prode [*Vespri*-Verdi]
Io vengo o domandar [*Don Carlo*-Verdi]
Pur ti reveggo [*Aida*-Verdi]
Gia nella notte densa [*Otello*-Verdi]

MC+GDS 25.10.73   **Hamburg recital**   *Eklipse CD 33*
O nuit d'amour [*Faust*-Gounod]
C'est toi? [*Carmen*-Bizet]
O mio babbino caro [*Gianni Schicchi*-Puccini]

MC+GDS 26.11.73   **Royal Festival Hall, London** with Ivor Newton [piano]
Divina DVN-5

MC   27.02.74   **Boston recital** with Robert Sutherland [piano]   *Ombra*

MC   21.03.74   **Dallas recital** with Robert Sutherland [piano]   *Ombra*
MC+GDS 02.03.74   **Chicago recital** [*Tu qui Santuzza*] with Robert Sutherland
[piano]

MC   Aug '77   **Paris**
Madre, pietosa Vergine [*Forza*-Verdi] with Vasso Devetzi

MC+GDS 21.03.74   **Miami Beach recital**   *Ornamente Fe 124*
Quale, o probe [*Vespri*-Verdi]
Habanera [*Carmen*-Bizet]
C'est toi? [*Carmen*]
Voi lo sapete [*Cavalleria rusticana*-Mascagni]

MC+GDS 09.04.74   **Westbury, New York recital** with R Sutherland [piano]
Legato LCD137-1

MC   15.04.74   **Carnegie Hall, New York recital**   *Ornamente Fe 109*
Addio notre petite table [*Manon*-Massenet]

MC+GDS 18.04.74   **Cincinnati recital**   *Ornamente Fe 124*
Suicidio [*Gioconda*-Ponchielli]
Habanera...C'est toi? [*Carmen*-Bizet]
Air des letters [*Werther*-Massenet]
Voi lo sapete...Tu qui Santuzza [*Cavalleria*-Mascagni]
Una parola, O Adina [*L'elisir*-Donizetti]

MC+GDS 13.05.74   **Montreal recital** with Robert Sutherland [piano]
Fonovox VOX 7812-2

GDS   2-4.09.74   **Duets with Montserrat Caballe**   *Forlane UCD 16557*
Et je sais votre nom [*Manon*-Massenet]
Leila! Leila! [*Pecheurs*-Bizet]
E cosi vada [*Francesca da Rimini*-Zandonai]
Il faut nous separer [*Werther*-Massenet]
Sento una forza indomita [*Il Guarany*-Gomes]
Una parola, O Adina [*L'elisir*-Donizetti]

MC   3.03.76   Ah Perfido! Op.65 [Beethoven] piano [self accompanied]
Gala GL 320

GDS   1982   Love is a Many Splendored Thing [S. Fain]
Dutch Records   DGCD 129D
Malafemmena [de Curtis]
Canto d'amore indiano [*Rose Marie*-Friml] with Monica Curth

Arrivederci Roma [Ranucci]
Non c' e stella come te [Bartoli]
Tristessa [Chopin]
Io senza te non vivo [Mariano]
Senza eta [Mariano]
E dimmi che non sogno [Bartoli]
Una donna come te [Facchini]

ၢၢ

COMPILATIONS

of miscellaneous recordings listed above

MC	Maria Callas Live in Concert	*EMI CZS 572030.2 [2CDs]*
[includes controversial *Un bel di vedremo* 07.04 1935 US Radio Broadcast]		
MC	Ses Recitals 1954 – 1969	*EMI CMS 566618.2 [11CDs]*
MC	The Voice of the Century	*EMI CDM 566628.2*
MC	Opera Arias	*HMV Classics HMV 573449.2*
MC	Popular music from tv, film and opera	*EMI CMS 557062.2 [2CDs]*
MC	Popular music from tv, film and opera	*EMI CDC 557050.2*
MC	Romantic Callas	*EMI CMS 557205.2 [2CDs]*
MC	Romantic Callas	*EMI CDC 557211.2*
MC	Callas, de Hidalgo: Pupil and Teacher	*Fono 010*
MC	Callas, Tebaldi: Rivals	*Fono 013*
MC	My First Record	*Fono 006*
MC	Maria Callas: The First Documents	*Fono 012*
MC	Maria Callas: The Secret of a Voice	*Fono 011*
GDS	My First Record	*Fono 1007*
GDS	Heroes	*EMI CDM 566808.2*
GDS	Giuseppe di Stefano	*Disky DCL 704822 [2CDs]*
GDS	Voce 'e notte	*Replay Music RMCD 4032*
GDS	Mama	*Replay Music RMCD 4050*
MC & GDS Italian Opera Duets		*EMI CDM 769543.2*

VIDEOS & DVD

MC   19.12.58   **La Callas...toujours [Gala Concert, Paris 1958]**
EMI MVD 9912583 & DVD DVB 492502.9

MC   18.05.59 & 16.03.62   **Maria Callas in Concert [Hamburg]**   *EMI MVD 491711.3*
& DVD DVA 492246.9

MC   **Life and Art**   *EMI MVD 991151.2 & DVD DVA 492248.9*

MC   04.11.62 & 09.02.64   **Covent Garden**   *EMI MVD 49'12833*

MC   **Callas Reveals Herself**   *Bel Canto Society 0197*

GDS   05.11.63   Ah fuyez [*Manon*-Massenet] TV Bell Telephone Hour, New York
VAI DVD 4201

GDS   **La Voce del Cuore**   *Hardy Classic Video 1008*

GDS   **Canto Per Te** [film 1954] with 'Autunno' and 'Canta pe' me' [1991–de Curtis]
BCS 0409

GDS   **Pavarotti and the Italian Tenor [Caruso, Schipa, Gigli, di Stefano]**
Decca 071 168.3

MC+GDS The Art of Singing [09.02.64 *Tosca*-Callas; 26.01.58 *Pagliacci*-di Stefano
NUC ARTS 0630-15898-3

MC+GDS 12.10.74 Tokyo recital   *CIN CIN CCCD 1037-38*
TOSHIBA EMI TOLW 3762

NOTES

Prologue

1. Peter Hutchinson: Preiser records 2001

Chapter 1

1. Jurgen Kesting: Maria Callas [Quartet Books, London 1992] pp.143-4]
2. Opera News [David A.Lowe: Callas As They Saw Her, Robson Books, London 1987] p.159]
3. Opera Vol.5 No. 3 March 1954 p.168
4. Ibid.Vol.5 No.2 February 1954 p.106
5. Giuseppe di Stefano: L'Arte del Canto, Rusconi 1989
6. Ibid.Vol.5 No.3 March 1954 p.169

Chapter 2

1. Gramophone Vol.58 No.694 March 1981 p.1234-5
2. Opera Vol.47 No.10 October 1996 p.1138
3. Ibid
4. Ibid p.1139

Chapter 3

1. Corriere della Sera [Lowe p.134]
2. 15.10.47 La Voce del Padrone to HMV
3. 14.11.47 HMV to La Voce del Padrone
4. 05.12.47 HMV to La Voce del Padrone
5. Gramophone Vol.25 No.297 February 1948 p.139
6. Ibid Vol.25 No.299 April 1948 p.171
7. Ibid Vol.26 No.305 October 1948 p.76
8. Ibid Vol.26 No.312 May 1949 p.195

Chapter 4

1. Il Gazzettino 31.12.47
2. Musical America March 15 1948 p.40/44
3. Ibid April 1948 p.44
4. Ibid September 1948 p.9
5. La Lavoratore [Lowe p.135]
6. Corriere del Popolo [Lowe p.135]
7. Il Messaggero [Lowe p.135]
8. La Nazione [Lowe p.136]
9. Il Gazzettino [Lowe p.136]
10. Mario Nordio [Lowe p.137]
11. Il Quotidiano [Lowe pp.137/8]

Chapter 5

1. Musical America January 1949 p.13
2. Ibid February 1949 p.256
3. Ibid April 1 1949 p.9
4. Ibid April 15 1949 p.11

5. Ibid February 1949 p.252
6. Ibid February 1949 p.260
7. Ibid February 1949 p.258
8. Ibid June 1949 p.23
9. Ibid March 1949 p.8
10. La Prensa [Lowe p.138]
11. Ibid
12. Musical America October 1949 p.8
13. Hanine-Roussel: Simionato [Baskerville 1997] p.96
14. Ibid p.178

Chapter 6

1. Opera Vol.3 No.4 April 1952 p.238
2. Musical America December 1 1949 p.3
3. Ibid January 1950 p.13
4. Ibid January 1950 p.8
5. Ibid April 1950 p.23
6. Ibid May 1950 p.27
7. Ibid January 15 1950 p.77
8. Ibid February 1950 p.325
9. Ibid February 1950 p.327
10. Ibid February 1950 p.328
11. Il Giornale [Lowe p.139]
12. Il Risorgimento [Lowe p.139]
13. Il Gazettino [Lowe pp.139/40]
14. Il Giorno d'Italia [Lowe p.140]
15. Corriere Lombardo [Lowe p.141]
16. Opera Vol.1 No.6 November 1950 p.40
17. El universal [Lowe p.141]
18. Excelsior [Lowe p.141]
19. Ibid [Lowe p142]
20. Ibid

Chapter 7

1. Musical America November 1950 p.3
2. Opera Vol. 2 No 3 February 1951 p.139
3. Ibid Vol.2 No.9 August 1951 p.453
4. Musical America December 15 1950 p.9
5. Ibid January 1 1951 p.9
6. Ibid January 15 1951 p.9
7. Ibid February 1951 p.252
8. Ibid p.250
9. Ibid April 1 1951 p.5
10. Ibid p.22
11. Gramophone Vol.30 No.359 April 1953 p.299
12. Musical America February 1951 p.257
13. Opera Vol.8 No.2 February 1957 p.116
14. Gramophone Vol.34 No.403 December 1956 p.259

15. Ibid Vol.30 No.353 October 1952 p.114
16. Opera Vol.3 No.12 December 1952 p.732
17. Ibid Vol.6 No.1 January 1955 p.48
18. Gramophone Vol.51 No 603 August 1973 p.381
19. Opera Vol.2 No.11 October 1951 p.590
20. Tito Gobbi: My Life [Macdonald & Janes's Publishers 1979] p.92

Chapter 8

 1. Musical America December 15 1951 p.17
 2. Opera Vol.3 No.3 March 1952 p.164
 3. Musical America January 1 1952
 4. Ibid January 15 1952 p..23
 5. Ibid
 6. Ibid April 1952 p.17
 7. Ibid January 1 1952 p.17
 8. Ibid March 1952 p.27
 9. Opera Vol.3 No.5 May 1952 p.280
10. Ibid Vol.3 No.4 April 1952 p.233
11. Musical America 1952
12. Opera Vol.3 No.7 July 1952 p.416 & Lowe p.149
13. Musical America 1952
14. Opera Vol.3 No.7 July 1952 pp.391-2
15. Musical America September 1952 p.18

Chapter 9

 1. Opera Vol.3 No.10 October 1952 p.628
 2. Ibid Vol 4 No.12 February 1953 p.95
 3. Ibid p.96
 4. Ibid Vol.4 No.3 March 1953 p.167
 5. Corriere della Sera [Lowe p.154]
 6. Opera Vol.4 No.4 April 1953 p.232
 7. Ibid Vol.3 No.8 August 1952 p.494
 8. Ibid Vol.4 No.4 April 1953 p.230
 9. Gramophone Vol.31 no.366 November 1953 p.198
10. Opera Vol.5 No.1 January 1954 p.38
11. Musical Times Vol.95 No.1333 March 1954 p.132
12. Musical America January 1 1954 p.16
13. Opera Vol.4 No.7 July 1953 p.391
14. Corriere Lombardo [Lowe pp.156-7]
15. Opera Vol.4 No.1 January 1953 pp.37-44
16. Ibid Vol.4 No.7 July 1953 p.436
17. Ibid Vol.4 No.8 August 1953 pp.507-9
18. Ibid Vol.4 No.7 July 1953 p.415
19. Ibid Vol.4 No.8 August 1953 p.504
20. Gramophone Vol.32 No.377 October 1954 p.212
21. Opera Vol.5 No.12 December 1954 p.759
22. Musical America August 1954 p 21
23. Gramophone Vol.30 No.355 December 1953 p.172

24. Opera Vol.5 No.3 March 1954 pp.174-5
25. Musical America January 1954 p.16
26. Musical Times Vol.95 No.1334 April 1954 p.193
27. Gramophone Vol.74 No.887 April 1997 p.37
28. Ibid Vol.32 No.379 December 1954 p.314
29. Opera Vol.9 No.1 January 1958 p.53
30. Gramophone Vol.35 No.416 January 1958 p.328

Chapter 10

1. Gramophone Vol.31 No.370 March 1955 p.390
2. Opera Vol.5 No.5 May 1954 p.301
3. Musical Times Vol.95 No.1336 June 1954 p.315
4. Musical America May 1954 p.17
5. Opera Vol.5 No.3 March 1954 p.189
6. Ibid
7. Ibid Vol.5 No.5 May 1954 p.310
8. Ibid
9. Ibid pp.310-11
10. Ibid p.311
11. Ibid
12. Idid Vlo.5 No.7 July 1954 p.442
13. Ibid p.443
14. Ibid
15. Ibid Vol.5 No.2 February 1954 p.108
16. Ibid Vol.5 No.4 April 1954 p.237
17. Ibid Vol.5 No.6 June 1954 p.362
18. Ibid
19. Corriere del Teatro [Lowe p.160]
20. Opera Vol.5 No.6 June 1954 p.362
21. Corriere della Sera [Lowe p.161]
22. High Fidelity [Lowe p.161]
23. Opera Vol.5 No.6 June 1954 p.362
24. Ibid Vol.5 No.7 July 1954 p.428
25. Ibid Vol.5 No.6 June 1954 pp.345-6
26. Gramophone Vol.33 No.388 September 1955 p.146
27. Opera Vol.6 No.11 November 1955 p.718
28. Musical America August 1955 p.17
29. Opera Vol.10 No.1 January 1959 p.29
30. Gramophone Vol.33 No.385 June 1955 p.26
31. Opera Vol.10 No.6 June 1959 p.39
32. Musical America November 15 1959 p.28
33. Gramophone Vol.36 No.421 June 1958 p.41
34. Opera Vol.6 No.4 April 1955 p.259
35. Gramophone March 1955 p.455
36. Musical America December 1 1954 p.10
37. Chicago Tribune (Lowe p.162)
38. Ibid (Lowe p.163)
39. Ibid (Lowe p.163-4)

40. Musical America December 15 1954 p.10
41. Opera Vol.6 No.3 March 1955 p.160
42. Ibid p.161

Chapter 11

1. Music and Musicians (Lowe p.164)
2. Corriere della sera (Lowe p.164)
3. Opera Vol.6 No.3 March 1955 p.174
4. Ibid
5. Ibid p.176
6. Corriere del Teatro (Lowe p.165)
7. Opera Vol.6 No.3 March 1955 p.177
8. Ibid Vol.6 No.4 April 1955 p.154
9. Ibid
10. Ibid Vol.6 No.5 May 1955 p.318
11. Ibid p.133
12. Musici + Dischi (Lowe p.182)
13. Chicago Tribune (Lowe p.183)
14. Musical America October 1957 p.9
15. Music and Musicians (Lowe p.165)
16. Opera Vol.6 No.6 June 1955 p.382
17. Musical America August 1955 p.15
18. Opera Vol.42 No.4 April 1991 p.476
19. Gramophone Vol. No.393 February 1956 p.361
20. Opera Vol.7 No.4 April 1956 p.251
21. Musical Times Vol.97 No.1357 March 1956 p.140
22. Gramophone Vol.79 No.944 p.97
23. Opera Vol.7 No.11 November 1956 p.689
24. Ibid Vol.8 No.10 October 1957 p.636-8
25. Ibid Vol.7 No.4 April 1956 p.250
26. Gramophone Vol.33 No.394 March 1956 p.393
27. Opera Vol.6 No.12 December 1955 p.769-70
28. New York Times 01.11.55
29. Opera Vol.7 No.1 January 1956 p.34
30. Musical America November 15 1955 p.3
31. Opera Vol.7 No.3 March 1956 p.154
32. Ibid p.155
33. Musical America December 1 1955 p.7
34. Opera Vol.7 No.3 March 1956 p.155-6

Chapter 12

1. Musical America December 15 1955 p.29
2. Ibid January 1 1956 p.16
3. Ibid December 15 1955 p.29
4. Ibid February 1956
5. Opera Vol.7 No.4 April 1956 p.233
6. Musical America February 1956
7. Ibid January 15 1956 p.17

8. Musical Courier (Lowe p.169-70)
9. Corriere della Sera (Lowe p.170)
10. Opera Vol.7 No.4 April 1956 p.245
11. Music and Musicians (Lowe p.170)
12. Opera Vol.7 No.4 April 1956 p.307
13 Ibid Vol.7 No.6 June 1956 p.368
14. Ibid p.356
15. Music and Musicians (Lowe p.171)
16. Opera Vol.7 No.7 July 1956 p.435
17. Ibid
18. Ibid p.436
19. Ibid Vol.7 No.8 August 1956 p.476
20. Ibid Vol.7 No.6 June 1956 p.366
21. Ibid Vol.7 No.8 August 1956 p.489
22. Ibid Vol.7 No.9 September 1956 p.555
23. Chicago Tribune (Lowe p.171)
24. Gramophone Vol.35 No.414 November 1957 p.233
25. Opera Vol.9 No.1 January 1958 p.53
26. Gramophone Vol.35 No. 413 October 1957 p.190
27. Opera Vol.8 No.11 November 1957 p.718
28. Gramophone Vol.35 No.418 March 1958 p.417
29. Opera Vol.9 No.4 April 1958 p.261
30. Musical America 1958

Chapter 13
1. Opera Vol.8 No.1 January 1957 p.32 + p.34
2. Lowe p.172
3. Lowe pp.173 − 4
4. Lowe p.175
5. Lowe p.178
6. Opera Vol.8 No.3 March 1957 p.190–192
7. Ibid Vol.8 No.2 February 1957 p.103
8. Musical America January 15 1957 p.3
9. Opera Vol.8 No.4 April 1957 p.241
10. Musical America June 1957 p.8
11. Opera Vol.8 No.3 March 1957 p.177
12. Ibid Vol.8 No.6 June 1957 p.378
13. Ibid Vol.8 No.5 May 1957 p.302-3
14. Musical America 1957
15. Opera Vol.8 No.6 June 1957 p.344-350
16. Ibid Vol.8 No.8 August 1957 p.511
17. Ibid p.498
18. Ibid Vol.8 No.11 November 1957 p.712
19. Ibid
20. Gramophone Vol.37 no.433 June 1959 p.23
21. Opera Vol.10 No.6 June 1959 p.391
22. Gramophone Vol.36 No.424 September 1958 p.158
23. Opera Vol.9 No.12 December 1958 p.800

24. Gramophone Vol.37 No.439 December 1959 p.301
25. Opera Vol.11 No.1 January 1960 p.53
26. Ibid Vol.8 No.10 October 1957 p.650
27. Ibid p.633-4
28. Ibid Vol.9 No.2 February 1958 p.166
29. Musical America December 15 1957 p.5
30. Ibid
31. Ibid

Chapter 14

1. Opera Vol.9 No.3 March 1958 pp.179-81
2. Lowe p.187
3. Musical America January 1 1958 p.16
4. Opera Vol.9 No.2 February 1958 p.114-6
5. Ibid Vol.9 No.5 May 1958 p.378
6. Ibid p.389
7. Ibid Vol.9 No.7 July 1958 p.454
8. Ibid
9. Ibid Vol.9 No.8 August 1958 p.523
10. Ibid Vol.9 No.7 July 1958 p.468
11. Ibid Vol.9 No.8 August 1958 p.533-7
12. Ibid Vol.10 No.4 April 1959 p.214-5
13. Ibid Vol.10 No.8 August 1959 p.543

Chapter 15

1. Opera Vol.16 No.2 February 1965 p.130
2. Ibid Vol.15 No.3 March 1964 p.202-4
3. Ibid Vol.16 No.7 July 1965 p.491-2
4. Ibid Vol.16 No.8 August 1965 p.605
5. Ibid Vol.9 No.12 November 1958 p.725
6. Ibid Vol.9 No.12 December 1958 p.787
7. Ibid Vol.10 No.8 August 1959 p.524
8. Ibid Vol.11 No.8 August 1960 p.548
9. Ibid Vol.11 No.11 November 1960 p.761
10. Ibid Vol.12 No.3 March 1961 p.176
11. Ibid Vol.12 No.9 September 1961 p.595
12. Ibid Vol.13 No.12 December 1962 p.813
13. Ibid Vol.15 No.11 November 1964 p.746
14. Ibid Vol.16 No.12 December 1965 p.900
15. Ibid Vol.9 No.12 December 1958 p.781
16. Ibid Vol.10 No.12 December 1959 p.787
17. Musical America 1959
18. Opera Vol.10 No.12 December 1959 p.789
19. Ibid Vol.11 no.1 January 1960 p.28
20. Musical America 1959
21. Opera Vol.12 No.2 February 1961 p.115
22. Ibid Vol.15 No.3 March 1964 p.172
23. Ibid Vol.16 No.2 February 1965 p.108
24. Ibid p.118

25. Ibid Vol.16 No.3 March 1965 p.184

26. Ibid Vol.16 No.4 April 1965 p.267

27. Ibid Vol.12 No.12 December 1961 p.798

28. Ibid Vol.16 No.2 February 1965 p.130

29. Ibid Vol.12 No.7 July 1961 p.480

30. Ibid Vol.14 No.11 November 1963 p.765

31. Ibid Vol.11 No.3 March 1960 p.216-17

32. Ibid Vol.13 No.4 April 1962 p.262

33. Ibid Vol.16 No.6 June 1965 p.441

34. Ibid Vol.13 No.2 February 1962 p.122

35. Ibid Vol.13 No.3 March 1962 p.186

36. Ibid Vol.13 No.5 May 1962 p.323

37. Ibid Vol.13 No.11 November 1962 p.733

38. Ibid p.736

39. Musical America March 1959 p.8

40. Opera Vol.10 No.2 February 1959 p.118

41. Musical America March 1959 p.8

42. bid p.38

43. Opera Vol.10 No.5 May 1959 p.316

44. Ibid Vol.11 No.2 February 1960 p.147

45. Ibid Vol.11 No.5 May 1960 p.350

46. Ibid Vol.12 No.6 June 1961 p.381

47. Ibid Vol.15 No.6 June 1964 p.383

48. Ibid Vol.15 No.9 September 1964 p.600

49. Ibid Vol.12 No.2 February 1961 p.96–7

50. Ibid Vol.13 No.2 February 1962 p.97

51 Ibid Autumn 1961 Special Festival Number p.66-67

52. Ibid Autumn 1960 Special Festival Number p.76-80

53. Ibid Vol.15 No.8 August 1964 p.534–535

54. Ibid Vol.16 No.8 August 1965 p.586

55. Musical America January 15 1959 p.8

56. Saturday Review [Lowe pp.202-3]

57. Musical America January 1 1959 p.3

58. Opera Vol.10 No.11 November 1959 p.759

59. Musical America

60. Vienna Kurier 24.06.68

61. Opera Vol.13 No.12 December 1962 p.835

62. 04.06.53 Legge to Bicknell

63. Opera Vol.10 No.3 March 1959 p.188

64. Gramophone Vol.58 No.694 March 1981 p.1234-5

65. Gramophone June 1952 p.27

66. Ibid Vol.50 No.596 January 1973 p.1358

67. Opera Vol.10.No.8 August 1959 p.536

68. Gramophone Vol.39 No.460 September 1961 p.164

69. Opera Vol.14 No.10 October 1963 p.704

70. Gramophone Vol.41 No.481 June 1963 p.24

71. Ibid Vol.42 No.497 September 1964 p.145

72. Opera 1967 p.749

73. Ibid Vol.19 No.1 January 1968 p.32

74. Gramophone September 1975 p.525

BIBLIOGRAPHY

James Anderson: Dictionary of Opera and Operetta [Bloomsbury, 1989]

Giuseppe di Stefano: L'arte del canto [Rusconi, 1989]

Maria di Stefano & Francamaria Trapani: Callas Nemica Mia [Rusconi, 1992]

Stelios Galatopoulos: Maria Callas, Sacred Monster [Fourth estate, 1998]

Ed. Renato Garavaglia: Omaggio a Giuseppe di Stefano [Edizione del Teatro alla Scala, 1997]

Tito Gobbi: My Life [Macdonald and Jane's Publishers Ltd, 1979]

Jurgen Kesting: Maria Callas [Quartet Books, 1992]

Michele Nocera: Sempre libera … [Centro Culturale San Michele, 2000]

Richard Osborne: Herbert von Karajan, a life in music [Chotto & Windus, 1998]

Nicholas Petsalis-Diomidis: The Unknown Callas, The Greek years [Amadeus Press, 2001]

Ed. Aurelio de los Reyes: Maria Callas, una mujer, una voz, un mito [Instituto National de Bellas Artes, 2000]

Sergio Segalini: Callas, les images d'une voix [Editions Francis Van de Velde, 1987]

Michael Scott: Maria Meneghini Callas [Simon and Schuster, 1991]

Arianna Stassinopoulos: Maria Callas, the woman behind the legend [Weidenfeld and Nicholson 1981]

Robert Sutherland: Maria Callas, Diaries of a Friendship [Constable, 1999]

Andre Tebeuf: La Callas: [Assouline, 1998]

Ed. Silvana Turzio: Scala diva [Franco Cosimo Paanini, 1993]

Henry Wisneski: Maria Callas, the art behind the legend [Robert Hale & Co., 1976]

http://frankhamilton.org

INDEX

PHOTOGRAPH CREDITS

Centro Regional de INAH en Pachuca
28

Dhellentas archives
11

Theo Hernandez
29

Musical America
154

Piccagliani
Cover, frontispiece, 5, 48, 58, 59, 72, 73, 85, 86, 90, 106, 123, 128, 129

Unknown
12, 77, 79, 96, 109, 159

Record advertisements by kind permission of *Opera*